PILLARS of PURPOSE

Leadership Lessons for Achieving a Life of Significance

David A. Pickler

Praise for Pillars of Purpose

"Pillars of Purpose is a profound look at what it means to be a leader. Through a collection of personal stories, anecdotes and powerful quotes, David Pickler takes us step-by-step through the lifelong process of becoming a leader. As an educator, I wish I would have had his compelling roadmap to lead with love and empathy before I walked into Room 203 to teach the Freedom Writers. While the road ahead will always be full of challenges, David displays that it's how one confronts those challenges that separates good leaders from great leaders."

— Erin Gruwell, teacher, author and social justice activist

"Pillars of Purpose demonstrates that, while we are all on our own personal journey, the power of partnerships and empathy can, and will, bind us all together. This masterful step-by-step guide to becoming a great leader, no matter your job or skills, shows us anyone can achieve a life of true significance."

— Dr. Tammy Grissom, education executive and advocate

"Pillars of Purpose is David Pickler's gift to all of us, and its impact will be enormous. David writes from the heart, and in doing so, it stirs our own... Prepare to be wowed."

— Joseph Deitch, business executive and philanthropist

"Pillars of Purpose shows us that a life of significance is built upon purpose, empathy and a commitment to helping others. This book shows us how to push ourselves to achieve greatness, and will inspire readers to leave a positive, lasting impact on those around them."

— John S. Aitken, past superintendent

Copyright ©2023, David A. Pickler
Printed in the United States of America.
Title: *Pillars of Purpose: Leadership Lessons for Achieving a Life of Significance*

All rights reserved.
The author retains ownership of all intellectual properties and copyrights to the book. No parts of this book can be reproduced, stored in a retrieval system, or transmitted by any means (written, electronic, digital, photocopy, audio or video recording, stored in a database or otherwise), nor used in a presentation without prior written permission of the copyright holder and the authors, except as permitted under Section 107 or 109 of the 1976 United States Copyright Act.

The Author and Publisher specifically disclaim any liability, loss, or risk which is incurred as consequence, directly or indirectly, from the use and application of any of the contents of this work.

AUTHOR
David A. Pickler
Email: dpickler@PicklerWealthAdvisors.com
Tel: 901.316.0160
www.PicklerWealthAdvisors.com

COVER ART & ILLUSTRATIONS
Cameron Spann
Email: cspann@PicklerWealth Advisors.com

PUBLISHER
High 5 Communications, LLC
Email: info@high5communications.com
Tel: 435.750.0062

Hard Cover Books: $39.95 USD
ISBN: 978-1-945578-21-2
Soft Cover Books: $24.95 USD
ISBN: 978-1-945578-22-9

Pickler Wealth Advisors
1135 Halle Park Circle
Collierville, TN 38017
Tel: 901.316.0160

Securities Disclosure: Securities and advisory services offered through Commonwealth Financial Network®, Member FINRA/SIPC, a Registered Investment Adviser.

The views expressed in the recommended publications are not necessarily the opinion of Commonwealth Financial Network®, and should not be construed directly or indirectly, as an offer to buy or sell any securities mentioned herein. Commonwealth Financial Network® makes no representation as to the completeness or accuracy of information provided in this publication. Nor is the company liable for any direct or indirect, information and programs made available in reading this literature. The information that may be provided is not intended to be a substitute for specific individualized tax, legal, or estate planning advice.

This book contains case studies and is for illustrative purposes only. Actual performance and results will vary. Case studies do not constitute a recommendation as to the suitability of any investment for any person or persons having circumstances similar to those portrayed, and a financial advisor should be consulted.

Pickler Wealth Advisors are dually registered advisors: Registered Representatives and Investment Advisor Representatives. As Investment Advisor Representatives, they are required to act as fiduciaries. Whenever there are reference to "acting as a fiduciary" in this book, they are referring to acting in an advisory capacity.

Dedication

To Our Truest Heroes-Our Teachers

Teachers instill in the children they serve the love of learning and inspire their students to achieve success and significance in life. Through their dedication and passion for education, they spark the flame of knowledge that continues to illuminate our world.

Teachers empower students to fulfill their potential and pursue their dreams. As society's most supportive mentors, they encourage students to believe in the power of the possible.

Teachers also understand that while *learning* represents the "how" of our lives and *knowledge* is the "what," we should all aspire to reach the pinnacle of lifelong learning and knowledge to attain *wisdom*. That is the "why" of our lives.

God Bless our Teachers. Each of you touch eternity. The enduring influence of your passionate service is an inspiration for us all.

Acknowledgements

Each of us is an amalgamation of a lifetime of relationships, influences and experiences. None of us travel this journey of life alone. It is frequently noted that most "first" books are somewhat autobiographical. While I have made a conscious effort not to make this book about me, it is filled with stories about experiences, influences and relationships throughout my life. There are countless people who have been inspirational and significant in my life. For the sake of brevity, I would like to acknowledge and express my appreciation to those who have had the greatest impact on the success of this book.

First, I want to thank my family for a lifetime of love and support. The greatest role I have ever had in my life has been as a dad for my children and now as a "Poppy" for my grandchildren.

Thank you to my professional family at Pickler Wealth Advisors, The Pickler Law Firm, Pickler Accounting Advisors and the American Public Education Foundation. Together we bring to life my vision for building organizations that can make a difference for our clients and community.

Thank you to all our amazing clients. The opportunity to serve as your advocate and advisor every day has been an honor beyond parallel.

Thank you to my collaborators in taking the book from vision to reality:

- Cameron Spann who has been my faithful partner from the book's inception. Thank you for your creativity and your friendship. You have been an incredible soundboard as the project meandered across a wide range of approaches until we finally found our "voice" for this book. Thank you also for your artistic genius, not only as the illustrator of this book, but also for the more than 10 years of creative branding for our firms.

- The amazing team at High 5 Communications. Lyn Fisher, you have been such a tremendous partner, collaborator and editor. Together, we have been able to take a lifetime of stories and some fundamental beliefs about life to build a book that, I hope, will provide value to our readers. Gina Lauer, our editor, and Nicole Coulter, whose early work on this project was a tremendous aid.

- Our incredible group of friends and colleagues who wanted to review our book. Your feedback and constructive criticism was most appreciated. One of the greatest gifts one can give is the gift of time. Thanks to each of you for giving your time to help me in this process: Joe Deitch, you have lived your life with such purpose. You are an inspiration to all who are blessed to have met you. Paula Jacobs, your carefully considered feedback was so impactful. Your professional eye for content and editing was impeccable. Mike McGough, your words of encouragement and support were so appreciated. As an accomplished author and historian, I could only hope that this book will have a fraction of the impact your work has achieved. To my friends Erin Gruwell and Tammy Grissom, thank you for your contributions and kind remarks about our work.

Thank you to the people who have inspired me through the content of their character. To Barry Saunders, my first business partner and a dear father figure; Tracy Speake, one of the most genuinely good men I've ever met; John Aitken, a man who leads with his heart and inspires others; Ron Lollar, my "comrade in arms" in so many fights for public education; Joe Clayton, a man whose faith and purpose defined a life of amazing accomplishments; my friend Phil Shipley, a man who continues to serve Scouting at the highest level across America. Lastly, I'd like to acknowledge my friend, Larry Rice. When Larry wrote the definitive text on divorce law, he acknowledged me even though I had nothing to do with his book. Consider the favor returned.

Finally, thank you to those who will embark on your own journey of discovery by reading this book.

Table of Contents

Dedication vi
Acknowledgements vii
Foreword xi
Preface xiii

SECTION I: Bedrock Principles 1
    1. Power of the Possible 7
    2. Perseverance 19
    3. Passion 31
    4. Integrity 45
    5. Discipline 61

SECTION II: Pillars of Purpose 77
    6. Trust 85
    7. Peace of Mind 101
    8. Problem Solving 119
    9. Advocate & Partner 137
    10. Order & Control 153
    11. Objectivity 169
    12. Navigate Life 185
    13. Educate & Counsel 203
    14. Main Street Values 227

SECTION III. The Pinnacle of Success 247
    15. Accountability 249
    16. Leading a Life of Significance 259

Special Acknowledgements 273
About the Author 277

Table of Contents

Dedication vi
Acknowledgements vii
Foreword ix
Preface xii

SECTION I: Bedrock Principles 1
1. Power of the Positive 2
2. Perseverance 19
3. Passion 35
4. Integrity 46
5. Discipline 61
SECTION II: Pillars of Purpose 79
6. Trust 88
7. Peace of Mind 101
8. Problem Solving 119
9. Advocate & Team 137
10. Oneness of Mind 153
11. Objectivity 169
12. Thoughtfulness 185
13. Educator & Counselor 203
14. Main Street Values 227
SECTION III: The Pinnacle of Purpose 247
15. Accountability 249
16. Leading a Life of Significance 259

Special Acknowledgements 273
About the Author 277

Foreword

When David asked if I would read his book, *Pillars of Purpose*, and offer comments, I didn't quite know what to expect. Crafting a compendium of worldly wisdom is a daunting task. However, to also make it interesting, relevant, thoroughly enjoyable and enormously helpful is a heroic undertaking.

I say this from firsthand experience. Many years ago, I too felt compelled to organize my own hard-won life lessons (let's just say that I had a lot to learn), along with the most compelling advice of others, into a valuable reference manual—something I wish I had throughout my own life. Something that would have shown me the way, turned obstacles into opportunities, and opportunities into successes. And so, it was with enormous curiosity, and a bit of trepidation, that I started *Pillars of Purpose*.

From the very first page, David captured my interest, entertained and educated. Happily, and amazingly, that continued on every subsequent page throughout the entire book. What began as a task quickly transformed into a celebration of life and learning. I was delighted and enriched at every turn. Phew!

Personally, I have little patience for boring books. I'm also not a fan of big books that should have been brief articles. Why do some authors decide to drag it out, holding us hostage while they parse out the occasional nugget? Not so here! *Pillars of Purpose* is overflowing with fascinating stories and valuable advice.

David connects the dots so that we can better understand how problems can be transformed into possibilities. His strategies for success are invaluable. And, while some of the book focuses on wealth management, it's equally applicable to navigating the landmines and springboards that permeate medical, legal, business, personal and interpersonal endeavors. It addresses our universal desire to have safe, successful and fulfilling lives.

But it's so much more than a how-to textbook. David writes from the heart, and in doing so, it stirs our own. This is his love letter to his family, his clients, his community, his country and all humanity. I was caught off guard near the end of the book (in the chapter on Main Street Values) when I found myself clapping at one point. I literally wanted to jump up and give a standing ovation. Don't be surprised if you find yourself doing the same.

And, much to my delight, It's also brimming with wonderful quotations that augment and add color to his points. A great quote can quickly communicate complicated ideas with just a few well-chosen words. We all have our favorites, and you're about to discover a treasure trove to add to your collection. One in particular, from Denzel Washington, applies perfectly to David: *"At the end of the day, it's not about what you have or even what you've accomplished… it's about who you've lifted up, who you've made better. It's about what you've given back."*

Pillars of Purpose is David Pickler's gorgeous gift to all of us, and its impact will be enormous.

While I have known David for many years in a professional capacity (he is one of the more accomplished and respected financial advisors within Commonwealth Financial Network), I had little idea of the true breadth and depth of his passions and accomplishments. Prepare to be wowed. Plus, now he can add "celebrated author" to that list.

I also want to thank David for giving me this opportunity to learn from his experiences, and for sharing so openly about his life. That was the big surprise bonus of this book—getting to know David Pickler, a most extraordinary man, who shows us time and again what passion, purpose, perseverance and partnership can accomplish. He is a guiding light with a warm and wonderful heart. I can't wait to see what he does next!

Joseph Deitch

Founder and Chair of Commonwealth Financial Network® and The Elevate Prize
Author of *Elevate: An Essential Guide to Life*

Preface

"The purpose of life is not to be happy. It is to be useful, to be honorable, to be compassionate, to have it make some difference that you have lived and lived well."

– Ralph Waldo Emerson

While I agree with Ralph Waldo Emerson that the purpose of life is to be useful and to make a difference, I believe that these efforts to live such a life *will* lead to true happiness. True happiness is the result of living our lives with purpose.

Four years ago, when I decided to write this book, my initial plan was to share some of my life experiences and philosophies of life with the hope that they could be instructional and helpful for my children and grandchildren. But as I began the actual composition of this book, I found myself struggling to find the right approach to telling my story. The entire project felt uncomfortable. After several failed attempts to progress on this writing journey, I finally had an epiphany—a moment of clarity. The project was not achieving traction because I realized that I was focused too much on me and my story and not enough on the countless people who have shaped and influenced my life. I needed to change the conversation from "me" to "we."

I have been blessed with an inner voice that sets off alarms in my head if I believe I'm talking too much about myself. We've all experienced conversations with people who seem to relish every opportunity to talk about their favorite subject: themselves. While people with a healthy sense of self can be amazing leaders and accomplished achievers, somehow that singular focus on "me" can be off-putting. I would rather ask questions to learn about the lives and interests of others than to talk about myself. The good Lord gave each of us two ears and one mouth. We could all benefit from listening more and talking less.

When I changed the focus of the book from "me" to "we," an amazing transformation occurred. The words began to flow, my creative energies mobilized, and I began to find my "voice" for the book. My authentic messaging became clear. This would become a book about empowering people to find their passion, their purpose and, hopefully, provide some guidance toward building lives of true significance. I would try to take the lessons of my life—my life stories—to illustrate how others can achieve purpose and significance in their lives.

My life stories then became interwoven with those of other people whom I admire, conveying a bigger picture. I discovered a much larger purpose than I had initially anticipated. During the almost four years it has taken to write this book, it has transformed from a memoir into a how-to guide to help people better navigate their own life journeys.

Where Ordinary Becomes Extraordinary

There's only one thing that kept me from being the starting first baseman of the St. Louis Cardinals—a complete lack of talent.

As a youth, my baseball coach once told me he had never seen someone more determined to play the game, yet struggle so hard and still lack any significant talent for playing the game. But what I did possess was a dogged determination and perseverance to play the very best I could. I learned how to master the small elements of the game. Baseball is a thinking-man's sport, and while over the years I would almost never be among the most skilled players, I relied on my intellect to become a smarter player. This allowed me to play the game I loved into young adulthood.

You might say my true talent is my enthusiasm and ability to get things done in spite of the obstacles I've encountered. Fundamental to the philosophy I hope to share with you, I've always believed that ordinary people can do extraordinary things. And quite frankly, I'm living proof.

In my view, there is nothing unique or uncommon about me. Like so many others, I wasn't born into a family of wealth or privilege. I was born and spent the majority of my childhood in the small town of Jonesboro, Arkansas. My family was firmly entrenched in modest middle-class circumstances.

However, I have been blessed with extraordinary self-discipline and focus. I continually strive to expand my knowledge, or as I'm fond of saying, "to sharpen the saw." I haven't let fear of the unknown deter my ambitions and often have led the charge on new projects that some had thought unattainable.

My strong drive has allowed me to build my successful family of firms, Pickler Companies in Collierville, Tennessee, where we strive every day to put our clients' interests first, help them navigate life's uncertainties and empower their dreams—the things that truly matter. It has been the driving force behind my effort to support my family in their heroic volunteering activities. It's led me to fight hard for things I believe in: my community and nationally as an advocate for public education. While I've sometimes butted heads with entrenched forces, I've learned to seek alliances to help accomplish goals. (It's what got me through night law school shortly after beginning my career as a financial advisor.)

I've constantly felt the need to break free from the pack mentality, both professionally and in my passion for service. I've spearheaded capital-funding projects for schools and other non-profit projects that no one had been willing to see to a successful conclusion, and our team got them across the finish line. I've led my colleagues in tackling issues while serving on the school board that no sane person would want to touch with a ten-foot pole. You might suspect I suffered some kind of childhood head trauma given the battles I've voluntarily undertaken in my "second and third jobs." I've relentlessly pursued my passions—especially my passion for my clients and for public education. I hold myself to a high standard of accountability, and I push those around me to raise their level, too.

Why do I do it?

Some of my guiding principles include:

- **The first law of motion.** Newton nailed it. Objects in motion tend to stay in motion. Objects at rest tend to stay at rest. Throughout our entire lives we're engaged in a battle against inertia. It requires a catalyst to break free and to help others break free, as well.

- **A focus on greatness.** Most sales-training and personal development programs focus on finding ways to improve in the areas where you struggle. Instead, my focus has always been on finding the things I'm good at and then striving to maximize my capabilities. While I had great passion for the game, I knew I would never be a professional baseball player. Quite frankly, I didn't have the talent. It's about awareness. Look for the things you have an interest and talent in, then strive to become the very best you can be by taking your natural abilities and developing them—moving from good to great. If you encounter a pit and polish it with all your might, it's still a pit. If you encounter a lump of coal and apply enough pressure, over time you'll end up with a sparkling diamond. Don't polish pits, make diamonds.

- **Our measuring sticks**. Only compare yourself against yourself. You are the barometer. You are your own measuring stick for success and significance. Too many times we focus on how other people are performing. Instead, our focus should always be on becoming the best version of ourselves. The standards we use to measure our performance should only be dictated by the person staring back at us in the mirror. Once I figured this out early in my career, I never looked back. I learned to define success on my own terms, and almost universally adopted a higher standard of expectations, beliefs and passionate pursuit.

- **We all have time**. We all have 24 hours in a day. It's how we use those hours that counts. Time is a gift from God and is one of our most precious assets. How we invest this gift will make all the difference in our lives, both personally and professionally. It's easy to write checks, but we give more when we give our presence.

- **Find a need.** To be successful and significant, you must first be aware of opportunities to serve your family, your business associates, your clients and your community. Each of us has the ability to be truly engaged and present in our communities. Often through engagement and presence, we can discover opportunities and needs that we can contribute to and will benefit from our assistance.

Cementing Your Legacy

You'll soon notice in reading this book that I don't define the terms *success* and *significance* synonymously. Material success is just a part of significance. Living a life of significance requires digging deeper into your purpose.

In this book I hope to show you how to live your purpose. I share examples from the lives of impactful individuals throughout history while relating purposeful stories from my own life. The stories within the book—whether about my own accomplishments or those of others—reflect my values and beliefs. I'm a graduate of the "school of hard knocks." I share these stories to teach, advocate and inspire you to reach for the stars. I hope to give you the tools to make your life journey easier and more impactful.

Please know everyone's purpose is different. That's what makes us unique. People will be drawn to your authenticity if you pursue your purpose with passion. Your *why* is your ultimate differentiator.

My personality, vision and values reflect the things I believe in. Our wealth advisory business is personal. We're a Main Street firm, a so-called "mom-and-pop shop." We're not a Wall Street firm. Our businesses reflect my life and my family's. It's also a reflection of the people who share these responsibilities with us—our team. Our clients do business with us because they relate to who we are and why we do what we do.

As someone who naturally excels in the role of protector and advocate, I realized at a certain point in my career that many of my clients were women who were struggling because of the death or divorce of a spouse. Others are people who have experienced difficult transitions and losses and need an empathetic ear to help them weather the storm. I'm always grateful to be there for them, and to build trust and relationships with those who are going through these tough times. That's why, when we developed our Unique Value Proposition (UVP), we chose "Our family delivering solutions for your family."

By writing this book, I hope to assist those who aspire to make a difference in their families, professions, communities and in the world at large.

What initially started as a memoir project I could leave to my children and grandkids about the lessons I'd learned in life and the principles that mattered to me—how they could be more successful and significant—has become a passion to share these timeless truths with everyone.

As we progress through this book together, each step will move us closer to achieving the pinnacle of our life's journey. The Bedrock Principles in Section One help us identify our passions, and the Pillars of Purpose in Section Two turn our vision to reality through daily actions. In the last section, once we've adopted the Pillars of Purpose and embraced Accountability, we learn how we can become truly significant in others' lives. As Emerson said, the purpose of life is *"to be useful, to be honorable, to be compassionate, to have it make some difference that you have lived and lived well."*

It all starts with the WHY ...

SECTION I
THE BEDROCK PRINCIPLES

Power of the Possible

Perseverance

Passion

Integrity

Discipline

Pillars of Purpose

Section I
INTRODUCTION

*"The two most important days in your life
are the day you are born and the day you find out why."*
– Mark Twain

I've always believed that if you want to build a life of significance, you need to start with a vision—a blueprint.

That vision must be anchored to something you truly believe in, something that will give you the strength of conviction to weather adversity. Think of this powerful belief as being like the foundation of a building—the height and strength of the building depend entirely on the sureness of its foundation.

We've all heard the parable of the two men who built their homes, one on rock and the other on sand. When the rain came down, the streams rose and the winds blew against the houses. The house built on a foundation of rock did not fall, while the house built on sand "fell with a crash."

We see this powerful illustration of sound building techniques playing out in modern construction. While most of us stare in awe at the height of a skyscraper, the true engineering marvel occurs deep below ground level in the unseen foundation that supports the towering structure.

In Chicago, for instance, the massive 1,451-foot Willis Tower stands on 114 reinforced concrete caissons set into solid bedrock beneath the earth's surface, while the 1,084-foot Petronas Towers in Malaysia descend 180 feet into the bedrock. Without a strong foundation, skyscrapers might crumble in a storm or tumble during an earthquake.

So it is with our lives. Our vision or blueprint of life has to begin with a well-formulated plan built on a strong foundation. I call this foundation the "Bedrock Principles." The five principles listed on page 1 form the core fundamentals that will help us live a life of purpose. They help us tap into the *why* of our existence.

THE BEDROCK PRINCIPLES

In the next five chapters, we'll discuss each of these principles: 1) Power of the Possible, 2) Perseverance, 3) Passion, 4) Integrity and 5) Discipline. We'll explore how they can help you build a solid foundation for turning your vision into reality. As we do this, I'm asking you to reach deep inside yourself to answer these questions: "Why am I here?" and "What is my purpose?" As John Soforic, author of The Wealthy Gardener once said, "What matters most in a purposeful life is giving one's fullest strength to one's cause. Great efforts assure satisfaction, while common efforts can lead to regrets."

Once you know your *why*, you need to pursue it with determination and embrace it with passion. Remember, anything is possible if you have the courage to pursue it. You've just got to take the necessary steps to make it happen.

Overcoming Adversity

Remember the famous Biblical story where Goliath towered over David? The only weapon David had to fight this giant was a bag full of rocks, a sling and a strong arm. However, his strongest weapon was the strength of his belief. Instead of being intimidated by Goliath's large size, he faced the giant with courage and commitment and was able to overcome him.

Having a strong foundation doesn't mean you'll never face challenges.

Section I. Bedrock Principles

But like David, when you arm yourself with a strong belief that anything is possible and a commitment to make it happen, you can turn your goals into reality. The five Bedrock Principles are the foundation upon which you can build a successful life. The strength of that foundation will help you endure difficult times.

Viktor Frankl, an Austrian psychologist and Holocaust survivor, shared the secret for enduring challenging times in his brilliant memoir, *Man's Search for Meaning*. In it he writes:

> "(My) experiences of (Auschwitz) show that man does have a choice of action. There were enough examples, often of a heroic nature, which proved that apathy could be overcome, irritability suppressed. Man can preserve a vestige of spiritual freedom, of independence of mind, even in such terrible conditions of psychic and physical stress."

While Frankl couldn't control his physical environment or the actions of the people around him, he did control his reaction to external stimuli. Similarly, we can control how we react to life's hurdles. When the road we travel is rutted and strewn with rocks, knowing our *why* will help us step over or walk around life's rough spots.

Discover Your Purpose

We each have the ability to discover our purpose in life and to embrace it with every fiber of our being.

Discovering our purpose is a personal journey for each of us. Again, the foundation that prepares us for this journey will give us the strength to endure the storms. Just as the massive root system of the tree is its lifeblood and support, the Bedrock Principles support our vision of life, our belief in what is possible—they help make our dreams and aspirations a reality.

As we continue through this book, ask yourself:

- Do you seize opportunities instead of being haunted by "what ifs" or regrets? (Power of the Possible)
- Do you overcome challenges by staying focused on your goals? (Perseverance)

Pillars of Purpose

- Have you found what motivates you, fulfills you and makes you happy? (Passion)
- Do you stay true to your beliefs? (Integrity)
- Do you hold yourself accountable? (Discipline)

The above questions are an introspective review of what you are already doing right and what you need to improve. If you answered "yes" to each of the questions, you're on your way to building a life of purpose. You've discovered your *why*, and the *why* will hold you accountable.

While it's sometimes hard to be honest with ourselves about our weaknesses, growth occurs only when we acknowledge and strive to improve them. Remember, it's not about wanting "more," rather it's about treating every moment as a precious gift. You were created for a purpose and once you realize that purpose, you'll be set free to enjoy the life you desire.

Enjoy the journey.

Chapter 1
POWER OF THE POSSIBLE

"If you can dream it, you can do it."
– Walt Disney

Every great endeavor starts with belief. A belief in yourself. A belief you can do it. A belief that the endeavor is worth doing. Belief will help you find a way through difficult times. It is truly the most basic building block in life. You can't get anything off the ground unless you believe your endeavor is both *possible* ... and *essential*.

I call this first Bedrock Principle, "Power of the Possible." And it's where the magic begins.

When considering "Power of the Possible" and the other four Bedrock Principles that will be illuminated in the first section of this book, I'll be asking you to ponder the great *why* questions in your life: Why are you here on this planet? What is your purpose? What drives you? These powerful questions form your *why*. They are the basis of your belief system and define your core values. And those values help create an unshakeable foundation.

Pillars of Purpose

The expression *"what is my why"* is a shorthand I've developed over the years in my personal life and in my business to describe the powerful beliefs that motivate me and cause me to want to get out of bed each day. My *why* anchors and inspires me—much like that foundation of a skyscraper we talked about in the Introduction to the Bedrock Principles. It includes my family, my faith, my devotion to my firm, my staff, my clients, my community and my support for public education, as I'll explain later in this chapter and in this book.

What motivates you may differ entirely from my *whys*. But your *whys* will help you dig deep into the bedrock of your soul to create a life of significance. Your *whys* or beliefs will help you create a vision for what is possible in your life and will give you the strength of conviction to make your vision happen. Your *whys* give rise to Power of the Possible.

> *Your "whys" will help you dig deep into the bedrock of your soul to create a life of significance.*

From a Creative Mind to an Empire

I opened this chapter with a quote from Walt Disney that truly sums up this principle I call Power of the Possible. *"If you can dream it, you can do it."* Walt Disney surely epitomized turning possibility into action. We all know him as the iconic founder of an incredibly successful and innovative film studio and theme park empire. Over his long career, Walt Disney and his team of "imagineers" built some of the Happiest Places on Earth. But his dream started as a young boy peddling his artwork to neighbors. Then, as a humble animator in Chicago, he dreamed of bringing his cartoon characters to life. He was fired from his first newspaper car-

1. Power of the Possible

toonist job for what someone foolishly believed was his "lack of imagination." Still, he remained enthralled with moving sketches of mice, ducks and dogs.

Disney overcame countless failures, kept the courage of his convictions and used them as catalysts for his goals. He believed in continually stretching himself and turning his dreams into reality. With some help from his brother Roy, who was gifted with financial acumen, and other key individuals he met along the way, Walt's infectious enthusiasm for creating beloved characters and family entertainment led to unimaginable success that has blessed millions. His belief in the power of his own imagination and the power of personal connections enabled him to discover his *why*.

Overcoming Fear of Change to Embrace Possibilities

Just as Walt Disney started with a vision of bringing animation to life and watched these dreams grow in unimaginable ways over the decades, similar choices greet each of us every day in our lives and professions. You never know where a golden opportunity might arise, where your purpose will intersect with your destiny. Often, people who can lead you in the right direction will suddenly show up in your life—if you let them.

Life offers boundless choices and opportunities, and your only limitation is your own imagination. Some people limit the possibilities in their lives when they let fear interfere with their dreams. Failing to seize opportunities and fearing uncomfortable changes that might result, they let their unfounded fear of failure control their destiny.

Gustavo Razzetti, CEO of *Fearless Culture* and author of *Stretch for Change, Stretch Your Mind*, writes, "*We fear change because we can't anticipate the outcome. However, staying put can be riskier than changing. Fear is an emotion that gets in the way—we lose clarity about our potential.*"[1]

On a positive note, Razzetti says we can train our flexible and adaptive minds to actually thrive on change. Welcoming new horizons is an essential element behind Power of the Possible. We only fail when we fail to follow our dreams.

---

1 Gustavo Razzetti; *How to Overcome the Fear of Change,* Psychology Today, https://www.psychologytoday.com/us/blog/the-adaptive-mind/201809/how-overcome-the-fear-change

Pillars of Purpose

By envisioning where we want to be and what we want to do we can retrain our brains to recognize and enthusiastically embrace possibilities when they come our way. This retooling provides us with the courage we need to accept change as an inevitable and valuable part of life.

I've tried to live my life never looking back with regret, or asking those tragic questions, "What if I had only taken that chance?" "What if I had seized that moment?" "What if…?"

Actively saying "yes" to intriguing possibilities (with no fear of failure) has paid dividends for me time and again. I'm fortunate to have personally experienced Power of the Possible many times throughout my life. However, one of my favorite stories involved a series of small steps. With the "big picture" in mind, this experience forever changed my life and positively influenced many others.

This story started with my foundational belief in public education and led to an appearance on the Red Carpet at the Academy Awards as the guest of a celebrated director.

A Red Carpet Journey

So how did I wind up on the Red Carpet in Hollywood at the 86th Academy Awards on Sunday, March 2, 2014?

It certainly didn't start out in glamorous fashion, but it did start out with a powerful belief. In 1998, I ran for and was elected to serve as a member of the local Shelby County Board of Education, a position I ultimately held for 16 years, winning re-election four times.

I believe in public education. It is one of my core *whys*. I had seen how public education transformed my life, helping me rise above a challenging childhood and become successful in my own business. I had seen my own two children thrive in public school and believe every child in America deserves the opportunity to learn, no matter their race, creed, gender or socioeconomic status.

When I ran for the position, I knew I wanted to make a difference. Public schools face continual shortfalls in funding and challenges to maintain-

1. Power of the Possible

ing academic excellence. I served on the board with six other members of the community, and we, along with the superintendent, set educational policies, oversaw hiring and negotiated school budgets.

In 1999, just one year into my term, my peers on the county school board entrusted me to serve as our chairman. While serving in this leadership position, I became acquainted with an organization that would play a big role in my life, the Tennessee School Boards Association. TSBA provides training and legislative advocacy for the 141 school boards across my state. I served on their board and eventually became president of that organization while still running my business and presiding over the local school board.

After several years with TSBA at the state level, I took on even more responsibilities with the National School Boards Association (NSBA), a federation of state school board associations based in Alexandria, Virginia, and representing approximately 15,000 school boards and 54 million public school children. NSBA helps those school boards by shaping federal education policy, raising public awareness of critical issues such as school safety and championing the mission of public education to prepare our nation's youth for the future.

Starting out as a regional director of NSBA, I eventually became president. During my tenure, I logged hundreds of thousands of air miles traveling to all 50 states and several countries. In the fall of 2012, when my peers chose me to represent them as president, I had begun pondering how I could make a big difference in my new role.

My term began in March 2013, so in December 2012, I made a list of the various entities that care deeply about or benefit most from public education. I've always believed that partnering with the right people can lead to great accomplishments. I wanted my year as NSBA president to result in building an Army of Advocates that could create a resolute voice that would spread a profound message for public education, one that could change our world, one child at a time.

As you will see, tapping into the power of connections is essential to fully realizing Power of the Possible.

Pillars of Purpose

Building an Army of Advocates Creates Possibilities

If you want to build an Army of Advocates, I suppose you could call the Army. Instead, I decided to start with the Navy. Not far from my home in suburban Memphis resides one of the largest Naval bases in the country—the Naval Support Activity Mid-South Naval Base. This fact might surprise you given that Memphis is located on the shores of the Mississippi River, hundreds of miles from a major body of water. Opening its gates in the autumn of 1917 and known originally as Park Field, the Millington, Tennessee base trained pilots for World War I. It became one of the most important bases in the world, training both U.S. and allied troops. By World War II, and despite its landlocked location, the base served as a hub for naval aviation.

These days, the NSA Mid-South continues to serve as the headquarters for the Bureau of Navy Personnel, while providing logistic and operational help for additional command units there. Fifteen flag admirals serve at Millington.

As I considered which organizations might be natural allies for public education, I started thinking how joining the military remains a viable option for some high school graduates. *Wouldn't it be cool if we could build a partnership with the Navy Recruiting Command headquartered at the Millington base?*

I decided to be bold. I called and asked for the executive officer of recruiting. They connected me to the chief deputy to the admiral for naval recruiting. I told him who I was and that I was interested in forging a relationship between the Navy and public education. I explained that this alliance could provide rewarding career options to graduating seniors and would also be a source of quality recruits for the Navy.

This led to a conversation with the admiral himself who immediately expressed excitement in partnering with us. I told the admiral about our NSBA annual meeting coming up in five months in San Diego, a significant base of operation for the Navy, and invited him to speak at the event. Enthusiastically he accepted and arranged for the official Navy Band to perform as well.

In April 2013, thousands of association members attended the hugely

1. Power of the Possible

successful event. Afterward, Naval personnel escorted a few dozen of my NSBA board and staff members on a tour of a Navy destroyer in San Diego Bay. This incredibly unique experience inspired board members to seek out military partnerships in their own districts. But it also led to something I could have never predicted.

The Power of Just Saying "Yes!"

One of the keys to realizing Power of the Possible, is learning to say "yes" to opportunities.

As the destroyer tour ended, our guide, Al Hoy (A. Hoy, what a perfect Navy name for an Army guy) who helped the Navy with tours pulled me aside and said, "I'm gonna give you a call. No matter what I ask, you have to say 'yes.'" Now that's not normally how I do business, but I thought I would play along.

Three weeks later Al called me. "What are you doing on Wednesday?" he asked. "I need you to come to San Diego. Remember, you promised you would say 'yes.'"

On arrival, Al treated me to a VIP experience I'll never forget. We ate dinner at a Marine bar near the base and spent the night in the Navy Seals' barracks. We arose at 0500 (5 a.m.), received a briefing at Naval Base Point Loma, and suited up in full gear for what seemed like and was an actual military training mission. We boarded a Navy COD (Carrier Onboard Delivery) transporter, flew for an hour, and then completed an abrupt tail-hook landing on the USS Ronald Reagan in the middle of the Pacific Ocean. I've never experienced anything like it. Far from smooth, it felt like a head-on collision off a five-story building. Talk about an adrenalin rush!

From our position on the carrier, we observed F-16 pilots taking off every 30 seconds and I mingled with XOs and chief officers. I experienced a close-up view of our heroic Naval aviators that *Top Gun* fans could only imagine. In fact, at times it felt like the F-16s might sweep us out into the ocean if we didn't duck.

I was certainly grateful I had said "yes" to this opportunity.

Pillars of Purpose

The Power of Connections Fuels Even More Possibilities

But that was just the beginning. This whirlwind experience spurred even more opportunities to build my army of public-school advocates. While on the Navy training mission, I met a fellow VIP passenger, Ron King, an insurance executive from California. We discussed how NSBA could form partnerships with the insurance companies he represented.

A month later, Ron called saying a friend of his, Greg Bell, would like to meet me. A graduate of Notre Dame and former football star, Greg played 10 years with the Los Angeles Rams and Buffalo Bills.

We agreed to meet in South Bend, Indiana. After touring the Notre Dame campus, we attended a football game as VIP guests where he introduced me to the Fighting Irish coach, Brian Kelly. Watching the game on the sidelines, we discussed how we could build a partnership for public education, leveraging the famed Notre Dame alumni network.

About the same time, an acquaintance from Kentucky called to say he was trying to develop an educational partnership with Montel Williams, the TV talk-show host and retired Marine. Montel, like myself, has a passion for education. My friend knew of my work on the school board and suggested I meet with Montel to discuss how we could leverage this relationship on behalf of NSBA.

Two weeks later, Ron King, the insurance executive, invited me to attend a PGA golf tournament and education forum in Southern California sponsored by the Clinton Foundation. You may recall that I met Ron on the aircraft carrier, and he was aware of my background growing up in Arkansas. He also knew I had been deeply rooted in local politics, and I had worked on several of Bill Clinton's political campaigns, which I'll discuss further on in the book.

At the event, I was totally surprised to see Montel Williams coming toward me with his beautiful wife. I introduced myself.

"Wait, you're Pickler? We're supposed to be talking," he said, to my amazement.

He had heard about my work with public education from our mutual acquaintance. It was truly amazing that just one call to the Navy had cre-

1. Power of the Possible

ated all these connections.

To make a long story short, Montel told me about a movie director who wanted to make his historical movie available to schools across America. He phoned me a few days after we met and wondered if I could help make that happen. I explained that if the NSBA board agreed to distribute it, we would need thousands of copies of the book the movie was based on and curriculum materials for the teachers across America.

In a surprisingly short time, the production company created the required teaching aids and were ready to show the movie in 15,000 high schools nationwide. However, I still needed to get approval from the NSBA board members. We had star power on our side.

Sometimes Power of the Possible can feel like a snowball running down a hill, gathering momentum and size as it rolls. Similarly, this "unlikely" story swelled as it rolled on.

A Red Carpet Experience

Montel Williams joined me at the next NSBA board meeting in D.C. to tell them about the proposed project, *12 Years a Slave*, directed by British filmmaker Steve McQueen. Needless to say, the board approved the project. Soon after (January 2014), Montel appeared on CNN with Piers Morgan to announce the school partnership, crediting me and my work with NSBA as being instrumental in making it come about. The movie became a blockbuster, earning nine Academy Award nominations.

A few weeks later, Melanie Holloway, a studio assistant at Fox Searchlight Films, called me. "Steve (McQueen) wants to meet you."

I said, "Sure, let's make it happen."

She said, "You don't understand. He wants you to be his guest at the Academy Awards this Sunday."

While I was honored by this incredible invitation, I was also deeply conflicted. As you will learn later in the book, my team and I had been working for nearly a year on a leadership conference in Gettysburg, Pennsylvania, that same weekend. For me to be in L.A. Sunday night would not only require a massive logistical restructuring, but it would also require significant planning for the leadership workshop to continue, as planned, in my absence. Despite these overwhelming challenges, all the stakeholders involved in the event encouraged me to make every effort possible to be in L.A. and represent NSBA at the Academy Awards. It was an exercise in contingency planning and logistics that would have made George Patton proud.

My last act, before leaving Gettysburg at 3 a.m. Sunday morning, was to grab a handful of bright red "Stand Up 4 Public Schools" wristbands.

After a crazy series of cab rides, multiple flights, little sleep and the coordination of our tuxedos being delivered to the hotel, Cameron Spann, my chief branding officer, and I found ourselves in a limo heading to the Academy Awards. (Cameron had joined my team in May of 2013, just after I had become president of NSBA.) Arriving at the Dolby Theater in Hollywood, we were experiencing the *almost* out-of-body experience of walking the red carpet when my phone began to ring. It was Melanie from Fox Searchlight. "Steve wants to know where you are!" she exclaimed. Cameron and I made our way over to a separate area of the red carpet dedicated for Academy Award nominees. Upon arrival, the British-born Steve McQueen proclaimed, "Man, can I give you a hug?" After brief comments between the two of us, I offered him one of the red wristbands as a token of friendship and good luck charm for the ceremony.

The whole experience seemed like a dream. We continued to walk the red carpet and rubbed shoulders with Kurt Russell, Goldie Hawn, Amy Adams, Anna Kendrick and other movie stars we'd previously only seen on the big screen. It was surreal.

Shortly after the ceremony began, my phone began blowing up with messages saying, "Steve is wearing the wristband!" It was the red NSBA wristband I had gifted him earlier. That evening, Steve was nominated for two awards: Best Director and Best Picture. As the ceremony progressed, I started asking myself, "How cool would it be if Steve won and was pictured with my wristband on?" It came time for the Best Director category, and Alfonso Cuarón's name was called for his film *Gravity*. Then came time for the final award of the evening, Best Picture. In the blink of an eye, it happened … to thunderous applause, Steve won the hallowed award for his film *12 Years a Slave*. However, the ultimate pay-

1. Power of the Possible

off for me occurred when McQueen went on stage to accept the award. He as well as Brad Pitt, co-producer and one of the stars of the film, approached the podium to accept the Oscar. Steve lifted the award into the air in a display of triumph. Lifting the award exposed the bright red NSBA "good luck token" on his wrist to millions of viewers worldwide. My phone lit up in a flurry of excited messages as pictures from the event began to post online. Social media and entertainment reporters started picking up on this small promotional opportunity for public education. Even our local newspaper ran a story about it above the fold with the title "Pickler Wristband Oscar Worthy."

This story exemplifies Power of the Possible. How a simple phone call to a local Navy base and trying to build a partnership led to a series of steps that culminated into walking the red carpet and a securing a public-relations victory for public education. Each step along the way served as its own catalyst to continue the journey on Power of the Possible. If you're willing to take the risk to do something, there is no limit to how far your dreams will take you … perhaps even to the Academy Awards!

It all started with a belief—and a vision.

Vision and Courage = Endless Possibilities

> "The journey of a thousand miles begins with one step."
> —Lao Tzu, Chinese philosopher

My point in sharing this long story was to illustrate Power of the Possible, and how belief backed by small fearless actions can lead to huge opportunities. A journey that began with a simple phone call to a Naval Recruiting Command led to every school receiving a child-appropriate digital download and DVD of an award-winning film and copies of the book. Additionally, Montel Williams now serves as a board member of the American Public Education Foundation, my educational non-profit organization. This all happened during the 14 months leading up to and coinciding with my term as president of NSBA.

What if I had let fear deter me from reaching out to potential allies? What if I had said "no" to the impromptu trip to San Diego three weeks after our national board meeting there or to the inconvenient flight from Get-

Pillars of Purpose

tysburg to Los Angeles for the Oscars?

You cannot build a life of significance without a belief in Power of the Possible. It is a key ingredient for building a strong foundation to support your *why*.

Just as my belief in Power of the Possible has given me courage to overcome the numerous obstacles I've faced, it can do the same for you if you open yourself up to truly believing.

I encourage you to dig deep within your soul as you ask yourself:

- What possibilities am I leaving on the table in my life?
- Am I allowing "what ifs" to motivate me or are my "what ifs" filled with regrets?
- What steps do I need to take to ensure I am fully engaging Power of the Possible?"

By having a strong conviction of your *why* and believing in Power of the Possible, you too can turn a belief into reality, one step at a time. You have the power to make it happen!

Chapter 2
PERSEVERANCE

*"Success is never final and failure never fatal.
It's courage that counts."*
– Sir Winston Churchill

Once we envision what is possible, achieving our goals requires focus, discipline and the determination to make it happen. I like to think of this Bedrock Principle as Perseverance. It's what helps us achieve our goals. It's the high-octane engine that propels us toward life's purpose.

To achieve greatness, you need to steadily move the needle toward your goals. Perseverance requires grinding it out, working through brutal schedules, overcoming bitter disappointment and applying a never-say-die attitude. If you set high expectations for yourself and persevere, there's nothing you can't accomplish, as countless examples from history attest.

Consider Thomas Edison. Just three months into his formal education, his teachers told him he was "too stupid to learn anything." He would spend the rest of his life proving them wrong. Self-educated, he spent countless hours in the library reading mostly scientific books. He ultimately secured more than 1,000 patents as America's most famous inventor, and he liked to remind everyone that after approximately 1,000 unsuccessful attempts, he invented the light bulb on his 1,001st try.

Thomas A. Edison once said, *"Many of life's failures are people who did not realize how close they were to success when they gave up."*

J.K. Rowling, author of the popular *Harry Potter* series is another prime example of a person who refused to give up. A divorced, single mom, she couldn't afford a computer. Instead, she used an old typewriter to write her first novel. Publishers rejected the manuscript 12 times before one finally accepted it. Now, having sold more than a half-billion books, she is a best-known author and one of the richest women in the world.

Sharing her secret for persevering with others, she said, *"Failure is so important. We speak about success all the time. It is the ability to resist failure or use failure that often leads to great success."*

Of course, one of my favorite examples of perseverance and never giving up comes from the world of sports. As head basketball coach at North Carolina State University, Jim Valvano led NC State's Wolfpack in one of the greatest Cinderella victories in college basketball history. Prior to the game, Valvano told his team: *"If you think we have come all this way, won all these close games, and made it to the national championship game just to hold the ball in front of 50-million people you are out of your minds."*

True to his words, he and his team gave the sports world an example of perseverance they will never forget. With only four seconds remaining in the game and the score tied at 52, Wolfpack player Dereck Whittenburg fired up a 35-foot desperation airball. Grabbing the rebound, teammate Lorenzo Charles astounded viewers as he dunked the ball, sealing their destiny as winners of the 1983 NCAA Championship.

While Valvano was known for his ability to encourage exceptional performance in others and to persevere, he showed even greater courage after his coaching days. Diagnosed with cancer at the age of 46, Valvano announced during his speech at the inaugural 1993 ESPY awards that he would be launching the Jimmy V Foundation for cancer research. It was there that he uttered these iconic words:

2. Perseverance

"Don't give up, don't ever give up. That's what I'm going to try to do every minute that I have left. I will thank God for the day and the moment I have ..."

He died of cancer less than two months later. Today, his legacy lives on through his foundation, and every year the ESPY Awards presents the Jimmy V Award for Perseverance in his honor.

Every time I hear his speech rebroadcasted, I think of Winston Churchill's similar plea to his countrymen to "never give up" during the dark days of World War II.

None of these individuals allowed others to intimidate them or deter them from their path. They had the courage to keep pushing harder after a loss and to never surrender to despair. The world remembers those who persist, who show a fighting spirit and overcome adversity.

Persistence in Fighting for Educational Excellence

As Coach Jimmy V faced the "fight of his life" in 1993, I faced my most severe test of character in 2010, when a long-brewing local political battle threatened the future of public education in my county. As mentioned in the previous chapter, I'm passionate about public education and about creating a brighter future for school children.

When it came to this particular public education fight, lots of people were involved, and it took everything we had to win this fight. I can't think of a better example of persistence.

From my early years, I'd learned that if I were to achieve anything in life, I needed to make it happen through my own effort. My parents struggled with financial issues throughout their lives. Teaching us as children about financial accountability was never a priority. My siblings and I weren't taught to save or invest. But these negative examples ironically engrained in me the importance of holding myself accountable. Accountability is the glue that holds your dreams together in spite of obstacles. From a young age, whatever I set out to do, I wanted to excel at, to rise above difficulty. These life lessons served me well time and again in my life, and certainly as chairman of the board for the Shelby County School Board—a position I held for 12 years.

Pillars of Purpose

Like individuals, schools need accountability to thrive. Accountability becomes easier when you share a commitment to excellence with other civic leaders and volunteers. I felt so fortunate to find that on the Shelby County School Board.

I started serving on the Board in 1998. At that time, we prided ourselves in family and parental engagement and in our growing diversity. During my time on the board, we worked strenuously to overcome the racial animosities of the past while striving to maintain our high standards of academic excellence. Eventually we became the only school district in America to rate in the top 100 in district enrollment *and* academic achievement. Moreover, we strived to address the challenges of at-risk students. Nearly half of our students resided in homes that met the federal definition of poverty even though there was growing affluence in the suburbs as well. We created a successful blend of leadership, accountability and a commitment to excellence.

Unfortunately, right next to us the Memphis City Schools lacked those positive virtues. The members struggled when it came to creating positive learning environments for the students they served. Because of this, we began witnessing a growing rift between urban and suburban schools. Families started moving out of the urban center of the county into the half dozen bedroom communities we served, seeking better quality schools.

Persisting Through Continual Budget Wars

This migration that started as a trickle eventually became a flood, leaving only the poorest residents who couldn't afford to relocate. The Memphis City School System that previously had catered to the children of the wealthy elite in the late 1800s had seen its demographics change precipitously in the last five decades. The catalyst for this change was a combination of urban flight and increased mobility due to shifting socioeconomics, as well as racial polarization brought on by court ordered busing. It now served a population that was 90% poor and struggling academically. With 125,000 students and 200 schools, it remained among the most populated school districts in the country.

As more and more families with school-age children relocated to the suburbs, the Memphis City School board faced budget problems—similar to

2. Perseverance

the City of Memphis itself. Much of its budget problems stemmed from lack of leadership and accountability.

Each time Memphis faced a budget crisis, the mayor and city council would annex more land (and property taxes) from the smaller communities and unincorporated land into the municipality. During the time I served on the school board, Memphis engaged in six annexations—taking land, students, schools, and tax base away from the Shelby County School system.

That created a burden for us as suburban school board members. We were losing schools, but gaining students overall as population shifted. Each annexation took away some of our students and many of our buildings, but the population kept moving farther and farther into the suburbs. We were struggling to provide enough buildings for educating them!

We continually had to convince the county commissioners to allocate more money to build new elementary, middle and high schools in the suburban Shelby County District. Additionally, Memphis business leaders and large property owners were opposed to paying the city's special education tax when they were still seeing poor test results from Memphis City schools.

Something had to change.

The Biggest Threat Yet

Lurking just beneath the surface of this ongoing animosity was a potential death sentence for Shelby County Schools—the possibility that Memphis City Schools would vote to surrender their charter as a special education district—something they'd been threatening to do for decades.

Doing this would mean Shelby County Schools would have to absorb Memphis City schools. It would cause the Shelby County School District, as we knew it, to no longer exist. Memphis City still had the population advantage in our county. City residents and their elected representatives would be able to outvote us and to install their leadership on the unified school board. We, in the suburban communities, would lose our voice, our autonomy, our accountability, and quite likely, our academic excellence. We had been bracing ourselves for this possibility for awhile.

Pillars of Purpose

Over the years, as school board chairman, I'd worked with attorneys and local leaders and had gone to the state legislature on several occasions to get a special law passed that would allow us to retain our independent school board even if Memphis "surrendered" and tried to force us into a unified district.

For several years, I spent countless hours in multiple meetings every month trying to preserve our autonomy and to forestall the potential calamity of a "hostile surrender." I began to view the school board as my unpaid full-time job although I was still running my growing investment business!

Sooner than expected, the calamity arrived disguised in the form of the 2010 Midterm Election. On that November night in 2010 when Republican "Tea Party" candidates swept to power in D.C., a similar transformation took place in the Tennessee legislature. Democrats lost, Republicans won—signaling a seismic shift in state power.

The change created an opportunity for us on the Shelby County School Board because it meant that we might finally be able to get enough support among the newly elected Republican Legislature to get our independence codified in state law—something we'd tried for so long to do.

This seismic shift in power created a panic within the leaderhip of Memphis City School Board. While efforts to force consolidation of local governments failed during the 2010 election, local school board and political leaders saw an opportunity to pursue their goal of governmental consolidation by forcing a vote to give up their school district charter. In early December 2010, a school board election was held. As a result of this election, there would no longer be suffient support on the board for charter surrender. However, the city school board leadership pushed to hold a special meeting prior to the time when the newly elected board would be seated. On December 20, 2010, the Memphis City School Board held a lame duck meeting and voted 5-4 to surrender their charter. When Thomas Jefferson said, "You don't get great change by narrow majorities," he was right.

It was a hostile surrender leading to the largest school district merger in United States history.[1]

---

1 Sam Dillon; *Merger of Memphis and County School Districts Revives Race and Class Challenges*; The New York Times; Nov. 5 2011; https://www.nytimes.com/2011/11/06/education/merger-of-memphis-and-county-school-districts-revives-challenges.html

2. Perseverance

Regaining Our Autonomy

While I continued to serve on the new larger "merged" board, only nine members out of 23 represented suburban Shelby County. As predicted, from day one we were outvoted on every single issue. In giving up their charter, Memphis City Schools erased the old Shelby County School board.

I believed the best interests of the 170,000 school children in all of Shelby County were being set aside to serve political interests. Not only had there never been a merger of this size in U.S. history, there had never been one that came about by a mere one-vote margin by a divided school board instead of as a negotiation. But for every action there is an equal and opposite reaction.

We came together with community leaders, municipal mayors and suburban legislators, and began working with attorneys (again) to draft legislation stating that if a certain type of merger took place, the affected communities could form their own municipal districts. After several re-drafts, we eventually passed the law and prevailed in court.

Thanks to our new legislation, six new suburban districts separated and broke away from the new Shelby County School System. Each suburban district formed its own school board and hired a superintendent. We were thrilled we would be able to retain our independence and academic excellence.

Through sheer perseverance and a passion for public education, I was inspired to devote untold time and energy to help achieve what, at times, seemed like an insurmountable feat. I applaud all those involved for working together to get the job done and their ability to persevere even when the odds were against us.

Talent is Overrated: Perseverance is Underrated

Some people are convinced it takes "talent" to be successful. To some degree everyone has talents and capabilities, yet not everyone succeeds. Too many people keep their talents buried, failing to explore opportunities availed to them. Others over-rely on their talents, while never having the dedication and persistence to fully develop them.

Pillars of Purpose

As a lifelong Dallas Cowboys fan, their recent failures are a painful reminder to me that talent is often overrated. History is full of stories of underdog teams rising to the occasion to win championships. We have seen many occasions where Super Bowls have been won by teams with less talent but more focus and dedication to their cause. How many times has the favored team lost the Super Bowl, while the less-likely team wins the game and the coveted Super Bowl ring with sheer persistence?

When we think of persistence, sports offers some tremendous examples. Gymnast and the winner of 32 Olympic and world medals, Simone Biles spends seven hours, six days a week honing her talent as she practices her gravity-defying stunts. Commenting on her grueling practice sessions, she said, *"Practice creates confidence. Confidence empowers you."*

> *"I don't do things half-heartedly. Because I know if I do, then I can expect half-hearted results.*
> –Michael Jordan

Similarly, six-time NBA Finals Most Valuable Player (MVP), Michael Jordan pushed himself to the limits of his endurance during every game and at every practice. Some say that Chicago Bulls practices were harder than the actual games because Jordan could be more physical without referees around. A role model for developing a person's talents with sheer persistence, he once said, *"I don't do things half-heartedly. Because I know if I do, then I can expect half-hearted results."*

Like Biles and Jordan, greatness exists in everyone. However, not everyone has the will to do what is necessary to achieve it. Just one loss, and they're ready to give up. It takes courage and persistence to overcome obstacles. It takes an intense belief in what is possible.

2. Perseverance

As a young boy growing up in Jonesboro, Arkansas, I had a vision of what I wanted my life to be like. Although the obstacles I encountered sometimes made the pathway difficult to maneuver, I was deeply influenced by the stick-to-it attitude of some great men I came into contact with. They showed me that by being open to opportunities and having an intense belief in what was possible, I would eventually achieve my goals.

Persistence in Politics

From an early age I was fascinated with politics and local leadership. In 1972, at the tender age of 12, I served as a page for the Arkansas State Senate and eventually met some impressive people, including Bob Riley, then Lt. Governor of Arkansas, as well as Bill Clinton, an Arkansas native and aspiring young politician at the time, who would eventually become the 42nd president of the United States.

In 1974, Clinton ran for a seat in the U.S. House of Representatives against Democrat incumbent John Paul Hammerschmidt, a northwest Arkansas legend who had won four previous elections. Everyone predicted that Clinton, a relatively unknown 27-year-old from Hope, a small town with a population of less than 10,000 at that time, didn't stand a chance of winning. However, Clinton enthusiastically accepted the challenge. While Clinton didn't win, he came close; Hammerschmidt, the heavy favorite, only eked out a 52-48 victory.

In his autobiography, *My Life*, Clinton recalls, "It seemed absurd on the face of it. I was young, single and willing to work all hours of the day and night. And even if I didn't win, if I made a good showing I didn't think it would hurt me in any future campaigns I might undertake."

True to his word, that first campaign gave him statewide exposure and his persistence eventually led him to becoming Arkansas' Attorney General, then Governor of Arkansas, and later, President of our country.

Clinton further explains in his memoir that his passion for politics began at age 17 when a service organization sponsored him to attend Boys State, an educational program that teaches high school students about leadership and government. In 1963, Clinton's peers at Boys State selected him to represent Arkansas as one of two delegates sent to Boys Nation, where he famously visited the White House and shook hands

Pillars of Purpose

MORE ABOUT BOYS STATE

American Legion Boys State is among the most respected and selective educational programs of government instruction for U.S. high school students. At Boys State, participants learn the rights, privileges and responsibilities of franchised citizens. The training is objective and centers on the structure of city, county and state governments. Operated by students elected to various offices, Boys State activities include legislative sessions, court proceedings, law-enforcement presentations, assemblies, bands, choruses and recreational programs.

Legion posts select high school juniors to attend the program. In most cases, individual expenses are paid by a sponsoring post, a local business or another community-based organization. While Boys State programs vary in content and method of procedure, each adheres to the same basic concept: teaching government from the township to the state level.[1]

---

1 https://www.legion.org/boysnation/ about

with President John F. Kennedy.

According to President Clinton, the experience was life changing. *"Boys State helped teach me from a young age that democracy requires us to get off the sidelines and into the arena... Imperfect as it may be, we can't take this system of ours for granted. And if we want to make it better and make a difference in people's lives, we need to stand up, show up, and speak up, day after day and year after year."*

When I learned of President Clinton's experience, I decided I, too, wanted to go to Boys State. The problem was, my parents weren't active participants in any service organizations, so the chances of one of the other parents choosing me to attend over one of their own kids was minimal. I knew that to make this happen, I needed to become involved with an organization.

At that time, the only service option for a 16-year-old was the Junior Chamber of Commerce (JayCees), an organization that provided a training ground for future leaders. This was my introduction to community service.

I've always said that luck is where preparation and opportunity meets persistence. The harder you work, the luckier you get. Al-

2. Perseverance

though our local Jaycee Chapter had never sponsored anyone to attend Boys State, they agreed to sponsor me. I don't know whether it was because they liked me or they were tired of me bugging them about it. But I like to think that my persistence paid off as they witnessed the intense passion I had for attending Boys State, and they knew I was willing to work hard to get there.

Connections I made at Boys State led to working as a staff intern for a congressman at the nation's capital in Washington D.C., and involvement in several political campaigns. The pinnacle of my youth involvement in politics was in 1980 when I was selected to the Democratic National Convention. While attending a social mixer, I met Witt Stephens, one of the most influential business leaders in our state and CEO of Stephens Inc, one of the largest investment banking firms off Wall Street. To my shock and surprise, he stated, "Boy, I've been watching you for some time. You're going to be alright, kid."

The next day, the governor of the state, Bill Clinton, and two United States senators nominated me to represent the state of Arkansas as a delegate at the 1980 Democratic National Convention.

Those experiences have led to other opportunities that continue to this day, all of which I attribute to my decision to take a risk and my persistence in pursuing my passion.

It's Your Life… Live It!

Life is too short to sit on the sidelines and let your dreams float on by. Instead, I encourage you to enthusiastically grasp every opportunity that comes your way. When you look in the mirror at the end of each day, be confident in knowing you did everything you could to fulfill your purpose with passion–to make your dreams come true.

At one time or another throughout our lives, all of us have to climb over obstacles in our pathway. It's our level of commitment to our *why* and our ability to persevere that allows us to overcome them.

As I alluded to earlier, Winston Churchill, former Prime Minister of the U.K. who led the British to victory in World War II, famously summoned his countrymen's courage in the midst of terrifying German air raids:

Pillars of Purpose

"Never give in. Never, never, never, never—in nothing great or small, large or petty—never give in, except to convictions of honor and good sense."

Perseverance propels us toward our purpose. That and an intense belief in what is possible can lead us to a life of significance. Reaching your goals can take time. Be patient with yourself. Remember the riddle, "How does a mouse eat an elephant?" One bite at a time.

When your challenges seem insurmountable, ask yourself:

- Why do I "need" to win the battle?
- Why do I "want" to win the battle?
- Do I have the will to do it?
- Am I willing to expend maximum effort to achieve success?

As you answer these questions, dig deep into your reservoir of conviction and remember: only with an intense belief in what is possible can you lead a life of significance.

I encourage you to live bravely so in the end you can loudly proclaim, "I did it!"

Chapter 3
PASSION

"Success demands singleness of purpose."
– Vince Lombardi, legendary football coach

The first two Bedrock Principles, Power of the Possible and Perseverance, can help you fulfill your life's purpose and lead a life of significance. However, without the third Bedrock Principle, Passion, our dreams often fall short. Without passion, your resolve can fade, much like a comet quickly blazing across the sky losing its glow with each cycle through the inner solar system.

Without sufficient passion, we may abandon our dreams just short of excellence. We may go along to get along, worry too much about making waves or avoid "breaking eggs" as I've frequently had to do in my life. In short, lack of passion can mean settling for something good, as opposed to great.

In his book, *Good to Great,* famed business author Jim Collins writes:

> Good is the enemy of great. And that is one of the key reasons why we have so little that becomes great. We don't have great

Pillars of Purpose

schools, principally because we have good schools. We don't have great government, principally because we have good government. Few people attain great lives, in large part because it is just so easy to settle for a good life.[1]

While each of us enjoys a precious but undetermined number of heartbeats in this life, some people wander through life half-heartedly. They give up on their dreams and approach each day with indifference or a fatalistic "whatever will be will be" attitude. They settle for a life of mediocrity as opposed to maximizing their limited time on this planet, fueled by purpose and passion.

When you combine your purpose with the principle of Passion, it can sustain you for the long haul. It can fuel you with an unquenchable desire to pursue greatness for as long as it takes and as long as you have. Passion provides the heart, the flame and burning desire to achieve—like the pursuit of a win drives elite athletes at the highest levels of competition. The best athletes aren't happy with settling for anything less than championships.

So, I ask you, is your day just good, or is it great? Are you pursuing your life with zest and passion? Or, are you settling for just "a good life" instead of making it "great?"

Passion means chasing your dreams to the fullest, challenging everything and energizing your soul. It means summoning the boldness to live an uncommon life.

The legendary Vince Lombardi, coach and general manager of the Green Bay Packers, exemplified passion. Considered one of the greatest coaches in football history, he dominated the league, leading his Packers' teams to three NFL titles in five years as well as to victories in the first two Super Bowls in 1967 and 1968. He epitomized championship football, so much so that the Super Bowl trophy has borne his name since 1970, when he tragically passed away from cancer at age 57.

Lombardi left behind an unsurpassed legacy and many inspiring quotes. I especially like this one:

---

[1] Jim Collins; *Author Jim Collins Reveals the Enemy of Greatness; Legends Report*; https://www.legends.report/jim-collins-on-the-enemy-of-greatness/

3. Passion

"Once a man has made a commitment to a way of life, he puts the greatest strength in the world behind him. It's something we call heart power. Once a man has made this commitment, nothing will stop him short of success."

By "heart power," I truly believe he means "passion." As he proved throughout his career, purpose pursued with passion allows us to serve freely, commit willingly, and to act boldly. It's the bedrock of the legacy a person leaves behind.

Passion to Live an Uncommon Life

"A ship in the harbor is safe, but that's not what ships are built for."
– John Augustus Shedd, author of "Salt from my Attic"

The quote above reminds us that while passion powers us to live an uncommon life and to achieve greatness, it doesn't guarantee smooth sailing. In choosing this journey of significance you're not always going to enjoy a life of ease or universal popularity. In fact, you may even create enemies. You need to be comfortable with that risk. You have to be willing to leave safe harbors to sail boldly toward your dreams.

Throughout my life I have considered myself to be an advocate for the causes I believe in. To the best of my ability, I've been a gladiator in the arena. Whether it be for my clients, public education or the community, I have always been willing to take the arrows and the body blows to fight for the things I believe in—the causes for which I'm passionate.

Likewise, if you really want to become an advocate for your causes, you must consciously pursue real change, not mere window dressing. While I respect people who can compromise (they often make successful legislators), their job involves seeking middle ground and offending the fewest number of people. In contrast, pursuing a life of purpose and passion is not about seeking the middle ground or pursuing simple popularity. Instead, it's about fighting relentlessly for the causes you believe in and in making a powerful difference. Sometimes you'll need to become the bull in the china shop. In the pursuit of greatness, it's more important to be respected than loved.

Pillars of Purpose

Passionately Honoring America and Our Veterans

As previously detailed in Chapter 2, I've experienced significant pushback in my pursuit of noble causes, such as our fight to maintain the autonomy and educational excellence of our suburban school system—which we ultimately achieved in 2013. But back in 1999, while just beginning my service on the Shelby County School Board, I learned what it takes to push through inertia and stand up for what you believe in the face of indifference or outright hostility.

At that time, I felt honored to become acquainted with a fellow board member, Ron Lollar. Ron and I immediately bonded over a common passion—patriotism and love of country. As a retired Marine, Ron had worked as an underwater demolitions expert—a harrowing job. He later took an assignment at the Pentagon for five years, and ultimately served as an Honor Guard at the White House before retiring. With our shared passion for patriotism and traditional American values, Ron and I fought for some very important issues during our tenure on the Board, many involving how to properly honor the country we both loved so passionately.

For instance, during our first year, we identified several trends that seemed to be moving in the wrong direction. As our district had scrambled to accommodate student growth and create enough classroom space, we had overlooked a simple but significant daily exercise in our schools: the Pledge of Allegiance. Students no longer recited the Pledge. Even more shocking, we discovered there were few American flags in the classrooms or in communal areas.

To fix this omission, we set out to place American flags in each classroom in all 50 schools in our district, as well as on the school grounds, and to reinstate the reciting of the Pledge. With an average of 40 classrooms in each school, plus the common areas, that meant buying a lot of flags—more than 2,000 to be exact. To make it happen, we reached out to Memphis' own Fred Smith, founder and CEO of FedEx, who generously agreed to buy the flags, brackets and flagpoles. Then, by a unanimous vote, the board passed a policy that we would begin every day with the pledge. In accordance with that policy, we placed plaques in each classroom inscribed with the Pledge of Allegiance and our country's motto, "In God We Trust." Not only had we re-introduced patriotism back into

3. Passion

the schools, but we'd brought back God as well.

While we loved seeing our patriotic vision become reality, we weren't finished fighting for traditional American values. Our next battle arrived when the superintendent proposed the district's calendar for the following year and recommended dropping Veterans Day as an official school holiday. He argued that by sending kids to school that day, fall break could be extended an additional day.

A serious discussion ensued as he attempted to convince the seven-member board to approve this calendar modification. Ron and I passionately objected. We were deeply offended. After all, Veterans Day honors everyone who has ever served our country in uniform. Our country owes its existence and continued freedoms to our vets. We owe them a debt of gratitude that can never truly be repaid. Is it too much to take one day to honor them?

Ron and I decided to fight to preserve the significance of this important day. We knew our fight wouldn't make us popular with some members of the board or the superintendent. However, this was not about being popular. It was about doing what we felt was right.

In the end, our passion won. The board eventually voted unanimously in favor of retaining Veterans Day as a school holiday. At the same time, knowing that the number of World War II veterans was diminishing each day, we launched an initiative encouraging teachers to assign students to collect oral histories from vets as a Veterans Day project. Not only did the students learn about the sacrifice these men and women made to ensure their freedom, they helped preserve these stories for future generations.

The media picked up on our Veterans Day victory. Moreover, we knew members of the community shared our passion for this important day when Ron and I started getting calls thanking us for standing up for this important group of heroes.

Passionately Saying Thank You—The Rest of the Story

As a poignant addendum to this Veterans Day story, we took an opportunity to give back to vets in a way they did not expect. When our local schools began collecting oral stories from area vets, we learned many of them had never graduated from high school. Instead, when Pearl Harbor was attacked in 1941, many of them chose to leave school to serve our country in WWII. When they returned home from the war, the door to a high school education had closed for many of them as they married and took on jobs to support their families. We felt it was important to find these individuals and to rectify the situation.

The board worked tirelessly with the State Legislature to pass a bill allowing schools to thank vets by presenting them with official high school diplomas at a special graduation ceremony, solely for the purpose of honoring them. Unfortunately, because so many years had passed, finding the individuals to award these belated diplomas to proved to be extremely difficult. Each diploma had to be granted by the school they had attended; however, many of those schools had changed names and some had even changed locations making it very challenging, to say the least. Through an incredible process of researching school histories and reaching out to the community, we eventually found 28 veterans who had never graduated, but instead fought in WWII.

In an inspiring, locally televised Veterans Day ceremony at the Memphis Rock and Soul Museum, the Navy Band played, the Commanding Officer of the Naval Support Activity Mid-South (NSA Mid-South) spoke, and nationally acclaimed singer and songwriter, Reverend Al Green, sang the national anthem. After we shared some of the veterans' inspiring stories, I felt privileged, as chairman of the school board, to personally hand each of these heroes their diploma.

It truly connected each of us in attendance to the sacrifices made so long ago as these American patriots proudly walked across the stage to accept a diploma, awarded with the name of their original high school. Participating in this process marked one of the pinnacles of my life. Those men, who may previously have felt incomplete because they hadn't graduated, now held a real diploma that would fill that void in their souls. We witnessed many tears being shed in the room during this powerful ceremony.

Energized by this experience, we continued to award diplomas to the vets we discovered for the next few years. Then, when we found there were 10 to 15 WWI veterans still alive in our area, we again worked with the state

3. Passion

legislature to pass a bill to award them with diplomas as well. We felt ecstatic when other school districts in the state followed our lead, choosing to honor their veterans in the same way.

Passionately Living Your Dash

You will see opportunities to make a difference arise in your own life. Seize every one you can. As you travel through life, your passion for noble causes and for the people you care about can help you fulfill your God-given purpose. Just remember, everyone's purpose is as unique as his or her fingerprints or DNA. You can't compare yourself to others. People mistakenly get discouraged when another person's accomplishments, the size of their home or their wealth far exceeds their own. You need only worry about your own unique contributions and maximize the precious allotment of time you've been given.

In her beautiful and thought-provoking poem, author Linda Ellis describes this time between our birth and our death as "the dash" and poignantly reminds us that the dash is all that matters.[1]

> For it matters not, how much we own,
> The cars... the house... the cash.
> What matters is how we live and love
> And how we spend our dash.

In my younger years, I always competed with others. When I didn't make the National Honor Society in high school, I realized I wasn't working hard enough. I needed to step up my game. From that point on, I started working harder to be the best I could be. While I achieved almost every academic record in college, the problem was I was looking for external validation. I was using other people's measuring stick instead of my own internal judgment.

In my career, I competed against others in the same manner. Then one day I realized that the only measuring stick of success that truly mattered was the one in my own head, heart and soul. I decided to raise my standards and strive to become the best version of myself—regardless of another person's ambitions or success. I was the only person who could

---

[1] Linda Ellis; *The Dash*; https://lindaellis.life/

accurately assess if I was aiming high enough or settling. It was truly a journey of discovery, and it's made all the difference in my life.

Again, quoting Ellis' poem:

> "So, when your eulogy is being read
> With your life's actions to rehash...
> Would you be proud of the things they say
> About how you spent YOUR dash?"[1]

Passion for a New State-of-the-Art High School

When my longtime friend John Aitken, the superintendent of newly created Collierville Municipal Schools, called saying he needed my financial acumen and personal network to execute his vision for the new District, particularly for a new high school, I eagerly accepted.

He began by citing the positive attributes of the newly minted school district—passionate teachers, devoted parents and students, and a high school rated among the top 100 high schools in America academically and among the top three in Tennessee. But (and there's always a "but") the high school lacked adequate facilities. They eked along with existing infrastructure, cramming more than 2,500 high school students into an old middle school originally constructed for 1,600 students. They commandeered an elementary school field for football games and relegated the marching band to practicing wherever they could find a vacant parking lot. We all knew the kids deserved better.

John's grand plans didn't just stop with new facilities or even a new auditorium or football field. He envisioned a new type of high school where students could learn the skills needed to be competitive in a rapidly evolving marketplace. Along with technical skills, he wanted them to learn practical skills such as auto mechanics, welding, nursing, IT and aeronautics. To do this, he hoped to provide them with real-world experiences. This meant creating partnerships with business leaders in the community interested in workforce development.

John explained that while the school received the majority of its funding from the town and state, the budget would not cover the entire cost

---

1 Ellis; *The Dash*; https://lindaellis.life/

3. Passion

of the 250,000-square-foot building he envisioned. "We're going to need organizations to help us create the infrastructure and to help us build this amazing structure."

He asked me to oversee a capital-raising campaign for the new high school. We would need at least $1 million to reach our initial goal for the athletic and vocational training facilities and auditorium. We both championed educational excellence. It was the perfect combination of purpose and passion, and it made a big impact.

After months of hard work and long hours, our fund-raising team presented John with a check for $1.5 million raised from a multitude of donors. Using the funds to build out the infrastructure of this incredible program, 70 business leaders stepped forward to partner with teachers to create industry workforce groups that included internships, externships and other cooperative education opportunities for the students. This aligned with our goal of providing the broadest possible opportunities for students in suburban Memphis. We knew that nearly 70% of the jobs created in the next 10 years wouldn't require a traditional four-year college degree, but instead, some type of advanced certification. Our students would be well served.

You can imagine my pleasure when I learned the new auditorium was to be named Pickler Auditorium after me, my family and our firm—a lasting legacy.

Passion for Children with Profound Hearing Loss

As a wealth management business, we're passionate about our clients and community projects. We unite our team around our shared vision of service and giving back.

> "Our mission is to make a profound difference in our world and in the lives of the clients we serve. We believe in giving back and paying forward with passion and purpose."
> –Pickler Wealth Advisors' Mission Statement

It all starts with that passion for our clients. We're proud to be fiduciaries —gladiators who fight tirelessly for them in our daily work. At times this means we have to be willing to look clients in the eye and tell them when it's time to change course. Not so long ago, I somberly told an elderly client that his actions might cause him to not reach his goals. With tears in his eyes, he thanked me for caring enough to be concerned. While I didn't like being the bearer of bad news, we've now taken the necessary steps to get him back on course.

Along with looking out for the well-being of our clients, our team commits to community projects that will better the lives of others ... another shared purpose.

In 1996, my wife began championing the Memphis Oral School for the Deaf (MOSD), a local organization that helps young children with profound hearing loss function in a "hearing world."

This wonderful organization teaches profoundly deaf children oral-deaf education and offers other essential life training, including speech therapy. In 1999, they asked me to serve on their board and to help them find a permanent facility. At that time, the schoolchildren met in downtown Memphis in a less-than-ideal setting. Some parents opted not to send their child to the school fearing for their safety because of the shoddy location. The administrators and teachers hoped that as a new board member I could help them develop a long-term plan for finding the first permanent home in its 48-year nomadic history. And, of course, that would require fundraising.

For several years, we explored possibilities for a new school building for MOSD. Then, in 2005, MOSD's principal, Teresa Schwartz, made us aware of a church that might be open to partnering with another affiliation. Kingsway Christian Church had previously bought properties upon which to build and then later sell as the church's membership evolved. The profit they made from the sales helped them to move one step closer to their dream of constructing a permanent church sanctuary, office, wedding chapel and community building. Unfortunately for Kingsway, yet fortunately for us, after purchasing land in the perfect location, and constructing the sanctuary, office and wedding chapel, they ran out of money before their dream of a community building could be realized. This opened them up to the idea of partnering with a group who shared common values and a common mission to finish the job.

After 18 months of negotiations, in 2006 we finally came to an agreement.

3. Passion

Kingsway Church would provide the property and we (MOSD) would be responsible for raising approximately $2.5 million for the new facility. It was time to get to work. For the next two years our team, my family and I led fund-raising projects, giving freely of our time and talents.

After raising $3.5 million, we built the community building on Kingsway property. Under the terms of our agreement, MOSD would enjoy use of the building for a rate of $1 per year for the next 50 years. In August 2007, at the groundbreaking ceremony, our team posed for a picture as each of us held a shovel full of dirt. It was a proud moment. Of course, all the young school kids loved expressing themselves in the dirt as well, with and without shovels. Our passionate desire to ensure every child with hearing loss would have a safe place to listen, learn and talk led to this achievement.

As a gesture of profound appreciation, school officials named the main gathering building at the school Pickler Hall in honor of the work my wife and I had done. While we appreciated the accolades, the real reward comes from knowing our efforts helped improve many lives.

Passion for Purchasing a Permanent Home for MOSD

In 2018, after four years of negotiations, we helped MOSD purchase from Kingsway Christian Church the land and building that housed the school. It was a triumphant moment that permanently secured the school's future. However, it didn't happen automatically. Just like the initial 2006 deal, it took work. By 2011, Kingsway had begun hemorrhaging members and faced significant financial difficulties. Their pastor subsequently approached me as the MOSD board chair about whether MOSD would be interested in acquiring full ownership of the building. I believed Kingsway's financial concerns could eventually lead to their having to sell the entire campus out from under us and that such a contingency could undermine the stability of our unique lease relationship.

It took several years of work to secure the deal, during which time the school continued to grow, and the church's building usage shrank. Eventually we were able to reach an equitable agreement to acquire both the land and the building from Kingsway for approximately $500,000. Much of this was made possible through the growth of the $3.5 million endowment that was originally raised to build the building.

Pillars of Purpose

MOSD: A Worthwhile Cause

Memphis Oral School for the Deaf (MOSD) works to empower children with profound hearing loss to listen, learn, and talk. MOSD has been serving families from all over the Mid-South since 1959. At MOSD no sign language is used. MOSD helps profoundly deaf and hearing impaired children ages birth to six years old learn language during the most critical developmental stages of their lives. The school believe that through early intervention and diagnosis, speech and language therapies, and advanced technologies and audiological services, deaf children can develop necessary listening and spoken language skills to become a part of, rather than apart from, a world of sound.[1]

---

1 https://mosdkids.org/who-we-are/

An Inspiring Example of Passion

This chapter would not be complete without acknowledging a person who, for me, exemplifies passion—my wife, Beth. Beth spearheads most of our community involvement and philanthropic efforts. Along with serving one-year terms as PTA president on five separate occassions when our children were growing up, she was the one who introduced us to MOSD, inspiring our entire team's passionate embrace of this terrific organization.

In 1996, Beth joined Subsidium, a MOSD-support organization that during its existence raised money for the vital needs of the school. No doubt spurred on by her own background in special education and growing up in a family of special education teachers, Beth immersed herself in this non-profit entity and quickly rose to leadership roles. Now, over 25 years later, she still takes pride in caring passionately for MOSD. Along with organizing the school's largest annual fundraising event, Speakeasy, Beth plans the Christmas party for the kids, creating Christmas tree ornaments customized with each child's picture. She engages our team to donate their time and talents and to help Santa write letters to the children and hand out presents dressed as

3. Passion

Santa's elves. They also dress in costume to help at the Halloween carnival, and they assist at the graduation ceremony.

For the school's 50th anniversary, Beth designed, edited, and published a commemorative book preserving its history. Even more impressive, she spends hundreds of hours each year taking pictures of the children and creating a personalized memory book for each of them. Then, at graduation, she presents each graduate with an invaluable book recounting their years at the school.

In 2023, she was recognized by the school with the first ever MOSD Lifetime Volunteer Award. Never one to seek the spotlight, Beth believes her real reward comes from seeing others benefit from the work she does. Her passion inspires others, and she is the rock for me, our family and the projects she engages in.

Passion Means Keeping the Flame Lit

On April 1910, Theodore Roosevelt delivered his infamous "Citizenship in a Republic" speech in Paris, France.

> "It is not the critic who counts; not the man who points out how the strong man stumbles, or where the doer of deeds could have done them better. The credit belongs to the man who is actually in the arena, whose face is marred by dust and sweat and blood; who strives valiantly; who errs, who comes short again and again, because there is no effort without error and shortcoming; but who does actually strive to do the deeds; who knows great enthusiasms, the great devotions; who spends himself in a worthy cause; who at the best knows in the end the triumph of high achievement, and who at the worst, if he fails, at least fails while daring greatly, so that his place shall never be with those cold and timid souls who neither know victory nor defeat."

President Roosevelt, a celebrated man of action, who championed bold ideas such as the National Park System, describes in this famous quote a person with passion, directed by purpose. Whether victorious or defeated, if you dare to fight the battle, you're a winner. Teddy knew what he was talking about!

Teddy's passion for life and encouragement to "stay in the arena" reminds me of my experience in a batting cage not long ago. One year, as a long-time season ticket holder, I received a VIP invitation to Busch Stadium to participate in a St. Louis Cardinal's batting practice against one of their World-Series-winning retired pitchers. Thrilled, I invited several members of my family and a friend to accompany me, and in turn, my friend invited some college baseball players to this once-in-a-lifetime opportunity.

As a big-time baseball fan, I was shocked that none of these talented players accepted the challenge. Here I was, 62 years old and hadn't played for years. I definitely didn't have time to practice, yet I embraced the opportunity.

Why did they pass? Maybe they feared they would swing and miss. They didn't want to be humiliated. However, if you had asked any of them if they felt passionate about baseball, they probably would have enthusiastically exclaimed, "Yes!" Unfortunately, instead of feeding their passion they played it safe. How many of them will now look back and think ... "What if?"

I hope you're beginning to see that once you've identified your passion, it's important to commit to keeping it alive. Engage in activities that will help it grow. Stay in the arena despite any and all criticism—or potential for failure. That's the key to keeping your passion alive.

The ancient Roman poet Virgil observed, *"Fortune favors the bold."* This holds true centuries later. In the immortal words of Vince Lombardi, the coach who personified single-minded determination:

> *"There are people who make things happen, there are people who watch things happen, and there are people who wonder what happened. To be successful, you need to be a person who makes things happen."*

I encourage you to ask yourself each day:
- Am I making things happen?
- Have I made my best effort?
- Have I prepared myself to meet future challenges?
- Have I kept faith with my purpose and life goals?
- Am I pursuing my purpose with passion?

At the end of each day, can you rest knowing you didn't just settle for "good" but instead passionately battled for "great?"

Chapter 4
INTEGRITY

*"Integrity is telling myself the truth.
And honesty is telling the truth to other people."*
– Spencer Johnson, American physician and best-selling self-help author

At the end of the last chapter, I issued a challenge. I essentially asked you: will you allow your legacy to be defined by easy excuses, or will you be bold? Will you hold yourself accountable even when no one else knows, or will you abandon what you're striving for when life gets tough and settle for less?

I hope by now you realize, I'm not a fan of excuses. Excuses erode our character little by little, just like lies. In fact, excuses are the lies we tell ourselves. Integrity, on the other hand, fortifies our character and grounds us in absolute truth. Everything we've talked about so far in this book—vision, perseverance and passion—hinges on personal integrity.

Integrity is the fourth essential Bedrock Principle for building a life of purpose and significance, and it's worth noting that integrity makes you more reliable as you live in accordance with deeply held values. Integrity is the force within each of us that governs our actions and propels us to do the right thing even when no one is looking. It's our moral backbone and unflinching code of conduct.

A Reputation for Integrity

Webster's dictionary defines integrity as: *The quality of being honest and having strong moral principles, and moral uprightness.*

Character and integrity go together. We vote for leaders who exhibit integrity. We prefer working with honorable people, and we choose to be friends with people who are truthful and fair. We seek people out who stand firm for their beliefs and have unshakable morals and courage.

Throughout history, leaders with integrity inspire us. President Abraham Lincoln was a brilliant man who was famously known for his honesty, earning him the nickname "Honest Abe." As a young man, the future president helped a business acquaintance run his shop in New Salem, Illinois. Serving as the main clerk in the town's general store, Honest Abe amazed patrons with his integrity. A story was told about the time he accidently shortchanged a customer by less than a dollar. He quickly discovered the error, and as soon as he closed the shop, he walked several miles in the dark to return the excess payment. He knew he couldn't sleep before righting the wrong. This was not the only example of his character.

Knowing him to be a man of integrity, people often asked Lincoln to act as a mediator in various contests, fights or arguments. According to Robert Rutledge of New Salem, Illinois, *"Lincoln's judgment was final in all that region of country. People relied implicitly upon his honesty, integrity and impartiality."*[1]

People of integrity feel guided by a deep sense of purpose and passion for what they do. Some of them are your next-door neighbors, the person sitting in a desk down the hall, or even someone holding a national, state or community leadership position. People of integrity come from all walks of life, yet they never boast about integrity being their personal or professional brand. Instead, it's what makes their brand believable. They're recognized as being true to their beliefs and sticking to their

---

1 Gordon Leidner, *Lincoln's Honesty*; Great American History; https://greatamericanhistory.net/honesty.htm

4. Integrity

values and morals at all costs.

Hopefully with these examples I've given you, you're beginning to see the value of living in accordance with your deepest values. When you have integrity you are:

- At peace with yourself (never pretend to be something you aren't)
- Reliable
- A natural leader
- An inspiration to others
- A peacemaker

People of integrity often are natural leaders because of their exceptional self-confidence and humility. That's not a contradiction! Humility and true self-confidence flow naturally from the same place. When you're motivated by and accountable to your own personal beliefs, you have nothing to fear and can proceed boldly. In turn, these same beliefs keep you humble.

As I scan the list of attributes above, I can't help but think of an esteemed acquaintance of mine, Civil War historian Mike McGough. I first met Mike during my year as president of the National School Boards Association (NSBA). I was attending the New Jersey School Boards Association (NJSBA) conference where both Mike and I had been invited to speak.

I was fascinated by Mike's presentation on "Leadership Lessons from the Battle of Gettysburg" and wanted to know more. Seeking him out, I introduced myself. I learned that Mike taught in the Education Department of a college in Pennsylvania. However, what really impressed me was his passion for the Battle of Gettysburg. His passion made him an incredible resource for anyone eager to learn more about the history of one of our nation's most famous battles.

I was blown away by all the knowledge he had gained through tireless reading and research. He'd learned not only the expected historical facts about Gettysburg, but also could share many unique stories that had never been included in any of the history books I'd read. He told how a battle with an estimated 51,000 casualties over a three-day period hinged on

Pillars of Purpose

A Little History

The Battle of Gettysburg marked the turning point of the Civil War. With more than 51,000 estimated casualties, the three-day engagement was the bloodiest single battle of the conflict.

While the carnage was overwhelming, the Union victory buoyed Lincoln's hopes of ending the war. Gettysburg ended Confederate General Robert E. Lee's ambitious second quest to invade the North. The loss there dashed any real chance of the Confederate States of America becoming an independent nation.

President Lincoln used the dedication ceremony at the Gettysburg's Soldiers' National Cemetery to honor the fallen and reassert the purpose of the war in his historic Gettysburg Address.

dozens of seemingly small decisions and turning points that won the battle and likely changed the course of American history.

Mike's stories came alive as he offered glimpses into the character and integrity of the men who decided our nation's fate in those critical moments. Whether talking about a general, a corporal or a foot soldier, he reflected on how their character influenced the decisions they made, and ultimately, how their courageous actions became deciding factors in the battle that turned the course of the arduous Civil War.

Eager to share his leadership stories with others, I invited him to speak at the upcoming NSBA conference. I knew anyone who heard his presentation would learn valuable life lessons. Later, when Mike invited me to attend his seminar at the Gettysburg battlefield, it was an offer I couldn't pass up.

Leadership Lessons from the Battlefield

During his fascinating seminar, Mike discussed leadership characteristics of participants in the Battle of Gettysburg, as well as the integrity demonstrated by President Lincoln. Whether you are a business professional, a parent raising a family, or a member of a re-

4. Integrity

ligious or social group, you can study and learn from these attributes. For example:

- **Be open to different opinions.**

  Confederate General Robert E. Lee first devised his plan to draw the enemy into a battle in a time and place of his choosing in Pennsylvania. On the third day in the battle that resulted in the Battle of Gettysburg, Lee decided on an assault against the center of the Union line. One of his corps commanders, General James Longstreet of the First Corps of the Confederate Army, advised against it. Understanding the Union Army had strategic and numerical advantages, he counseled Lee to take a more defensive stance. However, Longstreet's argument did not prevail; Lee instead chose to attack.

  The Confederates went on to lose the Battle of Gettysburg, which represented a turning point in the Civil War. Afterward, Lee took responsibility for the defeat, but at the same time tacitly faulted Longstreet for offering less than total support for the attack plans on July 3.

  While good leaders hold firm to their convictions, they are open to hearing different opinions as they carefully weigh their options. Success isn't built with an army of "yes" men, but requires the knowledge and energy of a team. Furthermore, as evidenced by Lee, ethical leaders take responsibility for their decisions—right or wrong.

- **Build a strategic vision for your organization or family.**

  From July 1 through July 3, 1863, the Union Troops battled and ultimately defeated the Confederate Army of Northern Virginia in Gettysburg. On November 19, with the wounds of battle still painfully fresh, President Lincoln stood in front of the war-weary audience to dedicate the Soldiers' National Cemetery. In fewer than 300 words, he delivered one of the most powerful and iconic speeches ever given. He succinctly laid out his vision for the nation's future:

  "This nation, under God, shall have a new birth of freedom, and

that government of the people, by the people, for the people, shall not perish from the earth."

In his speech he never:

- Used the words "I," "me" or "my."
- Talked about who was winning or who was losing.
- Said who was right, or who was wrong.
- Blamed anyone or gave credit to anyone.

Instead he focused on:

- The founding principles of the country: *"... a new nation, conceived in Liberty and dedicated to the proposition that all men are created equal."*
- The need to bind the nation and move forward together: *"It is rather for us to be here dedicated to the great task remaining before us."*
- A devotion to duty: *"The brave men, living and dead, who struggled here, have consecrated it ..."*
- Embracing a government *"of the people, by the people, and for the people."*

Not only is this historical speech revered as one of the greatest of all time, but also a true testament to Lincoln's integrity and his ability to be a leader for all the people.

- **Ability to adjust your views.**

Sometimes we need to be flexible and willing to change our minds. When Edwin Stanton began serving in Lincoln's cabinet as Secretary of War, as a Democrat he didn't particularly like or respect the president. After an earlier encounter in their legal careers, he allegedly referred to Lincoln as a baboon. While Stanton had a reputation for being bull-headed and often difficult to work with, when cabinet members recommended Lincoln consider him for the position of War Secretary, Lincoln did not hesitate to make him part of his cabinet.

The appointment worked as intended. Upon taking the helm of

4. Integrity

the previously dysfunctional department, Stanton's ruthless perfectionism and organizational skills paid dividends, ultimately commanding Lincoln's deepest respect, as he praised Stanton:

> "[Stanton's] position is one of the most difficult in the world. He is the rock on the beach of our national ocean against which the breakers dash and roar, dash and roar, without ceasing. He fights back the angry waters and prevents them from undermining and overwhelming the land. Gentlemen, I do not see how he survives—why he is not crushed and torn to pieces. Without him I should be destroyed. He performs his task superhumanly. Now do not mind this matter, for Mr. Stanton is right and I cannot wrongly interfere with him."[1]

In taking a position in President Lincoln's cabinet, Stanton proved to be a man of integrity. Confident he could be an asset to the war efforts, he pushed aside his first impressions of Lincoln. As he witnessed the strength and integrity the President exhibited, a mutual respect developed between the President and Stanton that eventually turned into a personal friendship. As Lincoln drew his last breath, Stanton reportedly said, "Now he belongs to the ages." At his funeral he pronounced, "There lies the most perfect ruler of men the world has ever seen."[2]

A Story of Healing

I've saved one of my favorite Civil War stories for last, as it requires a little explanation. As with history, there are several versions told and sometimes the storytellers themselves embellish on the truth. However, the purpose behind this story makes it worth telling:

> During the Battle of Gettysburg, Confederate General John B. Gordon and his troops engaged the Union soldiers and forced a retreat. It's said when he came across Union General Francis C. Barlow, who was badly wounded, he stopped to help him. His injuries were extreme. It was doubtful he would survive for long.

---

[1] Frank Abial Flower, Edwin MacMasters Stanton: *The Autocrat of Rebellion, Emancipation, and Reconstruction*, p. 369-370
[2] Michael Burlingame, et al; *Abraham Lincoln: the Observations of John G. Nicolay and John Hay*, https://ministry127.com/resources/illustration/the-best-man-for-the-job

Pillars of Purpose

As Gordon and his men carried Barlow to a shadier spot, Barlow asked them to destroy the letters from his wife that he carried with him. In addition, if Gordon were ever to meet Mrs. Barlow, Barlow asked him to assure her that he had died doing his duty for his country, and his only regret was never seeing her again.

Later that day, Gordon learned that Mrs. Barlow was with the Union Army. Under a flag of truce, he sent Barlow's message to his wife and told her where he lay. Unbeknownst to Gordon, she was able to find her husband and nurse him back to health.

Sixteen years later, Gordon, now a U.S. Senator from Georgia, was invited to a dinner party in Washington D.C. where General Barlow was also in attendance. Both thought the other one dead, and were surprised to learn of each other's survival. A friendship quickly formed between the two men, one that lasted the remainder of their lives.

It's a beautiful story; however, some historians suggest it wasn't actually Gordon who found Barlow. While Gordon may have been dishonest in sharing the story as his own, I like to think he did it to serve a purpose in those difficult times. It's a story that was embraced by the people, and his version encouraged social healing and a return to kindness.

Leadership: A Shared Vision

To say I was inspired by Mike McGough's stories about the Gettysburg battle would be an understatement. I told him, "I can't think of anything more amazing than to spend time with you." But true to my nature, I wanted to take it *one step further*. I suggested it would be equally beneficial for all 30 board members of NSBA to hear this inspiring leadership message. Joining him on the battlefield also would be a great team-bonding opportunity. He enthusiastically agreed.

We soon began planning how to bring all 30 members of NSBA's board to Pennsylvania. Not only did I have to figure out how to organize the event, but equally challenging ... how to fund it! We needed to cover the cost of flying 30 people into the tiny airport in Harrisburg, Pennsylvania. and setting up transportation from the airport to the town—about two hours away. In addition, we would need to line up meals and lodging in

4. Integrity

the small community. It seemed daunting.

In addition, I first had to convince the executive director of NSBA that my idea was feasible. Although he liked the idea, he explained there was no money in the budget for an event like this. I took that as a challenge. "So, you're telling me if I can arrange financing and take care of the logistics, we can make this happen?" I asked.

Nodding his head, we were on our way to making it happen.

We began the process of reaching out to our corporate partners to engage their support for the event. We explained this was not a boondoggle but an opportunity that could be transformational. With their company's support, we could sharpen our board members' leadership skills, and they could enhance their company's position as an advocate for public education—a win-win for everyone.

The estimated cost of the event was approximately $100,000. Over several weeks, we spoke with 15 different corporate partners and raised 75% of the required funding. Because of our dedication and passion to make this happen, my company contributed the remaining 25%. After all, if you believe in something, you must be willing to step up to make it happen. That required a personal commitment from me.

We set the date for a weekend in early March when Mike would be available, and lodging could be booked. By this time, my chief branding officer, Cameron Spann, and I felt like we were leading a small army all by ourselves to coordinate transportation, booking rooms and meals, and preparing an agenda complete with entertainment, starting on Friday afternoon and ending Sunday night.

Integrity Turns Dreams Into Reality

As NSBA board members descended on tiny Gettysburg, it didn't take long to realize the event was going to be a huge success. On the first night, our team brought in an 80-year-old gentleman dressed as President Abraham Lincoln. In full costume, including the stovepipe hat, he delivered an inspiring speech about leading during challenging times.

On Saturday morning our group joined Mike for his mesmerizing battlefield seminar, replete with the stories of courage and integrity.

Along the route, a gentleman dressed as a Union general joined us on a rocky hill overlooking the battlefield—a delightful surprise.

Speaking of generals, a few weeks prior, I had begun assembling an authentic Robert E. Lee uniform from boots to western hat, and I even acquired a military sword. During lunch on Saturday, I appeared in full dress and beard as the famed Confederate hero—adding a bit of lighthearted playfulness to the event.

By Sunday, everyone on our board had bonded and learned valuable lessons on leadership and integrity. This was the end result I had envisioned, and it had required help from many individuals.

Note: As I mentioned in Chapter 1, my colleague and I had to leave Gettysburg early on Sunday to catch a plane to Los Angeles for our Red Carpet adventure at the Oscars. Another opportunity to promote public education! Thankfully, I was able to witness firsthand the success of the Gettysburg event prior to leaving.

Integrity For a More Peaceful, Civil World

Just as we revere the war heroism of long ago, we also cherish peacemaking and the statesmen who have helped mend us after a conflict. Who can forget President Lincoln's famous healing words to a deeply divided nation near the end of the Civil War:

> "With malice toward none, with charity for all, with firmness in the right as God gives us to see the right, let us strive on to finish the work we are in, to bind up the nation's wounds, to care for him who shall have borne the battle and for his widow and his orphan, to do all which may achieve and cherish a just and lasting peace among ourselves and with all nations."

It's important to remember that the skill of peacemaking sometimes just boils down to how we treat other people every day. We can be true to our own values without being disrespectful to others. I often lament that as a society we seem to have lost the art of debate. We take grave offense when someone expresses an opposing opinion. Unfortunately, when we become

4. Integrity

insular in our thinking, we miss opportunities to grow. We need to remember that when we listen, we learn. That's one of the perks of civility.

At just 14 years old, George Washington wrote 110 Rules of Civility in his school tablet. This exercise helped him develop his character. His rules included guidelines for behavior in a wide variety of settings, "pleasant company, appropriate actions in formal situations, and general courtesies."[1] Washington, while a great military leader, was revered for his statesmanship, no doubt something he had honed throughout his life. He had the ability to bring people together.

Similarly, at the age of 20, Benjamin Franklin created a system to strengthen his character (page 56). It included 13 virtues or moral exercises he strived to live by. Plato and Aristotle also defined values to live by. Each one realized that creating his own set of essential virtues helped him become a better human being, a person of integrity.[2]

Perhaps we should all make a list of virtues to live by. As we face challenges in our ever-changing world, one thing remains constant: the need for more people of integrity who put the interests of their family, community, country and the world before their own.

Integrity to Last a Lifetime

While each of us likes to think we possess unassailable integrity, we can count on our integrity being tested throughout our lives. Headlines remind us every day of people who failed that test:

- *Employee of Kansas City Company Pleads Guilty to $3 Million Embezzlement*
- *Jury Convicts Dayton Businessman of Fraud*
- *Tyler Man Indicted for Using Stolen Valor to Defraud Investors*

As for the employee who embezzled money from the company she worked for, you can bet it didn't happen in one big swoop. Instead, it probably started with just taking a few dollars that she didn't think would

---

1 https://www.mountvernon.org/george-washington/rules-of-civility/1/
2 https://iulianionescu.com/blog/benjamin-franklins-life-virtues/#ftoc-benjamin-franklins-virtues

Pillars of Purpose

Benjamin Franklin's 13 Virtues[1]

"I included under thirteen names of virtues all that at that time occurr'd to me as necessary or desirable, and annexed to each a short precept, which fully express'd the extent I gave to its meaning." – Benjamin Franklin

1. Temperance: Eat not to dullness. Drink not to elevation.

2. Silence: Speak not but what may benefit others or yourself. Avoid trifling conversation.

3. Order: Let all your things have their places. Let each part of your business have its time.

4. Resolution: Resolve to perform what you ought. Perform without fail what you resolve.

5. Frugality: Make no expense but to do good to others or yourself: i.e., Waste nothing.

6. Industry: Lose no time. Be always employed in something useful. Cut off all unnecessary actions.

7. Sincerity: Use no hurtful deceit. Think innocently and justly; and if you speak, speak accordingly.

8. Justice: Wrong none by doing injuries, or omitting the benefits that are your duty.

9. Moderation: Avoid extremes. Forbear resenting injuries so much as you think they deserve.

10. Cleanliness: Tolerate no uncleanness in body, clothes, or habitation.

11. Tranquility: Be not disturbed at trifles, or at accidents common or unavoidable.

12. Chastity: Rarely use venery but for health or offspring; never to dullness, weakness, or the injury of your own or another's peace or reputation.

13. Humility: Imitate Jesus and Socrates.

---

1 https://iulianionescu.com/blog/benjamin-franklins-life-virtues/#ftoc-benjamin-franklins-virtues

4. Integrity

be missed and eventually grew into thousands of dollars over time.

All of us will have our integrity tested at some time or other. While some tests may be small, such as letting the cashier know she gave us too much change, bigger tests, such as spreading untruths about a person, can actually destroy lives.

During my five terms on the school board, the 2010 election was by far the hardest test of my integrity to the extreme. I had run unopposed for several of the previous campaigns, but with this one my opponent was ready to fight with fire. Our school district was dealing with incredible growth, and he drew ammunition from the fact that instead of supporting the needed renovations for our local Germantown High School, I had voted to build a new high school in Arlington, a neighboring community. While I fully understood the need to renovate the aging Germantown High School, building a new school in Arlington would alleviate overcrowding in two other schools as well.

When I voted for the new school in Arlington, I knew many of my constituents would be angry, but I was confident with the decision I had made. It all came down to making a choice to be a politician and keep voters happy, or do what I thought was the right thing. Then, all hell broke lose. I started getting angry phone calls from the public and was bombarded on social media. Although I was able to eventually get funding to renovate the Germantown High School campus, people were still angry. My political opponent accused me of not making Germantown a priority. It turned into a bloody campaign.

As the campaign intensified, I sought refuge with one of my closest confidants, my dog. Our nightly walks around the block kept getting longer and longer, but it was my only escape from the chaos. With the support of my family, I pledged to move forward with my re-election campaign. However, my integrity was again put to the test when, for the next eight months, my opponent spread lies and misleading information about me and my family. Deciding whether to lower myself to his level or continue running an honorable campaign was truly a test of moral integrity.

Already committed, I knew I had to get my story out there. I knocked on thousands of doors, encountering many angry constituents. Some barraged me with personal insults, while others engaged in name-calling. I visited nursing homes, retirement centers and churches to share my platform and to refute the lies that my opponent continued to spread. On Election Day, I was at peace knowing I had run a positive campaign. When the last ballot box was counted, out of 21,000 votes, I had won by 167 votes.

If I had lost the election, the next dozen years of my career could have been significantly altered. I probably wouldn't have served on and been president of the Tennessee School Boards Association or the National School Boards Association, and the American Public Education Foundation most likely would never have been founded. I believe my deep sense of purpose, ability to persevere and my need to keep my integrity intact has helped me to accomplish far greater things than I otherwise would have.

"With integrity, you have nothing to fear, since you have nothing to hide. With integrity, you will do the right thing, so you will have no guilt."

– Zig Ziglar, American motivational speaker

When You Look in the Mirror

I share these stories to show how integrity flows from your values, and your values guide your actions. Integrity comes down to saying you are going to do something and then doing it. That's why people are drawn to leaders who say what they'll do and do what they say. In turn, leaders seek out team members and partners with integrity as allies.

Integrity consists of making daily choices that reflect your deeply held values and staying true to ethical principles that govern your life. For many of us, it's doing what our parents always told us: tell the truth regardless of the consequences; say you're sorry when you're wrong; be incorruptible; and above all, be honest with yourself.

In Gettysburg, on a boulder overlooking the battlefield, you'll find an eight-foot-tall bronze statue of Father William E. Corby. Father Corby, a staunch Catholic, gave comfort to the wounded during the Civil War. However, he was saddened to think that so many soldiers would die without receiving last rites—a Catholic tradition that cleanses a person of his

4. Integrity

or her sins. On the second day of the battle, he mounted the large boulder and said rites for all the soldiers who might die in battle, giving them provisional or general absolution. By doing this, he matched his integrity to his faith and his duty to the troops.

Great leaders find ethical solutions to problems. They do so in the service of others and for the benefit of others.

You might ask yourself, "Am I a person of integrity?" Here are a few thought-provoking questions to help you take an introspective look at your daily actions:

- Do I live in harmony with my deepest values and beliefs?
- Am I dependable, and do I follow through on commitments?
- Am I open and honest when communicating with others?
- Do I hold myself accountable for my actions?
- Do I admit when I make a mistake?
- When I look in the mirror at the end of the day, do I like the person looking back at me?

Hopefully, you are able to answer "yes" to these questions. If not, today is a new beginning. Set a goal to demonstrate integrity in all your actions, whether with family, in the workplace or in social situations. When we hold ourselves to higher standards, we contribute to making the world a better place.

Pillars of Purpose

Chapter 5

DISCIPLINE

"With faith, discipline and selfless devotion to duty, there is nothing worthwhile that you cannot achieve."

— Muhammad Ali Jinnah, lawyer, politician, first governor-general of Pakistan

In these first chapters I've laid out four important Bedrock Principles: Power of the Possible, Perseverance, Passion and Integrity. Drawing inspiration from historical figures and reflecting on stories from my own life, I hope I've shown how certain attributes form the foundation for a successful life, and how they give us the best shot at realizing our dreams—our *whys*.

In this final chapter of our first section, we'll explore the fifth principle—Discipline—an essential character trait that can further strengthen our foundation and help us achieve whatever our mind can imagine.

Teacher, philosopher and religious leader Buddha wisely said: *"To enjoy good health, to bring true happiness to one's family, to bring peace to all, one must first discipline and control one's own mind. If a man can control his mind, he can find the way to enlightenment, and all the wisdom and virtue will naturally come to him."*

Pillars of Purpose

Discipline is the mental strength that pushes a person to make things happen. Through discipline, we hold ourselves accountable, not just for our actions but for our lives. It affects our ability to be independent, punctual, focused and organized, and brings stability and structure to what otherwise would be chaos.

There are two types of discipline:

- Self-discipline. The ability to control your feelings and overcome weaknesses. It's your ability to pursue internal objectives.
- External discipline. Drawing strength from accountability partners, mentors or coaches, as well as the ability to follow rules and laws that create structure in your life.

Developing self-discipline gives us inner strength and a sense of freedom—freedom from laziness, weakness and fear. It makes us mentally tough.

Once again, I point to legendary coach Vince Lombardi as an example of both self- and external discipline. A national symbol of determination and discipline, he inspired others to reach their full potential. Prior to Lombardi taking over as coach, the Packers were considered an underperforming, moribund team. He imposed tough, stringent practice sessions (external discipline) and expected members of his team to show consistent improvement—or be replaced. He sincerely believed that *"winning becomes a habit, and so can losing."*

The team came to love and respect him for his tough leadership and high expectations. In Lombardi's second season, the Packers made it to the championship game. The team didn't win, but the following year they did. It was their first step toward a winning dynasty that would continue throughout his tenure with the team. In all, the Packers won a total of five NFL championships in seven years and the first two Super Bowls (1966 and 1967), an impressive feat.

Lombardi epitomized mental toughness and understood that mental toughness requires discipline.

> *"Mental toughness is many things and rather difficult to explain. Its qualities are sacrifice and self-denial. Also, most importantly, it is combined with a perfectly disciplined will that refuses to give in. It's a state of mind–you could call it character in action."* – Vince Lombardi

5. Discipline

The late entrepreneur, motivational speaker and coach Jim Rohn, claimed, *"Discipline is the bridge between goals and accomplishments."* A self-made millionaire at the age of 30, Rohn ended up losing everything he owned. Sharing this devastating experience, he said, *"Somewhere in the deep fathoms of my mind, not only did I find the will to survive, but I also mustered up the energy to instill an enormous amount of self-discipline into my life."*

Upon his death in 2009, at the age of 79, Rohn was worth $500 million, had mentored numerous entrepreneurs to guide them on the pathway to success and had written dozens of books—all proof that his tremendous willpower and self-discipline paid off.

Discipline is the accountability bridge between our goals and accomplishments. It governs the thoughts, emotions and actions leading to our destination. It gives us the ability to reach our "goals" on the other side of the bridge without sliding off the edge.

Discipline in Goal Setting

I firmly believe in setting goals. For me, a goal not written down is just a hope. Written goals solidify our commitment and help us maintain a long-term focus and disciplined habits.

For instance, everyone knows Michael Phelps was a darn good swimmer, the most decorated swimmer (and Olympian) of all time with 23 gold, three silver and two bronze medals across five Olympic games. But less well known was the fact that he also excelled at goal setting. At just 11 years of age, Phelps wrote down a bold goal: to win a spot on the U.S. Olympic team in the next Olympics. Despite his young age, he immediately set out to reach that goal.

His youth coach, Bob Bowman, who acted somewhat like a drill sergeant to the developing athlete, said he could see immense potential and determination in young Phelps. Continually pushing him with increasingly rigorous training sessions, Bowman watched as Phelps outraced older and more experienced swimmers. Seizing on Phelps' penchant for goal setting, Bowman challenged him to pick three of his favorite races, and to write down the times he wanted to achieve at each as his goal for the year.

"He was just 11, but six months later he swam those exact times, to the

Pillars of Purpose

one-hundredth of a second," Bowman said.

Phelps' determination far exceeded that of other swimmers. When he found out other swimmers practiced six days a week, he knew he had to practice seven days a week. Just as water is hot at 211 degrees, but at 212 degrees it boils, similarly, that extra day of practice gave Phelps the one-degree advantage in his heats to reach his goal.

At just 15 years of age, Phelps' self-discipline and focus earned him a trip to Sydney, Australia, with the Olympic team. He was the youngest male swimmer to qualify and compete for the United States in an Olympic Games in seven decades. While his medals would come later, he had achieved his initial goal.

As an adult, Phelps explained that he has always written down his goals and put them where he could see them. *"I have to see something for **why** I'm getting up in the morning and what I'm doing that day."*

Discipline to Run the Race

Daily discipline creates habits. As children we learned self-discipline: we rose each morning, brushed our teeth, combed our hair and went to school. At school we practiced external discipline. We refrained from hitting the bully in the nose because it was against the rules. We attended the required classes and completed homework assignments.

As adults, we enjoy more freedom. While we must abide by certain external rules and laws that help us live together in social harmony, we face internal choices: Do I want to eat healthier foods? To exercise regularly? To have a bigger house? To get a better job?

As we determine our priorities, we set goals to accomplish them. Sometimes our goals arise from external motivation, e.g., your spouse wants a bigger house, and you want to make your spouse happy. Or you need a better job because you find your boss difficult to work with.

In my life, I've benefited from both internal and external discipline. I've frequently risen to challenges presented to me … like the time my daughter Katie invited me to join her in a 13-mile run through an amusement park for charity. I would not have chosen that goal for myself, but I didn't

5. Discipline

want to disappoint her. It also would be a fantastic opportunity for us to spend time together.

Discipline to Meet the Challenge

Just understand, I think I'm a lot like other people when I tell you ... *I hate running.*

Whether you call it jogging or fast walking, running for me combines the sensations of *boredom and pain*—neither of which I find amusing. So, for the first 58 years of my life, I avoided running ... with the exception of a few so-called fun runs sponsored by non-profit organizations. Mind you, those races usually took only 45 minutes or so to complete, and they required no serious cardio training outside of my regular racquetball games. I tell people my "fun run" strategy was to start slowly and taper off from there. That always produces a few laughs, but it's the honest truth.

However, when Katie proposed we take part in a half marathon, my distain for running was put to the test. In her fundraising work with the Juvenile Diabetes Research Foundation (JDRF), she'd learned about Disney's Marathon Weekend held every January in Orlando. Being the organizer she is, she'd pulled together a JDRF team to race and raise money for the cause. (Sponsors donated funds for each runner who completed the race.) Marathon weekend was nine months away. We had plenty of time to prepare.

As a 58-year-old participant, I would be taking on something I really hated. At 13.1 miles, this race would cover more ground than any of my previous races. It might take three or four hours to complete. Could I do it?

I have always believed that with pure determination and a heap of self-discipline, a person can accomplish anything. My daughter, a chip off the old block, didn't like to run either. But it was a challenge we couldn't refuse—a chance to overcome our bodies' natural inertia and to do something together for a good cause.

In August I started training for the race by running the equivalent of five kilometers (about 3.1 miles) nearly every day. While I still didn't like running, this time my feet hit the ground with a sense of purpose.

Pillars of Purpose

Race Day Arrives

After five months of training, in January our family arrived at Walt Disney World in Orlando, Florida. We felt physically and emotionally prepared. Unfortunately, a massive thunderstorm with lightning had blown through the area the previous night and was expected to continue into the next day. Race officials informed us they had canceled the half marathon scheduled for Saturday, but explained we could still receive our medals without running.

Even to me, a non-runner, that didn't sound right. I had signed up for the half marathon, and I couldn't accept a medal without earning it. Talking to other runners, I found they too felt disappointed they couldn't run the 13.1-mile course. All of us were determined to earn the medal through our own efforts. Thankfully, we persuaded race officials to let us run our half marathon with the full-marathon runners on Sunday. We ran the half marathon and proudly earned the right to wear the medals we received.

After completing the race, my ever-cheerful Katie suggested, "Next year, let's go all the way!"

All the way, of course, referred to a grueling four-day test of endurance people call the "The Dopey Challenge" after Disney's sweet, dimwitted dwarf. The entire weekend consisted of a 5k race on day one, a 10k race on day two, a half marathon on day three, and a full marathon on day four, a total of 48.6 miles. Soon to be 59 years old, I knew running that many miles would strain my capacity, and I knew I had to be freaking goofy to even try to do it. Determined, I would have to prepare for it all year long by substantially increasing my daily training.

The Biggest Test Yet

For a solid year, we trained for The Dopey Challenge. Five months prior, I began competing in races every weekend. I ran 5ks in August and September, 10ks in October and November, and in December I ran my first marathon at a charitable event for St. Jude Children's Research Hospital.

In January 2019, our entire family traveled to Orlando for the big event. My daughter, son Chris, daughter-in-law Amy, and I arose at 3 a.m. on the first day to join nearly 30,000 other people at Walt Disney World.

5. Discipline

Shaking in our shoes because of the chilly temperatures, we awaited the start of our race in designated sections or corrals that made us feel like we were farm animals being led to the slaughter. In my heart, I wondered if we actually were.

For the first two days, during the 5k and 10k, we jogged with litle difficulty through the world-renowned amusement park, surrounded by picture-perfect Disney-styled landscapes. However, after the third day, the half marathon, Katie developed severe blisters on her feet. We worried whether she would be able to run in the full marathon the next day.

Motivated by her cause (a cure for Type 1 diabetes) and in spite of the agonizing pain, she willed herself to run on the final day. My son, Chris, a more devoted athlete and runner, finished the marathon in an impressive time of 3.5 hours. I finished a while after that, using my last reserve of energy to sprint across the finish line. A symbolic push to show I gave it my all.

As we waited near the finish line, we saw Katie limping toward us. Her blisters had broken open making every step incredibly painful. But she finished. I was so proud of her. Even less of a runner than I am, Katie overcame challenges and persevered, inspiring all of us. A true example of sheer determination, Katie was the hero of the day.

Katie, Chris and I did not compete in those races to achieve great finish times, but simply to cross the finish line and achieve the goals we had set for ourselves. We accomplished something we never thought we could do. My kids and I now share a memory we'll cherish forever.

Discipline Reveals Character

I believe we show character when we conquer challenges and act in accordance with our values and beliefs. If "who you are" and "how you act" aren't in sync, your life won't feel right. You'll know you're not living the life you should be ... or could be. Even if you don't know it consciously, you'll feel it deep within your soul. However, to stay true to who you are, you have to be disciplined and have determination.

I stayed true to my character when I accepted my daughter's challenge to run a marathon. What if I had let my dislike of running cheat me out

Pillars of Purpose

of this experience? What if instead of preparing myself by running each day, I had vegged out in front of the television? I can't say it was always easy to put on my running shoes and step out the door, but I knew that if I were to reach my goal, I had to be disciplined, and I had to let my determination lead my actions.

In an earlier chapter, I mentioned how I vowed in my life never to look back with regret and say, "what if?" I've always been determined to never let fear stop me from acting. Some people are so terrified of not succeeding that they never try; but failure won't kill us, instead it helps us grow. From the first step we take to the final one, we experience risk, a vital element of life. We fall down, we make bad choices; however, in the end what matters is that we get back up and try again.

"Failure won't kill us, instead it helps us to grow."

The Journey to Reach a Goal

Just as young Michael Phelps knew at an early age he wanted to become an Olympian, many of us feel called to our occupations in our youth. In some cases, an encounter with a coach or mentor—or just a stirring within our souls—can start us on a long journey to becoming the person we aspire to be. When I was 14, my mother gave me *The Defense Never Rests,* a book authored by F. Lee Bailey, the famous defense attorney. After reading it, I knew I wanted to be a lawyer—to defend people, to present positions and argue cases. It became my dream, one that would require self-discipline to achieve through many twists and turns over decades.

Entering college at Arkansas State University in Jonesboro. I majored in political science, plan-

5. Discipline

ning to attend law school after graduation. I worked three jobs while carrying a full load of studies. I also became heavily involved with student government. I found I had an inclination toward politics when working on several political campaigns, including Bill Clinton's 1978 gubernatorial race. In 1980 I was the youngest delegate at the Democratic National Convention in New York City.

Not long into my college studies, however, I suddenly felt a crisis of confidence in my chosen path. How do I make a living with a political science degree if I don't go to law school? What if I don't become an attorney as I'd planned? I needed a backup plan.

I decided a political science degree wouldn't afford me many career options outside of politics or law. So, after my first year in college, I changed my major to industrial management, a course of study heavy in high-level calculus, math and accounting. In spite of my aversion to math, I graduated at the top of my class with a 3.9 GPA. While I felt ready to enthusiastically pursue my new path with passion, I still hoped to become a lawyer someday.

In 1981, life was moving along. I started working a full-time job at Xerox and was attending evening law school. For the next four years, my wife and I endured a crazy schedule. I worked all day, attended law school from 6 p.m. to 9:30 p.m. and then went home to study, which consisted of reading and briefing 100 to 200 pages of legal cases every night. Somehow, in spite of this insane schedule, my wife and I were blessed with our first child.

In 1984, I left Xerox to begin a career in the financial services industry, working for Paine Webber, Jackson & Curtis Inc. This required me to take a semester off from law school. Returning in the fall, I graduated from the Cecil C. Humphreys School of Law at the University of Memphis in 1985, with a Juris Doctor (JD) degree. I took the bar exam in February 1986 and became licensed in May. I had fulfilled my dream of becoming a lawyer.

While attending law school, I had begun to build a successful financial advisory practice working at PaineWebber. I asked the corporate manager how I could obtain approval to operate a separate law practice while still building my advisory practice. He replied that once I graduated from law school and passed the bar, all I would have to do is submit a request for outside business activity. He assured me it would be approved. Everything seemed perfect; I could have my proverbial cake and eat it too.

Once I passed the bar, I submitted the required documentation to management. After being ignored for nearly a year, in May 1987, the answer came. My request was denied. At that moment, all the trust I had built with PaineWebber was completely destroyed. The promise that had been made to me had no basis in fact. If I couldn't trust the word of the people with whom I was working, then we had no foundation for a long-term relationship. That breach of trust set into action a series of events that led to me leaving PaineWebber within three months to work with another advisory firm.

Over the next two decades, my ability to practice law was severely limited by the organizational constraints placed on me by the Wall Street firms for which I worked. However, I knew the time would come when I could fulfill my dream to establish a law practice that would make a difference in the lives of the clients we would serve. Until that time, I was responsible for preparing myself to embrace the opportunity when it came.

I continued sharpening the saw by increasing my knowledge and honing my skills as an attorney throughout those years. I maintained my law license by completing the required continuing education (CE) as well as ongoing professional development in estate planning, tax law and other related topics. I also did some legal work for family and friends, and in 2000, I joined a select group of attorneys admitted to practice before the United States Supreme Court.

In the summer of 1999, the firm I was working for was sold to UBS Financial, a global powerhouse in banking and finance. This sale represented a huge shift in the firm's philosophy in client service. They viewed financial advisors as distribution sources for their products and seemed less interested in customized client service and individualized solutions. This was in total opposition to the direction I wanted to go.

While I loved being a financial advisor, I had carried this dream of establishing a law practice for several decades. I wanted to do both. Over the

5. Discipline

next several months, I began to realize that my career was at a crossroads. I could continue as a successful wirehouse stockbroker, or I could take the risk to pursue an independent course that would allow me to build a firm of true significance and substance. If I took the second option, I would be risking everything I had built up to that point, as well as assuming a tremendous financial obligation. I truly was at that proverbial fork in the road, described so eloquently by the poet Robert Frost in his famous poem. I decided to choose the road less traveled.

> I shall be telling this with a sigh
> Somewhere ages and ages hence:
> Two roads diverged in a wood, and I,
> I took the one less traveled by,
> And that has made all the difference.

I knew I wanted to start an advisory firm that would compare to Wall Street's "big boys" when it came to the products and services I could offer clients. But I also wanted to create a unique business model, one that was client centric. For the next five years, I honed my skills, raised the necessary capital, hired a tech consultant to create state-of-the-art software platforms, found a location and built a building. Then, in March 2005, after five years of intensive research and planning, we opened the doors to Pickler Wealth Advisors.

While my short-term focus was on building the financial advisory practice, my long-term plans included opening a law practice and an accounting firm. For the next few years I continued to strengthen my knowledge and gain the experience that would give me the confidence, capability and ability to someday develop these two additional businesses.

Finally in 2008, 22 years after first obtaining my license to practice law, we opened the doors to our law firm. It was the culmination of my adolescent dream. I'm proud to say we went on to receive recognition as "Best Law Firm in Memphis" four years in a row.[1]

---

[1] 2019–2022 Best Law Firm in Memphis, created by Commercial Appeal, based on popular vote and not specific to the financial services and does not imply an endorsement, recommendation, or otherwise reflect the performance of the advisor. https://commercialappeal.secondstreetapp.com/2022-Memphis-Most-Awards/. Law services offered through The Pickler Law Firm are separate from and not offered through Commonwealth.

Pillars of Purpose

In 2012, we launched an accounting firm. Then, in 2014, we founded our non-profit organization, the American Public Education Foundation. Its mission is to support programs in financial literacy and workforce development. The organization promotes the power of public education to transform lives, grow economies and strengthen America. It strives to serve the interests of America's public schoolchildren, who are our nation's future.

Where would I be now if PaineWebber had followed through on its promise to let me practice law? It matters naught; I'm confident the road I took was the right one. Has my journey to get here been easy? Of course not. Going from being a young man just starting a family, working a full-time job and attending law school in the evening while starting new businesses was taxing on both my family and me. However, with their support, our shared sacrifice, and sheer determination, we reached our goals.

Living With Determination and Discipline

We gain discipline by setting goals, particularly written goals. Greg Reid, author of *The Millionaire Mentor*, described why written goals matter:

> "A dream written down with a date becomes a goal. A goal broken down into steps becomes a plan. A plan backed by action makes your dreams come true."

While in many ways I'm just an ordinary person, I do have an extraordinary amount of focus and discipline: I strive to hold myself accountable and use my time wisely. For more than four decades, I've written my New Year's resolutions on a nice piece of stationery and reviewed them throughout the year. It's always rewarding when, at the end of the year, I'm able to see what I've accomplished, and it gives me renewed motivation when I see things that I haven't yet completed.

I'm also an avid list maker. I was only 12 years old when I started writing a "to do" list, and I've now been doing this for 50-plus years. However, my lists have expanded to include my daily, weekly, monthly, annual and life goals written on yellow legal pads. I've filled a lot of these pads over the years. Before retiring each night, I review the list and then craft a de-

5. Discipline

tailed plan for the next day. If there is something I didn't get done, I write it down again for the next day … and again, and again until I complete it.

While some people may think I'm too regimented, writing my goals down and prioritizing them frees me from the stress of not knowing what I'll be doing that day and whether or not I've accomplished what I needed to do. When waking each morning, my day is laid out and I know which tasks to tackle first.

Frequently, life will happen, and it's easy to lose track of your goals. Sometimes I have to adjust my goals, but my objective is to hold myself accountable for accomplishing what I've written down. The list making allows me to maintain focus, even when life happens. The reviewing and assessing is an important part of my list-making process, as I never have to worry about something falling through the cracks. I feel immense satisfaction when I accomplish my daily goals and can cross each item off my list.

Discipline Through Bucket Lists

As a major "list" person, I also have a bucket list of goals and dreams that I wish to experience or accomplish before I literally kick the bucket … and it's exhaustive. On it, I list my top five goals in a variety of categories; for example the challenges I want to tackle and any fears I want to overcome.

I constantly add items to my bucket list and currently have more than 100 items on it. Some of them revolve around acts of service, while others will contribute to my personal growth. Many are adventures, such as going on an African safari, visiting the great pyramids in Egypt or watching a tennis match at Wimbledon. Others are downright idiotic, such as skydiving with the U.S. Army's Golden Knights parachute team or flying with the Navy's flight demonstration squadron, the Blue Angels.

Will I accomplish all the things on my bucket list? Probably not, but a person can dream, right? I do refer to my bucket list when I write my annual goal list. Once an item makes it to that list, it's almost guaranteed to become a reality.

Pillars of Purpose

Accountability

So often I hear people say, "I don't have the time …" I always laugh a bit when they say this. In reality, it's an excuse. All of us enjoy the same amount of time—86,400 seconds a day, 604,800 seconds a week and 331,449,600 seconds per year. However, we never know how much time we actually have on Earth. While none of us can petition for more time, we can control how we use the seconds we're given.

> *"I believe every human has an infinite number of heartbeats. I don't intend to waste any of mine."*
>
> — Neil Armstrong, American astronaut and first person to walk on the moon

I'm blessed that I don't require much sleep. For me, I can't think of anything worse than lying in bed for seven or eight hours when I've been given such a limited time on Earth. I feel it is up to me to maximize that time. Each morning when I wake up, I'm excited for the day and focused on what I need to get done. I've built structure into my workday and I'm deadline driven.

My team members are my accountability partners. In fact, between us, we've created a shared culture of accountability. We hold regular meetings to ensure nothing falls through the cracks, that we're on schedule to meet the deadlines we've set and on track to reach our goals. It's a culture where we all enjoy our work, have mutual respect for each other and even have fun times together. As part of our commitment to physical health, we built a on-site gym for our employees. We also take advantage of a mile-long walk around the lake by our office. It makes it so much easier to do these things as a group.

In addition to my work schedule, I've set a goal of walking 10,000 steps or more each day. If I haven't completed my goal before leaving the office, I don't allow myself to go home until I do. No matter if it's light or dark outside, or if I have to battle snow, sleet, rain or a thunderstorm, I put on my walking shoes and head to the trail around the lake. I can't say it's easy after a hard day at work; but for more than seven years or 2,500 days, I've held myself accountable for making it happen. I've kept the pledge and held true to my personal covenant: *"Do the right thing for the right reason, even when no one is looking."*

5. Discipline

Benefits of Lifelong Learning

While staying in shape physically has made a dramatic difference in my life, my commitment to rigorous mental workouts may be even more important. By now you know, I'm an advocate for lifelong learning. In our ever-changing world, it's more important than ever to keep sharpening the saw to become the best version of yourself. Doing this takes personal commitment and determination.

While external discipline is sometimes the motivating force behind continued learning, such as increasing our skill set to get a better and higher paying job, we get more mileage from internal or self-motivation.

In the previous chapters, we've talked about the importance of discovering your *why*—the driving force that makes you do what you do. Ongoing education becomes the fuel that will help you realize your full potential. As you learn more about the world you live in, you're enlivened to learn even more, and you're open to the free exchange of ideas and viewpoints, all of which will contribute to a more enriched and happier life. It may even keep you feeling young.

Henry Ford, the founder of the Ford Motor Company, once said, *"Anyone who stops learning is old, whether at twenty or eighty. Anyone who keeps learning stays young."*

In the 1990s, research commissioned by the U.S. Congress showed that the brain continues to grow and thrive as long as it is challenged and stimulated. According to Nancy Merz Nordstrom, M Ed., author of *Learning Later, Living Greater: The Secret for Making the Most of Your After-50 Years*, "One of the best methods for doing this, is through lifelong learning." She goes on to cite non-credit academic study, educational travel and community service as tools for stimulating the minds of older learners.

I'm convinced that an active brain is a healthy brain, and I've made it a goal to pursue additional knowledge or certifications every year. During the last three years, I've earned designations and certifications from The Wharton School of the University of Pennsylvania and Yale University. I've also taken programs at Harvard University, American College of Financial Services, College for Financial Planning, and The Investment & Wealth Institute. I've studied and passed exams to become a CERTIFIED

Pillars of Purpose

FINANCIAL PLANNER™ practitioner, a Certified Private Wealth Advisor® (CPWA®), Chartered Advisor in Philanthropy® (CAP®), a Chartered Financial Consultant® (ChFC®), and a Certified Divorce Financial Analyst® (CDFA®) practitioner. I've even taken a class in behavioral finance to better understand and address the challenges that clients face.

Overcoming Inertia

Again, I'm just an ordinary person who hopes when I get to the end of my journey, I can say with confidence that I have emptied the tank, having used all my God-given talents to the fullest.

To make things happen, we all need to overcome inertia. Maybe it's the inertia of a poor family environment, unexpected roadblocks or our fear of the unknown. Or maybe it's just our reluctance to get off the couch and make things happen.

It's helpful to recall Newton's first law of motion. In simplified terms it states, "A body at rest stays at rest, a body in motion stays in motion." In life, you're never standing still. Either you are moving forward or falling back. That's why it's important to take that first step … and then the next, and then another.

If you want your dreams to come true, you can't wait for life to happen. You must live life with enthusiasm and unstoppable determination.

As you adopt a disciplined approach to self-improvement, you'll find value in:

- Writing down daily, weekly, monthly and yearly goals.
- Reviewing your goals on a regular basis.
- Pursuing lifelong continuing education.
- Seeking accountability partners to help push you toward accomplishments.

With a disciplined mind and daily habits, you'll be programmed for success and primed to make it happen.

SECTION II.
PILLARS OF PURPOSE

Trust   Order & Control

Peace of Mind   Objectivity

Problem Solving   Navigate Life

Advocate & Partner   Educate & Counsel

Main Street Values

Pillars of Purpose

Section II
INTRODUCTION

"When the why becomes powerful, the how becomes easy."
– Jim Rohn, author and motivational speaker

In the first section of this book, we explored five Bedrock Principles that help us awaken our deepest sense of purpose and realize our greatest potential. Through Power of the Possible, Perseverance, Passion, Integrity and Discipline we have begun to build a solid foundation for turning visions into reality and for realizing our purpose.

I often refer to my life purpose as being my *why*. You might even think of it as your life calling. As Oprah Winfrey wisely said, *"There is no greater gift you can give or receive than to honor your calling. It's WHY you were born. And how you become most truly alive."*

Your "calling" or purpose is the reason you exist. It's the heart of who you are and why you are here. It defines and anchors your life. It can also represent a future goal—an objective to pursue throughout your life.

In this section, we'll dig more deeply into the "how to" for achieving our

Pillars of Purpose

life's purpose by building on that rock-solid foundation. We'll explore nine pillars—skills and ideals—that provide a well-designed template for leading a life of significance and influence. The pillars are the actual blueprint for building a life of significance. They include:

- Trust
- Peace of Mind
- Problem Solving
- Advocate and Partner
- Order and Control
- Objectivity
- Navigate Life
- Educate and Counsel
- Main Street Values

Each of these ideals and skills is vitally important in helping us reach our destination. While we may have already mastered a few, we're never too good for improvement. I'm reminded of a line from songwriter Reverend Burke Hudson's song, My Soul: *"Perfection is a road, not a destination."*

When we internalize or personalize knowledge, it motivates us to act. Action forces us out of our comfort zones so we can make a difference in our own life and the lives of others, and it enables us to gain even more knowledge.

Again, to share Hudson's soulful chorus:

> "... Everytime I live, I gettin' education.
> Every different situation forces me to grow
> And every different manifestation lets me know that
> Perfection is a road, not a destination."

Education is a life-long process. In this section, I hope to provide you with the education (knowledge) from some of my life experiences and to share the motivating actions of individuals who have significantly impacted my life. Most importantly, I want to provide you with the tools you'll need to accomplish your purpose—the *how*.

Section II. Pillars of Purpose

I'm not saying this process is necessarily easy, nor does it happen overnight. It takes perseverance. It requires you to act, and then make those actions a habit. While the motivation to do the right thing can get you started, habits keep you going. Then faith ultimately propels you to succeed.

> "He who has faith, has ... an inward reservoir of courage, hope, confidence, calmness and assuring trust that all will come out well."
> — B.C. Forbes, founder of Forbes magazine

Winning the Race

In considering the role of faith and perseverance in pursuing our purpose, I'm reminded of the astounding story of Rich Strike and his stunning victory at the 2022 Kentucky Derby. Just a year prior, his owner had given up on him after he finished dead last in a preliminary race as a two-year-old. Placed in a "claiming" competition for a quick sale, he was claimed by veteran trainer Eric Reed who hoped for another chance to train a winner after a tragic barn fire in 2016 had killed 23 of his horses. Trainer and horse both needed a lucky break.

And they got it. After failing to qualify to be among the final Kentucky Derby participants, Rich Strike was given a last-minute opportunity to run when the horse ahead of him scratched. His odds of winning were set at an impossible 80 to 1, the second-longest odds in Derby history. No one expected anything special from this unknown, inconsequential participant on his last chance as a three-year-old to compete in the event.

As the race began, nobody paid much attention to the chestnut-colored colt with a white-striped face and two white marks on his hind legs. Halfway through the race, Rich Strike fell 16 horse lengths back from the lead. It looked like the odds would prove correct.

But then he made his move.

He worked his way through the crowded pack, almost invisibly. Then, seconds before the finish, he miraculously overtook the two front-runners.

The stunned announcer barely noticed him before he crossed the finish line. Struggling to find his name, he breathlessly exclaimed: *"Rich Strike is coming up on the inside ... Oh my goodness! The longest shot has won the*

Pillars of Purpose

Kentucky Derby!"

With faith, there is always hope. Anything is possible with determination and persistence.

Just as Rich Strike and Eric Reed overcame long odds, so can you. By discovering your purpose, designing and implementing a plan, and staying true to your purpose, you can live a life of significance.

The Power of Purpose

At times you may feel like you're on your last chance, and the competition is blowing you away. By committing to being the best you can be, you'll overcome any adversity or challenge in your path. I like to call this the Power of Purpose.

We can unleash the Power of Purpose in our lives by:

- **Creating a vision.** As I've navigated my personal and professional paths, I've learned that a well-crafted vision of what I want to achieve helps me stay focused and gives me the determination to accomplish my goals. Do you have a vision of what you want to achieve personally and professionally? Does your home, workplace, social culture and the activities you pursue personify that vision?

- **Discovering your purpose.** For purpose to develop, you need to know your *why*, and be able to express it in your own words. Your purpose is the reference point for all the decisions you make and the actions you take. Do you have a stated purpose?

- **Being authentic.** How you implement your "purpose" matters. Are you being authentic? Is this truly something that stirs your heart? Your soul? Is your stated purpose consistent with your beliefs and your actions?

- **Pursuing knowledge.** According to Malcolm Forbes, founder of *Forbes* magazine, *"The purpose of education is to replace an empty mind with an open one."* As wealth management advisors and counselors, we continually strive to educate our clients and ourselves. We see lifelong learning as essential to a life of significance and success. Are you continually seeking knowledge with an open

Section II. Pillars of Purpose

mind? Are you a life-long learner?

- **Being purpose driven.** Your *why* defines your purpose. Are you motivated to actively pursue it? As author and spiritual leader Bishop T.D. Jakes once said, *"If you can't figure out your purpose, figure out your passion. For your passion will lead you right into your purpose."*

- **Connecting others to your purpose.** We should always fight for the things we care about and bring others to our causes. In the iconic film, *Field of Dreams*, Ray Kinsella hears a voice whispering, *"If you build it, he will come"* so he plows under his cornfield to construct a baseball diamond and recruits others to help with his vision. Does your passion for your purpose spread to others? Have you invited them to follow your lead?

- **Unleashing positive energy.** Fueled by purpose, we experience massive energy that propels us forward.

"A positive attitude causes a chain reaction of positive thoughts, events and outcomes. It is a catalyst, and it sparks extraordinary results."

– Wade Boggs, Hall of Fame baseball player

As you explore the next nine chapters, notice the common threads that run between them: being present, listening, demonstrating clarity of mind and ingenuity. Also remember, your current position is not your final destination. Life continually changes, and so can you. I encourage you to pursue lifelong learning and to love and support the people in your life. Most importantly, be kind to yourself and realize that as life evolves, so can you. Simply strive to be the best you can be *today*.

"The goal is not to be better than the other [person], but your previous self."

– the Dalai Lama

Pillars of Purpose

Chapter 6
TRUST

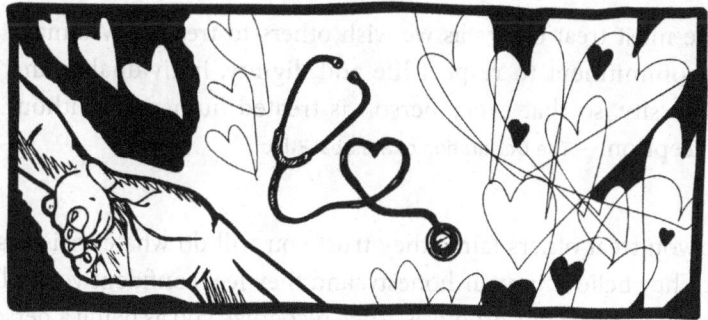

"To be trusted is a greater compliment than to be loved."
—George MacDonald, Scottish author, poet and Christian minister

Of the fundamental forces that hold our world together, perhaps the most important is trust. This small word, *trust*, carries enormous weight. It's the glue that holds our society together. It preserves and cements relationships, whether in a marriage, with family members, friends, social acquaintances or business associates. It provides a sense of safety. It empowers people to bond together to accomplish great deeds and creates the structure to help overcome adversity. When we foster trust, we can accomplish anything.

And while you may spend a lifetime building trust, you can lose it in an instant. Once you break trust, it can take years to repair … if ever.

> *"To earn trust, money and power aren't enough: you have to show some concern for others. You can't buy trust in the supermarket."*
>
> —Dalai Lama

Pillars of Purpose

Trust is built by doing right by someone ... over and over and over. In the Sermon on the Mount, Jesus taught his disciples the Golden Rule: *Do unto others as you would have them do unto you.* (Matt. 7:12) His timeless counsel on treating others fairly offers true hope for mankind to live in harmony. It's interesting to note that some version of the Golden Rule shows up in almost every religion and culture throughout history. In September 1993, more than 140 leaders of the world's major faiths endorsed the Golden Rule as part of the 1992 "Declaration Toward a Global Ethic."[1]

> We must treat others as we wish others to treat us. We make a commitment to respect life and dignity, individuality and diversity, so that every person is treated humanely, without exception. – The Declaration of a Global Ethic[2]

When you treat others fairly, they trust you will do whatever is best for them. They believe in your honesty, and they feel confident you will follow through with your promises. They recognize you as being a person of high integrity, one whose character aligns with your words and actions.

Trust = Character and Competence

In business, as with our personal lives, trust must be earned, never given.

In the investment industry, we encounter the absence of trust quite frequently. Far too many people in financial services call themselves advisors but act more like salespeople. They justify their transactional approach asserting the product or service they provide is "suitable" for the client's needs; it meets the minimum requirement. But is it truly the right product for clients' needs? Maybe they feel they are being technically truthful about the transaction, but are they really being *honest*? Is the transaction based on the client's best interest or their own?

Earning trust requires more than just being technically truthful, it means acting in an honorable way. As mentioned in previous chapters, as a financial advisory practice, we're proud to say we act as fiduciaries

---

1 *Towards a Global Ethic* (An Initial Declaration) ReligiousTolerance.org. – Under the subtitle, "We Declare," third paragraph, 09/04/2993; The first line reads, "We must treat others as we wish others to treat us." http://www.religioustolerance.org/parliame.htm
2 ibid

6. Trust

for our clients. We have an absolute commitment to put their interests above our own. We want our clients to know we'll always do the right thing for them.

I'm reminded of the movie, *The American President*, starring Michael Douglas as President Andrew Shepherd. After initially ignoring his opponent's personal attacks, he recognized the damage being done to his reputation and to those he cared about. At the next press conference, President Shepherd delivered this memorable response:

"For the last couple of months, Senator Rumson (his opponent) has suggested that being president of this country was, to a certain extent, about character. And although I have not been willing to engage his attacks on me, I've been here three years and three days, and I can tell you without hesitation: Being president of this country is entirely about character."

We feel the same about our responsibility to our clients—being a financial advisor is ALL about character, and character makes trust possible.

Stephen R. Covey, the late businessman, author and educator, once said, *"Trust is a function of two things: character and competence. Character includes your integrity, your motive and your intent with people. Competence includes your capability, your skills and your track record. Both are vital."*[1]

Trust, but Verify

On December 8, 1987, President Ronald Reagan met with his Soviet counterpart General Secretary Mikhail Gorbachev to sign the INF Treaty, agreeing to abolish several shorter-range nuclear weapons systems. After signing, President Reagan delivered his signature line, "Trust but verify" in Russian: "Doveryai, no proveryai," reminding everyone of "the extensive verification procedures that would enable both sides to monitor compliance with the treaty."[2]

Gorbachev reportedly said, "You repeat this at every meeting."

To which Reagan responded, "I like it."

---

1 Stephen R. Covey; AZQuotes.com, Wind and Fly LTD, 2022. https://www.azquotes.com/quote/657907, accessed April 10, 2022.
2 David K Shipler; *"Reagan and Gorbachev Sign Missile Treaty and Vow to Work for Greater Reductions"*. New York Times; (9 December 1987.

Pillars of Purpose

A responsible person must verify facts before acting on them. Sometimes you'll meet a person you feel is trustworthy; however, trust should never be so blind that you fail to verify the facts.

Daniel Kahneman, a Nobel prize-winner in economic sciences, introduced the concept of WYSIATI: *What you see is all there is*, meaning we tend not to look beyond what we see, creating massive blind spots. These cognitive biases, innate to all of us, can help us navigate our daily lives. However, they also can cause us to overlook relevant facts.

Throughout history, we have seen detrimental outcomes arising from a failure to verify. For instance, Bernard Madoff, the American financier, defrauded thousands of investors out of tens-of-billions of dollars. For 17 years or more, he conducted one of the largest Ponzi or investment fraud schemes in history. Paying earlier investors with funds received from more recent investors, he covered his illegitimate actions with fraudulent client statements showing higher returns. Eventually, during the 2008 economic crisis, the scheme fell apart as clients started taking more money out than Madoff could replace with new accounts.

Madoff's investors lost more than $65 billion in total, and he hoodwinked them all. Victims included Hollywood celebrities, banks and hedge funds, universities, charities and ordinary investors, some of whom lost their entire life savings. What makes this horrific crime even worse is that Harry Markopolos, a private financial-fraud investigator, had repeatedly warned the Securities and Exchange Commission (SEC) about his suspicions that Madoff was operating a massive investment scam.[1]

So how did Madoff manage to scam so many people, institutions, firms and organizations? He created a front of respectability: his returns were high but not outlandish, and his investment strategy was plausible.

However, the late Stephen R. Covey wisely said: *"Strategy is important, but trust is the hidden variable. On paper you can have clarity around your objectives, but in a low-trust environment, your strategy won't be executed."*[2]

---

1 History; *Billionaire conman Bernard Madoff arrested*; July 20, 2011; History.com editors; https://www.history.com/this-day-in-history/billionaire-conman-bernard-madoff-arrested
2 AZ Quotes; Stephen Covey; https://www.azquotes.com/quote/1286737

6. Trust

The people Madoff scammed weren't stupid. Instead, they were victims of a man who presented himself well. In today's world, we're faced with scams regularly. In fact, the FBI reported that senior citizens alone lost nearly $1 billion to financial fraud or Internet schemes in 2020.[1]

So how can these things be avoided? Education, fact checks, and verification are key, along with reporting occurrences to the proper authorities. Of course, a bit of common sense goes a long way as well. Sometimes when things look too good to be true, they are!

A Childlike Trust

Unfortunately, all of us at some time will come in contact with deceptive individuals. In fact, I'm a firm believer that if someone says, "trust me," it's an immediate sign you should run as fast as you can in the opposite direction. A trustworthy person never has to ask for your trust. Instead, they know it has to be earned—not just today, but in their everyday actions. To earn it, they know they must be honest, admit when they're wrong and honor their commitments. Trust means doing the right thing, even when it's hard.

The most basic example of the importance of trust is a newborn baby. Helpless babies depend on their parent or caretaker to provide for their needs: to change their diapers, feed and clothe them, and to protect them from harm. As children grow, they're taught to trust people in authority, such as the police, doctors and educators. Eventually that trust extends to friends, employers and mentors. That works … until it doesn't. At some time or other, they'll experience someone lying, cheating or stealing from them. They learn they can't trust everyone. Instead, trust must be developed over time and through actual experiences.

This misplaced sense of trust can happen to anyone. For instance, actor Robert DeNiro sold 50 of his father's artworks using a middleman he thought he could trust. DeNiro never received the $88 million he was owed. Music legend Billy Joel lost $90 million by trusting his ex-brother-in-law, and music icon Sting didn't notice his financial advisor was stealing from him for 15 years, until he had lost nearly $10 million.

---

1 Luke Barr; *Senior citizens lost almost $1 billion in scams last year*: ABC News; FBI; June 18, 2021; https://abcnews.go.com/Politics/senior-citizens-lost-billion-scams-year-fbi/story?id=78356859

President Reagan's signature phrase, "trust but verify," is one all of us can wisely practice.

Giving Trust

While understanding the necessity of verifying facts, it's also crucial to remember the importance of giving trust to build healthy relationships. Again, to quote Stephen R. Covey, *"It's not enough to be trustworthy; you also need to be trusting."*

There are three basic elements for determining whether or not a person can be trusted. I call them The Three C's:

- **Caring.** Do they care about you and are they concerned with your general well-being? Or are they instead motivated by their own self-interests?
- **Competence.** Do you feel confident they can deliver on their promises?
- **Consistency.** Are they consistent in their actions? Do they say what they will do and then do what they say? Can you count on them being there when needed?

These three character traits are associated with good leaders. Leaders know that to be trusted, they must first give trust. Just as the business owner must have faith his workers will do their jobs well, and a parent trusts their children to make the right decisions, placing trust in others encourages them to perform at their best. While over time that trust may have been misplaced, it's the first step to developing a healthy relationship.

Giving and Earning Trust

I'm reminded of my time serving on the Shelby County Board of Education. In 1998, I joined five other first-time-elected board members to the seven-member board. Of the seven board members, two were holdovers from the old regime and included the board chairman. Throughout my first year, the chairman regularly showed his disdain and frustration for the opinions of the new members. His level of trust in us was minimal. This caused him to lose support and eventually create an environment that demanded change. Instead of collaborating with each new school

6. Trust

board member, building a team and earning our trust, he chose a different path.

Prior to serving on the board, I'd had the privilege of getting to know a gentleman named Joseph A. Clayton, another one of the new board members. I considered him to be one of the most Godly and decent men I'd ever met. Serving on the school board was the first foray into elective office for both of us, but Joe was no stranger to education. He had been a long-time advocate for schools as a teacher, coach and principal. During our first year on the school board, other members were equally impressed as they got to know him. They were struck by the integrity he exhibited as we resolved various educational issues. Everyone knew him to be a man of honor and someone we could implicitly trust to serve our constituents and to do what was best for the students and educators in our district. We all felt that if we were to choose a new chairman, Joe would be the ideal choice.

One day Joe called me unexpectedly with a request. "I want you to be our leader," he said, to my surprise. "I believe in you and have watched you in a lot of different situations. I believe you can provide the courageous leadership we need and can truly make a difference for our community." He went on to tell me he'd had an amazing career, and while he didn't want the chair position, he would support me every step of the way. Joe understood the concept of servant leadership and empowering others.

His support warmed me to the core. To have such an amazing man say those things about me, and for him to put his trust in me was the honor of my life. With his endorsement, I went on to be elected chair, a position I retained for the next 11 annual elections. During those years, I worked tirelessly to maintain and uphold the trust Joe placed in me as well as the trust I was able to earn from my other board colleagues. I had the ultimate honor of serving with him for the entire 12 years I served as board chair.

While I'm blessed to run my own businesses and serve in organizations that allow me to have a positive influence on the lives of others, none of this would be possible if people didn't feel they could trust me. Trust is the defining element that makes it all possible. It empowers me to solve problems and to be a catalyst for positive change.

Pillars of Purpose

Trust: A Defining Characteristic

Of course, trust doesn't just work in the business world as a defining principle; it's a pillar upon which you build a good life all around. Character and trust go hand in hand. In previous chapters I wrote about how Abraham Lincoln built his reputation as a man of integrity. In a speech he gave in Clinton, Illinois, on September 8, 1854, he addressed the importance of trust:

> *"If you once forfeit the confidence of your fellow citizens, you can never regain their respect and esteem. It is true that you may fool all of the people some of the time: you can even fool some of the people all of the time: but you can't fool all of the people all of the time."*

> *"Part of building trust entails surrounding yourself with people who hold the same standards as you."*

Part of building trust entails surrounding yourself with people who hold the same standards as you do. At the age of 13, I joined DeMolay, a youth organization that promotes character-building and leadership skills for boys between the ages of 13 and 21. At weekly meetings, we regularly learned about the importance of our "word being our bond" and of being worthy of trust. Our activities—small ones, big ones and even those in the middle—were designed to build trust with each other, in our families and within the community.

Throughout my career, I've had the privilege and honor of providing support to many women who are widowed or divorced. When their world came undone, we've been able to be the "rock in the storm" for them. Their trust in us has been expressed repeatedly as they honor us with ongoing referrals. They know we are com-

6. Trust

mitted to being there for them through thick and thin, and that we are always willing to help them overcome any challenges life sends their way.

Combining my experiences with DeMolay, Boy Scouts of America, in business and with other organizations I've been involved with throughout the years, I've developed my personal list of 13 defining actions for building trust:

1. **Be true to your word.** To build trust, it's important to not only talk the talk but to walk the walk. Back your words with actions. It's hard to build trust if you can't be depended on to follow through. That's why you need to be realistic about what you can do and straightforward with any claims or promises you make. It's much more valuable to under-promise and over-deliver, than to over-promise and under-deliver.

   In today's busy world, we often are consumed by the multitude of tasks on our plate, and sometimes we start weighing the importance of a promise we've made. However, if we think of the promise as being a sacred covenant, it will naturally rise to the top of our priority list. Make sure people can trust you to do what you say you will do.

2. **Communicate effectively.** Through communication we create understanding. If you can't communicate effectively, you're nowhere. Every communication carries the potential of being misunderstood. Judith E. Glaser's research on Conversational Intelligence®[1] reported that in nine out of 10 conversations, the other person fails to understand our intentions, resulting in miscommunication, conflicts and confusion.

   That's why it is so important to have clarity in your communication. Be clear about what you are committing to do and when you will do it. Sometimes trust is broken because of a misunderstanding: "You said you would …" or "I never said that!" Of course, communication is a two-way street. Always verify what you think you heard the other person say, and make sure the other person has a clear understanding of the message you are conveying. Speak to create understanding. Be

---

1 Judith E. Glaser; *Conversational Intelligence: How Great Leaders Build Trust to Get Extraordinary Results*; 2016; https://scholar.google.com/scholar?q=Judith+E.+Glaser%E2%80%99s+research+on+Conversational+Intelligence%C2%AE&hl=en&as_sdt=0&as_vis=1&oi=scholart

clear in your objectives and build trust by delivering true knowledge. As Brene' Brown, author of *Dare to Lead*, wrote, "To be clear is to be kind, especially in leadership."

3. **Trust is built over time.** Although I'm sure you're an honorable person, you can't assume other people will automatically trust you. Unfortunately, that's not the way trust works. Instead, it's built in a series of small steps (experiences). It's all about getting to know each other and experiencing the ethical (or unethical) behavior of the other person.

   I like to compare building trust to investing. You wouldn't invest in a stock before spending time to learn about it, nor do you immediately trust a person just because he has a nice smile, or she has money in her pocket.

   In our business, we host an introductory meeting with every new client where we answer any questions they have, and in turn, we learn about them. It's our process of "investing our time before we invest your money," and it's the first step in building trust. We know trust isn't built overnight; instead, it's a journey. We work hard for our clients and strive to develop a collaborative and thoughtful relationship with them. We want them to trust we'll always be there for them. We take pride in knowing our actions are congruent with our words. In reality, it's all about our clients. They know they can trust us to do what is best for them.

4. **Be realistic.** Don't over-promise and under-deliver. Part of being true to your word is being careful not to overestimate your ability to do something. Trying to be all things to all people is a recipe for failure. I'm sure you've heard the saying, "Engage brain before opening mouth." Words are powerful, and saying the wrong thing at the wrong time can have a damaging effect. Every word you speak should reflect positively on your character. If you say you'll do something, do it. If you can't do something, have the courage to say, "I can't do it."

   At times, we have prospects or clients with specific problems or requests come to our office asking for help. While I always want to be there for them, sometimes we don't have the skill set to help, and fail-

6. Trust

ing to admit it would actually exacerbate the problem.

While there are things we're extremely good at, stretching beyond our capabilities would put the client and us at risk, and it could have a damaging effect on our relationship. I don't consider our limitations to be weaknesses. Instead, clients know they can trust us to be up front with them. If we can't help them, we'll find the right person who can.

5. **Be consistent.** People appreciate consistency. Actor and director Woody Allen once said that 80 percent of success is just showing up. I like to think the remaining 20 percent is following up. Both traits I ascribe to being trustworthy. A client recently told me he had called his CPA about an important matter and had waited three days before he got a call back. "I'm not used to that," he said. "I call you guys, and you call me right back."

We set our standards high and strive to meet our clients' expectations. We know that it's the small stuff that can make a substantial difference. In baseball, the worst thing you can say about a pitcher is that he's "brilliant but erratic." You can't count on someone who strikes out 12 batters one week and gives up 12 runs the next. You want someone who provides more consistent results in his outings. Likewise, we strive to be predictable in the value we provide to clients.

6. **Actively trust others.** I've found there are four essential characteristics of a healthy relationship: mutual respect, honesty, trust, and communication. For a relationship to thrive, both parties must actively cultivate this high level of openness. If you're holding back, not willing to trust others, then how can they trust you? "Trust begets trust and untrust begets untrust. It's natural."[1]

Are you willing to share your personal stories with others, even when some may not portray you in the best light? Do you listen carefully while others are talking to ensure you "really hear" what they are saying? After all, there's a reason God gave us two ears and one mouth. Are you willing to trust the other person until proven otherwise? Are you respectful of other people's differences?

Sometimes clients come to our office with a concern about their in-

---

[1] Dhanpat Rai Srivastava, Pioneer of Hindi and Urdu social fiction, 31 July 1880-8 Oct. 1936

vestments or fear they will not have enough money to last through their retirement. While some of the fears are unfounded, we respect their feelings and address the fear or find solutions if there is a problem. No problem is too small or solution too large to deal with when we have open communication.

7. **Be honest.** *"And ye shall know the truth, and the truth shall make you free."* (John 8:32) While life hands us myriad challenges, one of the worst we have to deal with is *lies*. A lie is the death of a relationship. Every lie diminishes or destroys trustworthiness. Lies not only ruin relationships but have destroyed societies.

    Sometimes the absence of truth can be as deceitful and damaging as a lie. For example, when a person omits telling all the facts about something, that omission has dire consequences that alter the outcome of a situation. It takes courage to be truthful. It requires admitting to our mistakes.

    Truth is truth; only lies are invented. Always tell the truth.

8. **Be authentic.** Lyn Christian, coach, consultant and TEDx speaker, says, *"Your authentic self is who you really are deep down. The part of you that doesn't care what others think."* Continuing, she stresses that learning how to be your authentic self is an essential part of building meaningful relationships.

    Being authentic happens when your words, actions and behaviors consistently match your core identity.[1] Your brand should reveal the authentic you. To be authentic you must be dependable and then go the extra mile in everything you do. When talking with people, show you are engaged by truly caring about them. Be true to who you are, and in turn, you will build trust with those around you, and you'll feel a sense of self-satisfaction at the end of the day.

9. **Show emotions.** I don't know what could be worse than talking to someone about an emotional experience you've had, such as a death in the family, loss of a job, or end of a relationship, only to have them look at you with an emotionless, stone-cold gaze. Their lack of response sends a message of not caring.

---

[1] Lyn Christian; *How to be Your Authentic Self: 7 Powerful Strategies to be True*; SoulSALT®; Mar. 22, 2021; https://soulsalt.com/how-to-be-your-authentic-self/

6. Trust

More important than our intelligence quotient (IQ) is our emotional quotient (EQ). It's our ability to perceive, control and evaluate emotions. It's an important aspect for responding to the emotions of others. It's okay to be open with your emotions. If someone talks to you about a tragedy, it's appropriate to shed a tear with them. I keep a box of Kleenex in my office for just such times. While I cannot truly know the depth of their despair, I can sympathize with them. In turn, when I share my own experiences with them, a bond develops between us. Sharing will help strengthen your relationships and will help to build trust.

10. **Avoid self-promotion**. When you come to our office, you won't see awards sitting on the console or certificates hanging on the wall. Yes, we have plenty of them in the drawer or in our private offices, but I don't want clients to think it's all about us. It's not. Our focus is on them.

While it's okay to be proud of our accomplishments and to use them to build credibility, we want to put the emphasis on our clients. For instance, we have a fun promotional program called "Oh, the places you'll go." We give a flag bearing our name and logo to clients to take with them on vacation. After taking a selfie on location with the flag, they send it to us so we can post it on our social media pages. At the end of the year, we pick three of these "flag pictures" and donate $1,000 in the client's name to the charity of their choosing. It promotes our business, but the clients are the real heroes, they're the world travelers, and we enjoy recognizing them for their achievements and good works.

11. **Do what is right.** Never, never, never lower your standards. If you compromise your values, you're eroding trust. Again, it's important to walk the walk and talk the talk. Support what you say through your words and actions. It's about the little things. It's about being honest and respectful, and continually acting in a way that is consistent with your values.

Each day you're developing your personal brand. Is your brand known for being genuine and trustworthy? Are you known for being honest and respectful? Do you act in a way that is consistent with your values? Your character is revealed when no one is looking. When you look in the mirror at the end of each day, are you happy with the person looking back at you? Have your words and actions made you trustworthy? If so, it's been a good day.

12. **Admit your mistakes.** No one is perfect, and making mistakes is part of life. While admitting to them is an important first step, learning from and correcting them is even more critical. It allows you to live in harmony with your highest ideals. Correcting your mistakes means trying to do the right thing and in the right way.

It's quite simple. Own your mistakes. If you make a mistake, be straight up, identify and correct it, and then move on. This quote by the late Norton Juster, American academic, architect and writer of children's books, sums it up:

"You must never feel badly about making mistakes … as long as you take the trouble to learn from them. For you often learn more by being wrong for the right reasons than you do by being right for the wrong reasons."

No one expects you to be perfect, but they do expect you to be honest, to be an advocate and to fix your mistakes. They want to trust you'll consistently do what you say.

13. **Be Grateful**. A simple "thank you" goes a long way to developing a healthy and trusting relationship. It's interesting how the more you say it, the more you need to. Everyone likes to feel appreciated, and showing gratitude helps to raise a person's spirits and feelings of self-worth.

We have so much to be thankful for that it's never difficult to find someone you can thank. Often a simple, "Thank you for being you," works wonders to brighten a day.

The late Ray Kroc, founder of McDonald's, was famous for saying, *"When you're green, you're growing. When you're ripe, you rot."* Life is all about being green and growing. I hope these 13 tips will help you on your road to bettering your life and enriching the lives of those around you.

Managing the Small Details Makes a Big Difference

My job is all about making a difference and solving problems for people.

6. Trust

I know clients trust me to do what's best for them. As a board member of various organizations, and with family members and friends, I've often been able to help with the problems they've faced. I've found that if I help them manage small details, they trust me with larger matters, and that's really what I want. My goal is to be brilliant with the basics. I want people to feel they can come to me with all their problems, big and small. I want them to feel at ease sharing life's trauma and drama with me.

My wife, Beth, has a distant cousin in a neighboring state whose husband had cancer. Doctors told him unless he got a transplant, he would die. Of course, any surgery carries a risk, and this type of surgery even more so. Unfortunately, he didn't have a will drawn up and hadn't even assigned a power of attorney.

Beth found out about this just two days before the transplant surgery was scheduled. She asked me to get in touch with her cousin. After a conversation with the couple, my team and I drew up the required documents, and watched them sign the documents via FaceTime.

Of course, their next question was, "How much do we owe you?"

"Not a thing," I said. "Just repay me by getting well and enjoying your life together."

Fortunately, this man who was only given a few weeks to live received the transplant, and he now has a prognosis for a long and healthy life.

The reason our law firm was founded was to solve these types of problems, and I get satisfaction from helping someone in need almost every day. It keeps me fired up like a bolt of energy. After all, it's nice to be successful, but it's much more important to be significant, to have people trust you to do the right thing for them day in and day out and to truly make a difference.

I implore you to build your life around making good choices and doing the right thing. Be a positive influence in all areas of your life. As you earn the trust of others, no one will question your motives—even if the endeavor you embarked on together doesn't work out.

At the end of each day, ask yourself:

Pillars of Purpose

- Am I reliable?
- Do I keep promises?
- Can I keep a confidence?
- Am I honest? Are my words consistent with my actions?
- Do I put the interest of others before my own?
- Can people depend on me to always do the right thing?
- Am I trustworthy?
- Do I show appreciation by saying "thank you" a lot?
- Do I actually like the person I see in the mirror? If not, get back on course!

If you can answer "YES" to each of these questions, you're well on your way to living a life of purpose.

Chapter 7

PEACE OF MIND

"With faith, discipline and selfless devotion to duty, there is nothing worthwhile that you cannot achieve."
– Brian Tracey, author and motivational speaker

In the previous chapter, I talked in length about the importance of trust in any relationship. Relationships are strengthened by trust, and in turn, can be destroyed by lack of trust. However, when a person's trust is well placed, peace of mind follows close behind.

On a personal level, I feel peace of mind from helping our clients find solutions to their challenges and designing financial plans that will allow them to reach their goals. When trust is attained in any relationship, it becomes possible to do the things that empowers each individual to find peace of mind. We want them to come to us with their problems, both big and small, and we're happy to help them find solutions. We want to assist them in creating order out of chaos, thus allowing them to feel more confident in reaching their goals. In spite of the challenges life sends their way, we want them to trust we will be there for them today and every day.

Pillars of Purpose

We want them to experience tranquility in their lives.

> *"The life of inner peace, being harmonious and without stress, is the easiest type of existence."*
>
> – Norman Vincent Peale, author and Protestant clergyman

Peace of Mind Requires Flexibility

Peace of mind occurs when a person's course of action suits their personality and risk tolerance. We all have fears and triggers. Through the years, I've learned to pay close attention to a client's emotional and psychological makeup. We focus on what our clients want, the process they must undertake to get there and their ability to endure potential investment losses. It often takes time to find the individualized path they should take to reach their desired destination.

I'm reminded of a client whose husband had recently died, leaving this fairly young widow with a windfall of funds. While she was still working, she wanted to use her inheritance to grow a nest egg for early retirement. After talking with her about her dreams and aspirations, we created a portfolio of investments that would help her reach her goals.

While at the time she was happy with the plan, as months went by and she saw fluctuations in the stock market, she became nervous, calling us almost daily. We could see the turbulent market really upset her. Even though she had committed to long-term growth, it was becoming more difficult for her to be at ease with what we had established.

I asked her to come back in so we could address her concerns. When I suggested a new course of action, I could see the visible relief on her face. While she said she felt guilty making us do the additional work, we explained that there are always multiple paths and multiple solutions. "We just needed to find the right path for you."

Our goal was to ease her mind yet help her reach her goals. To do that, we needed to design a plan that could fit not only her goals, but also her personality—her heart and soul. By taking the time to understand her unique set of experiences, values and concerns, we were able to address her needs, both financial and psychological.

7. Peace of Mind

"If you don't make the time to work on creating the life you want, you're eventually going to be forced to spend a lot of time dealing with a life you don't want."

– Kevin Ngo, owner of MotivationalWellBeing.com

Listening: A Vital Skill

As shared in the previous example, true balance requires alignment between our goals, objectives and the amount of risk we are willing to endure to achieve those goals. While some amount of risk may be unavoidable, we also need to respect our own comfort zones so we can be comfortable with our decisions. In the case of our young widow, she initially indicated a desire to pursue the potentially high returns of riskier investments, but a volatile stock market soon made her realize she had stepped outside her comfort zone and needed to recalibrate.

Thankfully, we live in a world of almost unlimited options and opportunities. As life happens and the world changes, we should never be so doggedly committed to one course of action that we can't see different and possibly better solutions—especially when those solutions might afford us greater comfort.

As a young financial advisor, I quickly learned the importance of listening carefully to clients and then drilling even deeper to understand what they were *really* saying—their verbal and non-verbal communication. For example, a shrug of the shoulders can mean they are indifferent or don't really understand what I'm saying. A frown shows discontent or frustration. A smile goes a mile in saying they're on board. Usually, a few strategic questions about their willingness to accept potential losses can uncover their true thoughts and emotions and reveals what they can tolerate in terms of risk.

When we delve more deeply into their true comfort zone, we help our clients gain greater clarity and confidence, and we partner with them to:

- Make smarter financial decisions and feel more confident about those decisions.

- Prepare for a smoother transition into retirement.

Pillars of Purpose

- Develop more meaningful financial goals and then reach those goals.
- Feel confident their money is well managed.
- Become role models for financial responsibility for their children.
- Build necessary confidence to face major changes in life.
- Have a healthier relationship with money.

We advise them not to worry about a market that can't be controlled. After all, worry is a worthless state of mind. Instead, we help them control what can be controlled. We help them find the right path for their goals within the constraints of their comfort zone.

Avoiding a Mountain of Anxiety

So, what is your comfort zone? And how can you use it to your advantage?

To ascend to new heights in life, you'll frequently have to leave your comfort zone and step into a *growth* zone. However, just as important, sometimes our intuition tells us to hold steady. Perhaps it's not the right time or place to make a move, or perhaps we don't yet have the skills to proceed. Harkening to our gut feeling can give us peace of mind.

Former basketball coach John Wooden counseled, *"Success is peace of mind which is a direct result of self-satisfaction in knowing that you did your best to become the best you are capable of becoming."*

It's important to become the best we can be within our capabilities. Following your instincts is part of your natural comfort zone that can help you find peace in life—and avoid potential calamity!

I'm sure you've heard people say: "My gut reaction tells me …" or "My gut instinct is …" Both expressions describe the communication that takes place between your gastrointestinal tract and your brain. I call this the "tummy factor." If your stomach is churning, it's a signal that things aren't quite right in your life, and it could be a warning about danger. Being out of your comfort zone creates an uneasy feeling that disturbs our peace of mind.

Acknowledging your "tummy factor" can help you avoid many of life's pitfalls. Your reaction to various situations stems from firsthand experiences

7. Peace of Mind

and knowledge. Just as no two individuals share the exact same weight, height and facial features, our intuition can be just as individualized.

Suppose you have a mountaineering friend who invites you to join him in climbing Alaska's Denali, the tallest mountain in the United States. While he's excited about the adventure, if you've had no training or experience, you'd feel extreme apprehension.

Although you may feel comfortable enough hiking the trails at the base of the mountain, you might feel out of your depth climbing the 35-mile trail to the Kahiltna Glacier. However, that's nothing when compared to a climb that would take you to the stomach-churning 7,200-foot base camp on the Southeast Fork of the massive glacier. Now factor in spending an additional three days and nights camping and hiking the mountain's wild side to arrive 17 miles from the summit. Unthinkable, right?

If you're an inexperienced climber, your instinctive response to such an invitation would be, "No thanks!" And you'd be right. Human beings have depended on instincts for survival for millennia.

Debasish Mridha, American physician, philosopher, and author, suggests, *"Follow reason, but don't ignore that gut feeling. We create reasons with our limited knowledge and experience, but gut feelings often come from universal knowledge."*

We must all choose whether to follow our minds or our guts—or a combination of both. Every challenge you face presents an opportunity for growth. Bigger challenges create even more opportunity for growth despite seeming dire and overwhelming at first. So how do you conquer your own mountains? One step at a time, at your own pace and within your own capabilities.

By acknowledging your limitations and developing a sense of self-compassion, you'll find you are more at ease within yourself. Remember, Rome wasn't built in a day, and no job or task is done properly when rushed and lacking preparation. It takes perseverance, practice and patience to achieve greatness. Prepare for the unexpected so you're able to welcome whatever life throws at you. Stay unruffled by day-to-day worries.

Pillars of Purpose

The Search for Peace

All too often, people search for peace of mind in the wrong places. They trust people, companies or organizations that are incapable of delivering the results they want or need. Again, I encourage you to pay attention to the "tummy factor." If you feel overwhelmed, nervous, anxious or stressed when making a decision, no matter what the potential benefits might be, you won't be happy with them.

Along with paying attention to your emotional reactions, do your research before taking any action. In today's tech-savvy world, it's easy to check the facts when buying a car, moving to a new community or seeking professional services from a CPA, lawyer, financial advisor, insurance agent, contractor or realtor. With a simple online search, you'll find reviews and comments other people have posted, sharing their experiences about that person, product or service.

A Commitment to Clients

We always encourage prospects to check us out before making a decision to work with us. We want them to ask us questions until they feel comfortable with our process. We want them to feel they can come to us any time they have questions or if changes occur in their lives, both good and bad.

We believe a client's trust and confidence doesn't come from numbers or dollar signs. Instead, it comes from engaging with them. We consider our clients to be among our best friends, and we want it to be a mutual feeling. We are in the business of helping people solve problems by crafting plans to help them reach their goals and objectives, and we do it because we genuinely care about each and every one of them.

Over the past 40 years, I have been honored to witness some outstanding examples of professional relationships where the focus was on achieving confidence and clarity. Each of these elements strengthens the bond between the professional and the client and overtime can build an enduring relationship of trust. Any professional aspiring to build trust with their clients should incorporate the following elements into their professional practice:

7. Peace of Mind

- **Invest time to understand the client's needs.** Client relationships should be started and maintained through *stewardship*, not *salesmanship*. The same amount of time and care should be put into every relationship no matter how much business a client brings your way. This philosophy has provided outstanding professionals with a high rate of client retention and client referrals—something that should never be taken for granted.

- **Listen carefully.** There's a difference between *passively listening* and *truly hearing* what clients are saying. To build personal, lifelong relationships with each client, take time to understand their unique situations. Help them to realize their goals through individualized and professional counsel.

- **Be present.** Never see clients as just an account number or something to check off your daily to-do list. Truly engaging with your clients helps to create deep and rich friendships. Maintaining those relationships should be an essential part of your process. To build synergistic relationships with clients, make sure you are not just physically present but also emotionally there for them and conscious of their needs.

- **Take time to understand who they are, what their goals are and how you can help them reach their destination.** Once you learn what's important to your clients you can then develop an individualized roadmap to help them reach their destinations and turn their visions into reality. Be committed to excellence in client service and only consider yourself successful when you are viewed as significant in their lives. Consult with them and those they trust to ensure you've properly identified and targeted their goals.

- **Ask questions to ensure their plan reflects their goals.** Establish a deep understanding of your clients' current circumstances as well as their goals and dreams for the future. This process empowers them to more clearly identify their goals, whether financial, retirement-related objections or personal bucket list.

- **Build a plan to help clients fulfill their dreams.** Every person has unique passions and goals. Be committed to creating the right plan that reflects your clients' deeply held ambitions. Develop a clear

Pillars of Purpose

understanding of their family, interests and passions and create a customized plan that will help them reach their life goals.

- **Put their plans into action.** Execute plans that will help them achieve their goals. In this stage of the process, it's important to handle all the intricate, moving parts involved in actually putting a client's plan into action. A well thought through plan will eliminate the worry that small details might fall through the cracks.

- **Act as a fiduciary.** Always place your clients' interests above your own. Instead of making recommendations that serve *your* best interests, be obligated and passionate about delivering solutions that benefit your *clients*. Act as a fiduciary to give your clients a greater sense of confidence that you are always striving to do what is best for them.

- **Prepare for life's uncertainties.** Life happens. Life is not always smooth sailing and the challenges your clients face can cause them anxiety. Be your clients' lighthouse in the storm, and help them feel confident that you'll work even harder when the going gets tough. As a true partner, it's your responsibility to help clients navigate the ups and downs in life.

- **Be a problem solver.** Align firm resources to protect your clients' diverse interests and resolve client challenges. There is no greater joy for a true professional than the satisfaction received in helping a client solve a problem.

- **Keep your promises.** Above all, value accountability, transparency and consistency in everything you do. While it takes time to build trust, it only takes a moment to lose it. That's why the expression "a promise made is a promise kept" is paramount in the way you operate.

- **Have a communication process that is highly disciplined and will ensure clients are always in the know.** Client communication can distinguish your firm from your competition. Far beyond just the standard conference-room meeting, your communication process needs to flow into everything you do; it needs to be an essential part of your DNA. Dedicate yourself to connecting regularly with clients and providing clarity in all your interactions.

7. Peace of Mind

- **Walk the walk with the same passion as you talk the talk.** It's one thing to talk a big game and exchange niceties. It's another thing to actually follow through on promises. Take diligent care to not over-promise and strive to always do what you say you'll do.

- **Celebrate your clients' successes.** Honor their achievements! Every client has amazing stories, and you need to enthusiastically broadcast their stories knowing that success tends to reverberate and inspire more success.

Providing prospects with our written commitments goes a long way in assuring them about our future relationship. Likewise, when seeking the services of professional advisors in your life, you can benefit from gaining a comfort level with them before you initiate a formal working relationship. Here are some questions you might consider asking a professional you are considering working with:

- What is your background?
- How long have you been serving in your professional capacity?
- How do you continue to grow as a professional and as a person?
- What are your designations and credentials? Why are they important?
- What is your fee structure? How do you get paid?
- How do you determine which strategies/tactics are best to accomplish my long-term goals? Short-term goals?
- How often will we be meeting to re-evaluate my goals and assess progress toward achieving those goals?
- Can I contact three of your clients for references?

While knowing this basic information is important, it's only a small portion of the picture. You will also want to know what inspires and motivates the advisor's behavior, and to better understand their moral compass and the values that define their practice. The following questions can help you get to know your potential advisor on a deeper level:

- Why are you a (financial advisor, attorney, accountant, realtor, physician, contractor)?
- What motivated you to pursue this as a career?

Pillars of Purpose

- What are you passionate about?
- Tell me a bit about your background.
- What do you consider to be your greatest success in life?
- What professionally gives you the most fulfillment?
- How do you define success?
- What do you hope will be your professional legacy?

Once you begin to understand their *why*, their governing values and their work ethic, you begin to know the person behind the job title. Listen carefully to their responses (or lack thereof), especially since you'll be sharing confidential information with them. You need to feel confident they are trustworthy and will have your best interest in mind—always!

A Roadmap for Tranquility

"You're off to great places, today is your day. Your mountain is waiting, so get on your way."

– Dr. Seuss, from the book *Oh the Places You'll Go*

As I've described my career mission and shared my commitment to my clients' well-being, I want to reiterate that I passionately believe that having trusted professional advisors and enriched friendships in your life can lead you to achieve the confidence and clarity that you are pursuing the correct path in your life. We know this because it's what our clients tell us.

But I also want to acknowledge that finding that elusive peace of mind may take longer for some than for others. We all endure unique challenges, just as each roadway comes with its own potholes. In these instances, as you travel your personal highways and byways, sometimes you'll just have to focus on the journey, not the destination. Maintaining a cheerful outlook while on your journey will help you turn obstacles into opportunities for growth that can enrich your life.

As Mahatma Gandhi (1869-1948), the late leader of India, wisely advised: *"Keep your thoughts positive because your thoughts become your words. Keep your words positive because your words become your behavior. Keep*

7. Peace of Mind

your behavior positive because your behavior becomes your habits. Keep your habits positive because your habits become your values. Keep your values positive because your values become your destiny."

Gandhi took his own advice to heart as he famously helped gain India's independence from British rule through positive, non-violent resistance. He achieved international recognition for inspiring civil rights and social progress throughout the world. A legend in peaceful protest, Gandhi epitomized humility and frugality. His teachings transcend the ages as they continue to inspire to this day.

Just as other movements drew hope from Gandhi's actions, we all benefit from shared experiences, no matter our individual circumstances.

Here are seven fundamental principles of peace I have used successfully in my personal journey. It's my blueprint for tranquility in life, which you might find similar to your own. Feel free to share these principles with others.

1. **Think positively.** "This is the day which the Lord hath made; we will rejoice and be glad in it." (Psalm 118:24) Every day we have the power to make it a good day. Avoid hurtful, hateful and discouraging thoughts; instead, start your day with a joyful attitude and surround yourself with positive people. Choose to be happy!

2. **Take time for "you."** Whether you choose to spend time each day meditating, reflecting or praying, take some "you" time. It can help calm you as well as help you examine and better understand the challenges you face. Often upon reflection, instead of boulders, problems become grains of sand.

3. **Read every day.** Reading an enjoyable book can open a door to another world. It gives you the relief you need from worldly stresses and can brighten your day. This quote by the late Charles W. Eliot, former president of Harvard University, sums up my feelings about the importance of reading: *"Books are the quietest and most constant of friends; they are the most accessible and wisest of counselors, and the most patient of teachers."* Develop a habit of reading for pleasure each day.

Pillars of Purpose

4. **Relax expectations.** If you can consciously reduce your expectations of others, you'll rarely be disappointed. Often, we make unrealistic demands without considering whether the other person is capable of fulfilling them. This creates undue pressure on both you and the other party. Likewise, setting nearly impossible standards for ourselves makes life unnecessarily hard. Instead, set realistic expectations, and stay flexible with people in your life.

5. **Give yourself time.** We never seem to have enough time. We waste it and then wish we could make up for lost time. While time is one of our most precious resources, often we squander too much of it. Allocate sufficient time for the most important things so at the end of your life you'll feel peace in knowing you spent your time doing what you love to do with the people you love.

6. **Share your feelings.** Find that friend or family member you can trust and talk to them. Studies show holding in emotions such as anger, sadness, grief or frustration can put physical stress on your body, leading to a variety of ailments. Don't be afraid to show your emotions. Additionally, sharing with others helps them to be more open with you, and it strengthens the bond between you.

7. **Take a walk.** At the end of a stressful day, I find it therapeutic to walk. This simple exercise clears my brain, raises my spirits and energizes my body. Of course, the health benefits of walking are no secret. According to Melina B. Jampolis, M.D., author of *The Doctor on Demand Diet*, walking can do everything from lowering your blood pressure to reducing your risk of chronic diseases. It also is known to make your brain sharper and your heart happier.[1] Additionally, walking can relieve your stress. Often problems can be solved with just a half-hour walk.

When doing these things on a regular basis, you'll become more at ease with yourself and able to put day-to-day worries into perspective. You'll even gain a sense of self-compassion. In the end, you'll be better prepared

---

1 Meghan Rabbitt and Kaitlyn Pirie; *12 Biggest Benefits of Walking to Improve Your Health*; Prevention; 12/01/2021/ https://www.prevention.com/fitness/a20485587/benefits-from-walking-every-day/

7. Peace of Mind

to face whatever life throws at you with strength and confidence.

Bad News and Changing Plans

Peace of Mind is the result of discovering your life's mission and putting it into action. It's about being authentic and holding true to your values.

However, peace can be elusive. In our connected world, we're bombarded with "bad news" 24/7 that can shake our tranquility. Newscasts anxiously relay the horrors of war, homelessness and crime. Sometimes it's hard to rise above the clatter and find your inner calm. It can feel like we're living in a war zone. That's when we need to focus on what we can control: the present moment and our response to it.

Lao Tzu, a sixth century philosopher and father of Chinese Taoism, once said, *"If you are depressed, you are living in the past. If you are anxious, you are living in the future. If you are at peace, you are living in the present."*

I'm a big believer that to achieve true peace and fully live in the present we must tune out the noise and plan ahead, accepting that plans often change. It's how I maintain an even keel through life and endure all the unpleasant events around me. I actively plan my life so that the adverse conditions we so often hear about on the news won't harm me or my family, and it allows me to sleep soundly at night.

It's important to maintain flexibility allowing you to respond confidently to new challenges, much like how a warrior on the battlefield reacts to changing circumstances. However, don't skip the planning process. Failing to plan means planning to fail. Planning gives you that safe, quiet space apart from the confusion and chaos, and it creates a base of preparation to adapt to unfamiliar problems. Planning is how we tune out the clatter around us and focus on what matters most.

President Dwight D. Eisenhower, the illustrious war commander, famously said: *"Plans are nothing. Planning is everything."* It's a philosophy I encourage with my clients as we patiently and compassionately plan ahead for their futures amid constantly changing circumstances. This takes time and listening.

Awhile back, a woman who had been referred by a friend came to see me.

Pillars of Purpose

She was in her late 70s and had been married for more than 50 years. Late in life, her husband had developed a serious drinking problem and had become mentally and physically abusive. Giving her respect and dignity, which quite frankly she wasn't getting from her relationship, we spent several emotional hours as she vented, and I got to know her situation. (I keep a box of Kleenex handy for just such occasions.)

She explained she had tried to get help for him, but he refused. Now, at the end of her rope and feeling trapped, she wasn't sure if she had the financial resources to support herself should she divorce him. While it wasn't appropriate to talk about finances at that time, we agreed to explore her options. We wanted to shine a ray of hope on this life-changing event. Her life plan needed serious adjusting for her to regain her self-confidence.

During the next few meetings, my staff and I worked to create a safe place for her, one in which she knew her information would be kept confidential. Using the resources we have available through our law firm, we eventually were able to help her achieve an amicable divorce settlement with her husband that saved them thousands of dollars in court costs.

During our meetings, we created a trusting and open dialogue between all of us, and eventually both the husband and wife asked us to manage their finances going forward. As the couple regained respect for each other, they were able to create a healthier relationship.

The point is, bad things happen. In this case there could have been dangerous consequences, both financially and emotionally. However, because we took the time to listen and to gain a deep understanding of her fears and feelings, we were able to help this sweet woman plan for her future with confidence. Today she is a happily single, independent woman doing the things she loves, and her ex-husband is doing fine as well. We're pleased we could help these two people move to a happier and more positive situation—helping them both navigate through a failing plan to achieve a better one.

All in Time

As mentioned previously, finding the right plan can sometimes take con-

7. Peace of Mind

siderable time. I'm reminded of the race between the tortoise and the hare. When the tortoise challenged the hare to a race, the hare was sure he would win. Midway through the race he stopped to nap. Overly confident, the hare assumed he was far ahead of the tortoise and still had plenty of time to reach the finish line and win the race. As you know, the tortoise, although slower, was persistent. He passed by the sleeping hare and won the race.

In my personal life, I'm similar to the hare—I'm always fast-moving and active. Unlike the hare, however, I don't ever nap—I require very little sleep, actually. Also, unlike the hare, I suppress my natural instinct to make quick decisions and plans when managing my clients' business interests. In that regard, I compare myself to the tortoise. I like to take things slowly. I want to have a thorough understanding of what I'm facing before offering a solution. Just as doctors take the Hippocratic Oath promising to "first do no harm" in pursuing the best interest of their patients, we strive to be worthy of the role of trusted fiduciary for our clients.

I gained a valuable introduction to the "fiduciary path" early in my career as I searched tirelessly for new clients. In my early days as a financial advisor, the way you built a business was referred to as "smiling and dialing." For five straight years, I made more than 300 cold calls a day, a grueling introduction to success in the financial advisory business. On a good day, I would find 25 people who would talk to me. Out of that small number, only one or two turned out to be viable prospects. It was a tough way to build a business. However, my persistence and dedication ultimately paid off as I became one of the highest achievers in our group of rookie recruits. Ever the optimist, I knew that every "no" brought me one step closer to a "yes."

During those early years, my first manager, Jerry Moore, would walk past my desk each day to inquire about my progress. And tellingly, he never asked me how many calls I had made; instead, he would ask, "How many *needs* have you found today?"

It was a question I've never forgotten. He taught me that our job wasn't just about selling a product, but instead it was to identify and fill a need. I've carried this lesson with me to this day: my job is to build trust with clients so I'm able to provide solutions in sync with their financial, psychological and emotional well-being.

Finding Peace in Life

Just as I learned to take the defeat of each "no" response to lead me to an eventual new client, each of us has our own life story with day-to-day setbacks and opportunities. While we can't control some life events, others we can control. We each need to learn to recognize the difference and find the path that will lead us to a happy and peaceful life.

The well-known Serenity Prayer, attributed to the late Reinhold Niebuhr (June 21, 1892-June 1, 1971), provides personal and universal truths for living a happy and peaceful life. In fact, the word "serenity," itself, is defined as "the state of being calm, peaceful, and untroubled."

> "God grant me the serenity to accept the things I cannot change, courage to change the things I can, and the wisdom to know the difference, living one day at a time; enjoying one moment at a time; taking this world as it is and not as I would have it; trusting that You will make all things right if I surrender to Your will; so that I may be reasonably happy in this life and supremely happy with You forever in the next. Amen."

To gain peace of mind in your life, I encourage you and those you assist in finding peace of mind to reflect on this peaceful and calming prayer, and then consider the following:

- Are you at ease with yourself?
- Do you accept what you can't change or control?
- Do you strive to change the things that will improve your life and the lives of others?
- Do you faithfully take time to plan ahead so life doesn't constantly overwhelm you?
- Are you forgiving of the shortcomings of others? Of your own?
- Are you prepared to face anything life throws at you with a cheerful outlook and a determination to succeed?

At the end of the day, peace of mind flows naturally when our actions

7. Peace of Mind

reflect our values. It comes from learning how to control what we can and accept what we can't. We find peace of mind when we discover our life's mission, our *why*, and then pursue it passionately in the arena instead of just fretting and worrying from the sidelines.

Life offers a variety of paths, and it's up to you to discover the one that is right for you. I pray the one you take today, and every day, will lead you to a place of tranquility and peace.

Pillars of Purpose

Chapter 8
PROBLEM SOLVING

"A duty dodged is like a debt unpaid. It is only deferred, and we must come back and settle the account at last."
—Joseph Fort Newton, author and Baptist Minister

Everybody experiences problems; they're an unpleasant, unavoidable part of life. In the above quote by Joseph Fort Newton, I'm inclined to change the word "duty" to "problem": *A **problem** dodged is like a debt unpaid. It is only deferred, and we must come back and settle the account at last.*

Too often we ignore problems when they are small, hoping they will disappear. But they don't. Instead, small problems fester and become bigger problems, forcing us to deal with even larger issues. It's quite like owing money on your credit card. If you miss a payment (dodge a problem now), you get hit with a late fee. If you keep missing payments, more fees accrue, and the company eventually turns you over to a collection agency. Then, when the company reports your missed payments to the credit reporting agencies, your credit score plunges.

But that's not all. The problem continues to haunt you. When you attempt to buy a new home or car, the loan company turns you down because of your poor credit history. The minor problem, making a modest monthly payment, has now spiraled into an overwhelmingly larger problem that not only affects you, but also affects your family and their future.

As we see in this scenario, our problems don't just affect our own lives. Procrastination can lead to undesirable consequences for those we love and can leave them to deal with our bad choices even after we're gone. For example, failing to create a last will and testament or to take care of other estate planning needs, such as a living trust or durable power of attorney, can have dire repercussions should you be injured or die unexpectedly. Without these documents, the probate court must decide who gets your assets, who will care for your children or who will make decisions for you should you become incapacitated. If you thought proper estate planning takes time, you've never experienced the amount of time it can take to hash things out in probate. Do you really want your loved ones left with this scenario, dryly described by writer Ambrose Bierce?

"Death is not the end. There remains the litigation over the estate."

Sometimes a problem—like planning your financial future—can seem so huge, so overwhelming that it feels like it's swallowing you up. It becomes the monster in your head consuming your life. Fortunately, few imagined monsters warrant our irrational fears. The late Henry Ford, iconic founder of Ford Motor Company, once said, *"There are no big problems, there are just a lot of little problems."* So how do you deal with a large problem (or a pile of small problems)? Just as the mouse devoured the elephant—one bite at a time!

In Chapter 5, I shared how I ran the Disney Dopey Challenge with my son, Chris, and daughter, Katie. The weekend included a 5k, 10k, half marathon and full marathon races, and for me it was a huge challenge. However, after accepting Katie's invitation to participate, I didn't start running a 26.2-mile marathon on day one. Instead, I trained over many months, first doing a power walk, then light jogging and eventually running. Such it is with the problems we encounter in life. If we break them down into digestible bites, we can find solutions and tackle them one day at a time.

8. Problem Solving

Problem-Solving as a Trusted Friend

As a financial advisor, I genuinely believe I have the best job in the world: spending each day helping our clients solve their problems! I always say that while it's nice to be successful in a job or career, I'd rather be significant. Being significant means we are there for others in times of distress. We always want our clients to think of us as competent advisors who can help them with their financial and legal problems. But we also want them to recognize us as being trustworthy friends whom they can turn to for help during times of adversity.

Whenever our clients experience life- or career-changing events or other challenges, we want them to feel comfortable enough to pick up the phone and call us. No matter the size of their problem, we take it seriously. Life happens! And while it's not always smooth sailing, failure to plan for the future can cause needless anxiety. We try to put ourselves in our clients' shoes to fully understand every facet of the challenges they are dealing with, and how problems affect them emotionally. Then we work to find a viable solution. We are committed to being there for them.

> *"Our family delivering solutions for your family."*
> – Pickler Wealth Advisors' Unique Value Proposition

I like to think we create moments of clarity for our clients' lives and problematic situations. Singer-songwriter Joni Mitchell once wrote of the need for clarity: "You could write a song about some kind of emotional problem you are having, but it would not be a good song, in my eyes, until it went through a period of sensitivity to a moment of clarity. Without that moment of clarity to contribute to the song, it's just complaining."

Whether in a catchy folk song or a financial plan, looking at a problem from a different perspective or recasting it in a different light can better illuminate the source and lead to a solution.

In our business, we begin every relationship by building a comprehensive and customized plan that reflects the client's goals and addresses their fears. This in-depth analysis lays the foundation for a mutually beneficial, long-term relationship. While we don't charge for this service, we ask for something far more valuable than money—their time and cooperation—so we can make the best recommendation for their unique situation. We are truly investing our time before we ever consider asking our clients to invest their money.

As they share confidential information and answer personal questions about their hopes and dreams, a feeling of trust develops between us. As we dig deeper, we discover their specific goals for the future. Sometimes a client may say they want to retire at 65, but that's just a small part of the "retirement" picture. With further questioning, we're able to identify more specific information. Some retirees may want to downsize their home, while others want to travel or start a business. Perhaps paying for a grandchild's college education is at the top of their priority list. Each situation is unique and requires a different approach to ensure they reach their retirement goals.

As we engage in a meaningful dialogue, we build a bridge of credibility and care. Our prospective clients know we're not just concerned with signing them up as quickly as possible as a new account, but instead we're focused on learning about them, their future plans and helping them achieve their goals. We know they rely on us to use our best judgement to make the recommendations that best fit their needs, and we take that responsibility seriously. We strive to provide customized solutions while simplifying the process for them.

Simplifying a Multitude of Decisions

When in the midst of a demanding situation, people often feel hesitant to move forward, unable to commit to a course of action. Solving problems usually requires making tough decisions and then taking that first step—which may be why so many people avoid or put off solving them. Decisions, like the problems themselves, clamor for our attention. Every day we're bombarded with choices, large and small. It's estimated the average adult makes 35,000 decisions each day. It's no wonder people feel overwhelmed by decisions from the moment they wake up in the morning until they go to bed at night. All of us at some point wish we could just "turn on autopilot."

A study of 401(k) retirement plans, for instance, explored the correla-

8. Problem Solving

tion between how the number of fund options made available affected the likelihood of an employee enrolling in the plan. Using data collected from 800,000 employees, the results showed that employee participation decreased when the employer offered 10 or more funds compared to a higher participation when offering plans with just two options. Too many decisions stymied the decision-making process.[1]

Another study conducted by a condiment company—mustard, olive oil and jams—also attested to the fact that too many choices can be counterproductive to decision-making. In this study, the company set up two tasting booths, one offering six different jams and one offering 24. While 20% more passers-by stopped to taste the 24 samples, the six-sample booth sold 27% more jams. Again, people are more likely to act when fewer options are made available to them.[2]

An overwhelming number of choices are available in financial markets, too. In 2021, more than 2,529 stocks were listed on the New York Stock Exchange (NYSE) and a much higher 3,767 were listed on Nasdaq, which doesn't include the availability of nearly 8,000 mutual fund products. With that many investment options, investors would need to spend months, if not years, sorting through them to create a portfolio that would best fit their needs and allow them to achieve their investment objectives.

When I joined the financial services industry in 1984, it was in a transitioning phase. Up until then, there were limited investment options—stocks, bonds and a few mutual funds. Because information about these products was limited, investors relied on a "stockbroker" to obtain these products for them. Of course, a stockbroker did exactly as the name implied, they bought and sold products. In those days, stockbrokers had far fewer options to offer their clients.

Fast forward to today. Investors now can tap into a vast array of investment products, and they have unlimited data available to them outside the confines of a brokerage office. Accessing investment products and data is as simple as performing a Google search and opening an online account. Unfortunately, I often compare this approach to quenching your

---

[1] S.S. Iyengar., et el (2003); *How much choice is too much? Contributions to 401(k) retirement plans*; https://www.researchgate.net/publication/237792043_How_Much_Choice_Is_Too_Much_Contributions_to_401K_Retirement_Plans
[2] ibid

thirst by drinking from a fire hose. The abundance of water forced from the hose could drown you. Such it is with too much investment information. The abundance of available data can drown you! How do you know which products are right for *you*? The excessive availability of information without the proper application is useless. However, coupled with a true understanding of a client's needs and goals, that information becomes knowledge that can evolve into wisdom.

Our role as financial advisors is to synthesize all this information and then present clients with data that is relevant and meaningful for their purpose. By understanding their unique situations, we shorten and simplify the decision-making process for them. We help clients overcome inertia to achieve positive results.

A Career Conundrum

While writing this chapter, I'm reminded of decisions I made as a young man that changed my career path and forced me to make a difficult choice.

Prior to becoming a financial advisor, I worked at Xerox for three years. I loved the job and the opportunities it afforded me. I made good money, received great sales training and had many opportunities to refine my selling skills. However, at a certain point, I had to decide whether to accept a promotion they offered me, one that would require me to leave Memphis and drop out of law school, or whether I would instead transition to another phase in my career.

I was in a quandary. I knew whatever decision I made would have a long-term effect on my family and me. I needed to make the right one.

I had watched as several of my friends and Xerox colleagues left the company to enter the investment business. The financial advisory business was an unfamiliar world to me. To my knowledge, my parents never owned an investment account, and there had never been an emphasis placed on saving in our family. However, I felt confident that with my talent for sales and relationship building, I could learn the rest of the business.

In anticipation of my pending career change, I phoned seven different financial firms, got invited to participate in seven interviews and received seven job offers. Now, I had a problem. Which firm should I go with?

8. Problem Solving

Which one offered the best support as I pursued an entirely new career? It was a huge decision for a 25-year-old to make.

I was astute enough to know that I would need to receive the best training possible. During a series of interviews, I asked each interviewer extensive questions about their firm's training programs and the tools they would provide to help me succeed as a financial advisor.

In the end, I chose to go to work for PaineWebber Jackson & Curtis, one of the oldest investment firms in the United States, as they offered outstanding advisor/broker training at that time. Making that decision was not easy and required a thorough process that included weighing the pros and cons of each option. However, in the end, I made the choice that would allow me to stay in Memphis and continue to pursue my dream of becoming a lawyer. I felt confident I had made the right choice.

At some point in each of our lives, we have made or will yet make decisions that significantly change our life's direction.

The Four Stages of Competence

While we all have our own process for solving problems, our learning curve typically follows an interesting pattern discovered in 1969, by management trainer Martin M. Broadwell. The Four Stages of Competence is a system that has since been used by numerous trainers and has been identified as being an efficient guide for learning and problem solving. I use these with my clients as we work through their challenges, paying close attention to where they are on this continuum. The stages include:

1. Unconscious incompetence
2. Conscious incompetence
3. Conscious competence
4. Unconscious competence

In the first stage, *unconscious incompetence*, a person has a problem, but remains unaware that the problem exists. Alfred North Whitehead, British mathematician and philosopher, aptly identified this as: *"Not ignorance, but ignorance of ignorance ..."* Because the problem can only be fixed if the person knows it exists, they must first recognize the problem.

Pillars of Purpose

Only when someone or something draws attention to the problem (for example: a teacher, the media, a mentor or counselor) or a larger problem occurs making it impossible to ignore, will the person accept the fact there is a problem and move to the next stage of problem solving. An example of this could be when a husband gets blindsided when his spouse asks for a divorce, never having realized there was a problem.

In stage two, *conscious incompetence,* a person recognizes a problem exists, but he/she doesn't know how to fix it. Again, using the example of the troubled marriage, the husband now realizes a problem exists and decides to seek solutions. He knows he needs to acquire additional communication skills and tap into outside resources to appropriately address and solve the problem. He wants to get his marriage back on track, either by having a heart-to-heart talk to uncover exactly what the problems are or by seeking outside counsel.

In stage three, *conscious competence,* a person is not only aware of the problem, but is actively pursuing activities to learn skills and gain the knowledge needed to solve the problem. Sometimes the individual retains an outside resource to help fix the problem. In our continuing narrative, the husband learned why his wife is unhappy in their marriage. Together, they are seeing a marriage counselor who is giving them excellent advice on how to communicate more effectively and how to constructively deal with their problems. However, it takes a consistent and conscious effort to execute the suggestions. For a day or two after each session with the counselor, things seem to go well; but then the advice falls to the wayside as life gets in the way. While the couple now knows what needs to be done to save their marriage, actually doing it is far more difficult.

The final phase of problem solving, stage four, is *unconscious competence.* In this stage a person has practiced or implemented the skills consistently to the point they are now second nature to him/her. For our couple, they now have the skills they need and are experienced with implementing them. They continued counseling for one year to ensure the skills were consistently applied to their daily behaviors. They've learned how to more openly communicate with each other and have been pleased with the positive changes that resulted. Their newly developed skills have become part of their DNA. It's almost like riding a bike. Once you learn how to do it, you never forget. In the process, they've gained newfound

8. Problem Solving

respect for each other and feel their previous problems are no longer an issue. They're both content in their marriage and look forward to their life together.

Using these four stages of problem solving requires a concentrated effort. Arguably, stage one, *unconscious incompetence*, is the hardest as you don't know what you don't know. In such cases, it's important to listen carefully to what others are saying to become aware of any problems that exist. Also, increasing your overall knowledge can help you identify areas that need fixing. This might include reading self-help books.

Of course, if you have already identified the problem, then determining how to correct it is the next step. Then, with persistence and commitment you're well on the way to finding and implementing a long-term solution (stages two, three and four).

Becoming a Facilitator

Previously, I mentioned how fulfilling it is for me to be able to help others, especially our clients, solve their problems. I've learned that some of my happiest moments come when I can be there for others. In my experience, I've found there are skills a person can learn that can help them be a better facilitator.

For example, people feel drawn to a strong person with integrity. When people identify you as being a person of integrity, they'll respect you and trust you enough to share their challenges and concerns with you. In the past, I've had mere acquaintances ask me for help. Although our relationship had not yet reached the friendship stage, they had developed a baseline level of respect for me and felt they could trust me enough to ask for my assistance or advice.

Sometimes they come to me because another person has suggested they contact me. It's the most flattering kind of referral, being known as a problem solver. This happened shortly after I made the decision to become a financial advisor. The first step I had to take was to get my securities license (Series 7). The other "newbies" and I were given four months to prepare for this fairly difficult test. Day in and day out, we studied for the test knowing if we failed, we would be out of a job and miss a potentially life-changing opportunity.

Pillars of Purpose

Fortunately, studying has always come easy for me. However, this wasn't the case for Susan, a colleague of mine. One day my manager, Jerry Moore, said to me, "Your job is not to pass the Series 7 test. I know you are going to pass. Instead, your job is to make sure Susan passes it."

Now Susan was a bright young woman. While she had never gone to college (book study was not her forte), she did have tremendous street smarts. With Jerry's encouragement, I began mentoring Susan each day. As Jerry would walk by our door, he would make a swinging motion simulating a golf club hitting a ball. This action signified my responsibility for bringing Susan along with me as we strived for a successful completion of our mutual goal. "Hit the ball, drag Susan" became our unofficial tag phrase to describe my role in helping her achieve a great result.

I'm happy to report our collaboration was successful. We both achieved our goal of passing the Series 7 exam. More importantly, I learned that sometimes while a person may not ask for help solving their problem, if you can just be there to make it a little easier for them, it's like hitting a hole in one.

You're probably familiar with the biblical story The Good Samaritan (Luke 10:30-35).

> "A man was going down from Jerusalem to Jericho when he was attacked by robbers. They stripped him of his clothes, beat him and went away, leaving him half dead. A priest happened to be going down the same road, and when he saw the man, he passed by on the other side. So too, a Levite when he came to the place saw him and passed by on the other side. But a Samaritan, as he traveled, came where the man was; and when he saw him, he took pity on him. He went to him and bandaged his wounds, pouring on oil and wine. Then he put the man on his own donkey, brought him to an inn and took care of him. The next day he took out two denarii and gave them to the innkeeper. 'Look after him,' he said, 'and when I return, I will reimburse you for any extra expense you may have.' Which of these three do you think was a true friend to the man who had fallen upon hard times?"

Of course, it was the good Samaritan who genuinely cared and took time

8. Problem Solving

to help solve the man's problem. This parable teaches a valuable lesson. Never stop doing the little things, as sometimes those little things become the best things that occupy the biggest part of the heart.

Drawing from my experiences as a problem solver, I've made a list of four attributes that can help you be the kind of person others turn to as they deal with life challenges. They include:

1. **Be a person people can respect.** If you live a life true to your principles and convictions, people can trust you to do what you say—and say what you do.

2. **Learn to listen.** Not just listen, but *really* listen. After all, that's why God gave us two ears and only one mouth. It's hard to listen when you're talking or when you're thinking of a response. Instead, when talking with someone, put aside all the distractions, e.g., phones, television, interruptions, and clear your mind of clutter. Then look directly at them so they'll know they have your full attention. Listening is one of the sincerest forms of respect. Attentively listening can be part of the solution, if not the entire solution.

3. **Be empathetic.** Embrace and understand the person's emotions. Only when you listen with your heart and soul can you begin to feel the pain, concern or joy they are sharing with you. Don't just listen to the words they are saying, but watch their body language, and don't interrupt. Let them say what needs to be said, then respond with compassion, using statements such as: "I understand how you must feel" or "This must be difficult for you." This quote by Professor Brené Brown, author and researcher, succinctly summarizes my thoughts: *"Empathy is simply listening, holding space, withholding judgment, emotionally connecting, and communicating that incredibly healing message of 'you're not alone'."*

4. **Show you care.** People want to know you respect them enough to care. Often the conversations will be difficult; however, one of the greatest honors you'll ever receive is helping someone find a solution to a difficult challenge or problem. Handle their concerns responsibly and with gentleness.

Sometimes you may think the solution to the other person's problem is simple, and you're just in your own head as you think about it. At that point, you've stopped listening and you may be missing the core element of the problem. When this happens, the person sees you have disconnected from the conversation.

Instead, listen intently then paraphrase back their concerns, asking, "Did I understand you correctly?" or "Is there anything I missed?" As you define the problem, they'll feel reassured by how intently you are listening.

At this point you can move to the solution stage: "Have you thought about doing this …?" Or "Here are a couple of things you might consider …" Always offer the solution as a suggestion, and never as a "you have to do this." And never minimize their problems by saying, "The solution is simple …" Instead, respect the fact that they came to you for a solution, not because they were being foolish or simpleminded, but because they needed an outside perspective to help them solve the problem.

Author and activist Maya Angelou astutely observed, *"People will forget what you said, people will forget what you did, but people will never forget how you made them feel."*

How you make people feel says much about your character. When helping people with their problems, always leave them feeling better about themselves. Remember, people don't care what you know until they know that you care.

Big Problems = Big Rewards

When my son, Chris, participated in Cub Scouts and Boy Scouts, each October he attended a weekend camp at the Millington Naval Base called Scout Base. It was a fun experience for the boys as they got to hang out with young Navy or Marine recruits for the weekend. Unfortunately, in the mid-90s, Congress repurposed the base as a corporate headquarters for senior Navy officials. Since recruits were no longer trained there, the local Scout Council was forced to discontinue the camping weekend.

In the summer of 1998, I was serving on the executive board of the local Chickasaw Council when the council president and a Scouting executive approached me with a unique challenge: Would I help resurrect the Scout Base event that had now been defunct for five years? Could we build a new one?

8. Problem Solving

Always up for a challenge, I, of course, agreed. Collaborating with Council District Executive Phil Shipley, we instinctively knew we would have to bring the event back in a different format than the previous one. After several weeks of discussing options, we decided that if we were to resurrect Scout Base, we needed to assemble an incredible team and devote the time necessary to do it right. As a result, we set October 2000 as our target for the rebirth of Scout Base.

We were extremely motivated to make this event like no other. Knowing that a large percentage of the 30,000 boys in our district came from families that lacked the financial resources needed to attend Scouting's National Jamboree, held just outside of Washington D.C. at Fort A.P. Hill, Virginia, we wanted to create a National-Jamboree-type experience for them, just on a smaller scale. After building a team of 40 of the best and brightest volunteers across the district, we were ready to pursue our goal.

Our first job was to secure support of the Naval-base leadership to reestablish Scout Base as a bi-annual event. We approached the commanding officer at the base, Captain Diane Lofink, who happened to be the mother of a Boy Scout and a council volunteer. Captain Lofink became one of my strongest allies and one of the most essential members of our leadership team.

With Captain Lofink's support, we secured the Navy base for Scout Base 2000 as well as significant resources and volunteer personnel for our event. In the year leading up to the event, we first met on a monthly basis. As the event grew closer, we met twice a month and eventually weekly. Our diligent team of volunteers demonstrated incredible focus and work ethic.

Finally, in October 2000, we held our inaugural event, Scout Base 2000, at the new naval support activity campus. While the boys didn't have the experience of co-mingling with young Navy or Marine recruits, our 2,000 scouts and Scouters (adult leaders) reveled in the experience. It was a resounding success generating positive revenue for the council. In fact, it became the largest revenue contributor to the council budget. We soon had a commitment from the Navy to continue the event bi-annually.

Of course, our next challenge came as we planned the follow-up event for 2002. The world changed forever after the events of September 11,

Pillars of Purpose

2001, and all U.S. military bases immediately restricted civilian access. We would have to find a new venue for the event.

After extensive research and the continued cooperation of Captain Lofink and the Navy, we found a location north of the base that was occupied by the city of Millington. Even though our planning group had to make significant changes to the event because of 9/11, we still had the full support and volunteerism of the Navy.

Attended by 2,500 Scouters and scouts, the 2002 event was an enormous success. However, the week of the event brought some unique challenges: torrential rains so intense that the garbage bins sunk deep into the mud (some of which remain buried there today). Local Scouters affectionately referred to this wet weekend as Mud Base 2002.

In spite of the obstacles we faced in these first two newly re-organized scouting events, we knew we had provided an experience cherished by many inner-city scouts as well as thousands of scouts throughout our region, making it well worth the effort.

As American industrialist and father of modern shipbuilding, Henry J. Kaiser once said, *"Problems are only opportunities in work clothes."* We had successfully helped this event rise from the ashes, or perhaps more appropriately, the mud.

A few months later, the Navy informed us they would not be able to support the event any longer, and for 2004, we would have to relocate *again*. This time we found a venue south of Memphis in Tunica, Mississippi, at the Paul Battle Arena. The event attracted attention from all over the country, and we were pleased when more than 6,000 Scouters, scouts, venders and exhibitors attended, representing 20 states. Again, it was a huge success.

I'm proud to say that the event proved so successful that, in 2008, we hosted well over 15,000 Scouters and scouts representing every state in the union. Scouting magazine did a feature article proclaiming it "Scouting at its best." Our group of volunteers had worked tirelessly for 10 years to put on the largest non-Jamboree scouting event in the country, where we offered 280 events and skills training for 100 merit badges. We provided these boys experiences they may never otherwise have had,

8. Problem Solving

like sleeping in a tent, listening to Native American folklore and learning about aircraft mechanics, among others. They even got to see both the Army's and Navy's elite parachute units, the Golden Knights and the Leap Frogs, perform.

We had achieved our goal to create and deliver a National-Jamboree quality event. It was time for Phil and me to turn over the mantle to a new generation of problem solvers.

Becoming a Problem Solver

Anyone can become a problem solver. While some people possess natural critical thinking skills, anyone can develop these skills when following these seven steps.

1. **Define (or identify) the problem.** Albert Einstein, one of the greatest and most influential physicists of all time, wisely said, *"If I were given one hour to save the planet, I would spend 59 minutes defining the problem and one minute resolving it."* Clearly identifying the problem involves some or all of the following steps.

2. **Assess the threat.** A problem can occur in three distinct phases: the emergent phase where a problem is small, but can mushroom into a much bigger deal; the mature level where problems begin to impact our lives; and the crisis stage, which severely affects our lives and families.

3. **Separate cause from effect.** Continue to analyze the problem as Einstein suggested. Separate the cause from the symptoms. For example, you may continually worry about money and make late payments on your bills. While those are symptoms, the actual cause of the problems could be your lack of a budget, lack of time spent on paying bills or a lack of work opportunities. While attacking the symptoms may be a short-term solution, understanding and attacking the cause will ensure it's not going to reoccur.

4. **Fully describe (articulate) the problem.** When we're able to fully articulate a problem at its root cause, we're on our way to solving it. A solution may be a slight behavior change that can easily be fixed. Other times it may take the assistance of a specialist to help fix the problem.

Pillars of Purpose

After carefully assessing where we are in the process, we can begin to develop the appropriate response.

5. **Develop alternative solutions. What are your options**? Once you have done your research, it's time to explore solutions. To do this, ask yourself:
   - What are the challenges of implementing each solution?
   - What positive outcomes are possible? Negative outcomes?
   - What resources are available to help solve the problem?
   - Who will benefit from the solutions? How will they benefit?

6. **Implement the solutions.** Edwin Louis Cole, founder of the Christian Men's Network, once proclaimed, *"You don't drown by falling in the water, you drown by staying there."* Stand high above the rising waters ... act! In this step you need to select the best solution and move forward.

7. **Assess the results.** Measure the success of your actions. Did you accomplish what you were hoping to? Did you reach your goal?

I refer to the first several steps in this problem-solving process as "peeling the onion" or identifying, analyzing, describing and brainstorming solutions. With each level peeled back, we expose relevant facts about the problem and discover viable solutions. Then we must take the action to achieve the results we seek.

Unclutter Your Life

I'm always reminding people that problem solving offers an opportunity for immense growth. As Sir Winston Churchill once said, *"A pessimist sees the difficulty in every opportunity; an optimist sees the opportunity in every problem."*

Although some problems may seem insurmountable, I like to compare them to a house filled with clutter. When walking through an overstuffed house, we can easily feel intimidated by the chore of uncluttering and organizing all our belongings. However, if we focus on just one room, close the door and only clean that room, the task no longer seems insurmountable. So, it is with problems. If we look at them "one room at a time," we

8. Problem Solving

can simplify the process and more easily arrive at a solution.

Ignoring or running from your problems only increases the distance to the solution. The Chinese philosopher Confucius warned: "*A man who does not plan long ahead will find trouble at his door.*"

Problem solving is all about making choices and making them early enough so you still have the best options available to you. Face your problems head on and approach them with optimism. Then turn each of them into an opportunity for personal and professional growth.

Problem solving creates resiliency and confidence within us all. You can be part of the problem or part of the solution. Be a problem solver.

Pillars of Purpose

Chapter 9
ADVOCATE & PARTNER

"When the world is silent, even one voice becomes powerful."
—Malala Yousafzai, Pakistani activist for female education
and the 2014 Nobel Peace Prize laureate

In Chapter 7, we covered not only how we can achieve peace of mind for ourselves, but also how we can facilitate peace of mind for others. When we're looking out for others, we truly take on the role of advocate and partner. In these vital roles, we always strive to put the well-being of others above our own.

While fulfilling my obligations to a family member, client or group, I always ask myself if the actions I'm about to take are the right ones. Am I doing everything possible to defend and preserve the interests of those individuals and groups? Whether as a financial advisor, attorney, nonprofit board member, or as a father, grandfather or husband, am I standing tall in advocating for them?

While serving on the Shelby County School Board, I witnessed advocacy at its most elemental, raw level: the countless times when parents participated in school board meetings to advocate for the interests of their children. Sometimes their impassioned arguments missed the mark; and while I did not always agree with them, I could understand their instincts. They were defending their own children, who more often than not could not defend themselves.

That kind of passionate defense reminds us of our duty to those we would represent. The dictionary defines advocacy as "any action that speaks in favor of, recommends, argues for a cause, support or defends, or pleads on behalf of others." In building a life of purpose, we must defend and advocate for the rights of those we represent to achieve our goals.

Stand Boldly for Your Beliefs

While some people might question whether they have what it takes to be an effective advocate, everyone can agree that spirited advocacy has contributed to positive change throughout our nation's history, and it defines our individual character as well. As Dr. Martin Luther King wisely said, *"Our lives begin to end the day we become silent about things that matter."*

An eloquent advocate for racial equality, Dr. King inspired urgency among our elected leaders as he challenged the unjust laws and the appalling treatment of Black people. Boldly, in his impassioned "I Have a Dream" speech, he beseeched others to join his fight for equality:

> "Now is the time to make real the promises of democracy. Now is the time to rise from the dark and desolate valley of segregation to the sunlit path of racial justice. Now is the time to lift our nation from the quick sands of racial injustice to the solid rock of brotherhood. Now is the time to make justice a reality for all of God's children."

Encouraging others to join him as participants in non-violent sit-ins and protests, and with dogged determination, he won the allegiance of citizens throughout the United States and gained the support of two presidential administrations, Presidents John F. Kennedy's and Lyndon B. Johnson's.

In 1964, as the youngest recipient of the Nobel Peace Prize, Dr. King proclaimed in his acceptance speech, *"I accept this award today with an abiding faith in America and an audacious faith in the future of mankind."*

9. Advocate & Partner

Assassinated just four years later in Memphis, King, who died at the young age of 39, left a lasting legacy as a relentless advocate for equality. He successfully fought for the passage of the 1964 Civil Rights Act and 1965 Voting Rights Act. He also advocated for peace in the midst of the tragedies unfolding in the Vietnam War and lent his powerful voice to lifting Black and white Americans out of poverty.

Strategic Advocacy with Peaceful Results

Just as Dr. King advocated effectively for peaceful solutions to long-standing challenges, we need to be patient and purposeful when advocating for our personal beliefs and on behalf of others. We need to plan and then strategically adjust the plan as facts change, all while staying true to our convictions.

In my own life, I've seen the benefit of patient persistence when advocating for something I believe in. I've mentioned my advocacy for public education. It's what led me (strategically) into politics. I had made a promise to myself that if I ever ran for an elected office, it had to be something I was passionate about. I knew I could and would fight for anything that I genuinely believed in.

So in 1998, when I ran for and was elected to the Shelby County Board of Education, it was with the strong belief that every child deserves a quality education. However, my passion for quality education would soon collide with political reality—and lack of backbone among some of the other local leaders. It would test my own commitment to the cause.

At the time of my election, I had been told I had a bright political future … if I played my cards right. Local political leaders suggested privately that in a few short years I might find myself in the state legislature, then in a few more quite possibly the governor's office. Ultimately, I might find myself in Washington as a representative or a senator. Obviously, it was an ego-fulfilling prospect, one in which I just had to *go along to get along.*

I had to decide at that critical point in my life if I wanted to be a politician, willing to compromise my principles on critical issues. Or did I want to be an advocate? Being an advocate meant I would sometimes say things that would anger people and disrupt the equilibrium. To achieve change, I would need to be a catalyst for the causes my constituents and I believed in. I would need to break a few eggs, as they say.

Also coinciding with my arrival in local politics was a critical change in the way local school board members were selected, which put into action some of the battles that ensued. In 1994, the Tennessee Legislature passed a law requiring local school board members to be directly elected by local citizens by 1998. Up until that point, school board members had been appointed by the county commission, the local governing body.

In the wake of this significant change, we experienced a new conflict whereby the new class of independent school board members were no longer politically tied to the county commissioners and could now exert more independence without fear of losing favor with their bosses on the commission. However, the county commissioners still retained authority for funding the school districts. It was a marriage made far south of heaven.

That same year, 1994, Tennessee passed a law establishing the maximum number of children per classroom per teacher. We knew this change would require a tremendous capital investment for our district. At that time, our per-student funding put us near the bottom on the national scale, and we knew additional teachers would need to be hired to abide by the new law.

Giving us a few years to comply, we found ourselves in a quandary when our local county commissioners chose not to raise property taxes, which of course was where the vast majority of education funding came from. They feared voter outrage much more than they felt the need to champion the well-being of our students. I knew exactly what course the elected leaders were taking—the path of least resistance.

This was the defining moment of my career. As an elected official, I had to decide whether I would pursue a bright future as a politician or take the proverbial road less travelled and commit to being an advocate for public education. I chose the role of advocate, determined to be true to my beliefs and faithful to those for whom I advocated.

Approaching a friend who served as a county commissioner, we engaged in an exceedingly difficult conversation. I expressed to him my belief that the commissioners were "political cowards" for failing to vote for the needed funding. They weren't willing to do the right thing for the stu-

9. Advocate & Partner

dents in our district! As you might imagine, my friend took offense to my position. He was probably amazed that I would cast my lot as an advocate for education and not for a future as a career politician.

While both of us would have been considered fiscal conservatives, my belief was that underinvesting in public education would be devastating to our prospects for long-term economic growth and stability. Those on the board who shared my views knew we had to exercise patience and creativity. We had to develop a plan of action and advocacy to engage community leaders, parents and teachers in a collaborative effort to advocate for enough funding needed to fulfill the state's mandate for reducing student/teacher ratio.

Eventually we brought enough people to our side of the issue. We secured the seven votes needed on the board to approve enough funding to bring the student/teacher ratio in line. That proved to be the first of numerous times over the next 12 years as chair of the school board that I had to wage (and win) a funding war on behalf of our district.

The Endorsements in the Bag

Tennessee ranks among the lowest-taxed states in the country. Since we have no personal income taxes, we're completely reliant on sales and property taxes. Unfortunately, that low tax base can challenge school funding. At that time, Tennessee typically ranked among the bottom 10 states in per-pupil funding for public education, at just over $9,500 per student. As an advocate for public education, I tried to follow the example of change agents such as Martin Luther King who showed that peaceful engagement could win hearts and minds.

In one particularly challenging funding battle, we recruited more than 50,000 children and 100,000 parents in our district to help us create and send out "property tax increase" permission slips to every home in the district. Our efforts couldn't have been more successful.

Remember the movie *Miracle on 34th Street*? It's one of my all-time favorites. There's a scene at the end where they brought bags of mail addressed to Santa Claus to the courthouse and dumped them on the judge's dais to prove Santa's existence.

Similarly, we collected more than 100,000 individually signed permission slips from voting parents and other stakeholders. Then our parent advocates delivered bags filled with the slips to the county commissioner's meeting. Seeing more than 100,000 voters giving them permission to increase their taxes, as long as funds went to improving public education, no doubt gave the commissioners some extra courage. We got the votes. We freed the funds to more adequately provide for students in our district.

Delivering a targeted message to the right people at the right time was the most effective strategy for getting things done. On two other occasions, we secured funding for new $60-million high schools. In both of those situations, I was told it couldn't be done. However, both times we accomplished our goal by enlisting advocates and swinging the votes our way.

Early in my working relationship with our Shelby County School District Superintendent Bobby Webb, we agreed to a good cop/bad cop strategy to get things done. I, of course, played the bad cop. Bobby was a conciliatory guy, someone who everyone loved. He could be seen as the peacemaker, while I was known as the fire-breathing, red-meat-eating advocate for the district.

I often wondered if that's why my peers on the school board voted me to be board chair, simply thinking, "He's crazy enough to go out there and fight for this stuff. He's willing to get his hands dirty." It wasn't a job everyone was willing to do.

At the end of my time as chair, despite the fact our district remained one of the least-funded school districts in America per pupil, the Shelby County School District could boast of being the only district in the United States in the top 100 in size *and* academic quality. We also undertook an incredible process to improve the quality of our teacher training and educational excellence that empowered us to become the first district in the nation to receive system-wide accreditation.

Building an Army of Advocates

I have always believed that public education is the cornerstone of our democracy. More than a civil right, it's a vital national security imperative. The future of our nation depends on our ability to educate the 54-million

9. Advocate & Partner

school children for engaged citizenship and global competitiveness.

While public education is a national concern, it's really the state's responsibility, and it needs to be a local passion. Public education should reflect the values of our communities while preparing children to be equipped for a rapidly evolving global marketplace.

During my 12 one-year terms as chair of the Shelby County Board of Education, I also served on the Tennessee School Boards Association (TSBA) board of directors, and eventually became president. I also served as president of the National School Boards Association (NSBA) in 2013 and 2014. It was a remarkable learning experience.

Throughout my tenure as local school board chair, TSBA president and NSBA president, I became acutely aware that advocacy for public education would always be an uphill climb. Public education didn't have the same financial resources as the more well-funded advocates of private and charter schools, and the privatization of public schools. Furthermore, advocates for public education often were isolated from one another in their individual silos. Their focus was primarily on their own local or state needs and issues. Rarely, if ever, would you see all of the organizations in public education unite in advocacy.

As a state and national leader, I knew it would be pointless to actively engage in a tug of war with the privatization forces. There was no way we could compete dollar-wise in our lobbying efforts. So how could we deliver our message in the most impactful manner?

Then it hit me ... there were more than 54 million children who received their education through public schools and as many as 100 million parents of those children. There were another six million stakeholders in public education—educators, administrators, policy makers and advocates. Just as I had seen on the local level, if we could tap into those natural constituencies, we had the power of the people behind us, the power of the voters!

During my NSBA presidency, we cultivated this national Army of Advocates. We reached out to teachers' groups, parents' groups, even chambers of commerce nationwide to secure their support for public education. We created a manifesto, and had each organization take a vote within their membership to agree to join our Army of Advocates—to join our cause. Our goal was to combine and leverage our voices whenever we approached lawmakers and legislators.

We mobilized all these stakeholders to make phone calls and to reach out to their elected officials to lobby for our causes. In so many cases, we found that the most effective campaign for school support did not occur in the halls of the state capital, but at the local grocery stores when people are out doing their shopping, at the 4th of July picnic or at youth soccer, basketball or football games.

We had begun building an army of advocates community by community, state by state, and in the end received some incredible recognition and support for our efforts—a *Power of the Possible* movement. It was the same year we had the Oscar-winning director wear our red "Stand Up 4 Pub-

---

National Public Education

The right to learn is the most important promise we make to our nation's children. America's future is dependent on keeping the promise of a great public education for every child in every community. The investments we make today in weaving a strong tapestry of diverse, inclusive, and equitable public schools will create the fabric of our society and the world to come.

[The] mission [of public education is] simply stated is to promote the opportunity for all children to receive an excellent education from birth through college and career. This purpose is not the province of a singular organization, institution, or moment in time. It requires many hands—and hearts and minds—working together across generations to continually regenerate the power of public education as the engine for our social progress and economic vitality. It requires a dynamic ecosystem of community and parent leaders, educators, policymakers, advocates, and funding partners with a shared commitment to inclusive systems for schooling and supports that respect and engage students and families in all their diversity. [As an advocate] our strategy is to nourish that ecosystem and harness the power of our collective experience and resources to strengthen and sustain the healthy learning environments that all children deserve and need to thrive.[1]

1 National Public Education Support Fund; https://www.nsba.org/Advocacy/Public-Engagement

9. Advocate & Partner

lic Schools" wristband at the Academy Awards, and famed basketball star Earvin "Magic" Johnson led a pep rally and delivered a keynote address in New Orleans at our annual conference.

By the time we arrived in New Orleans for the annual conference, we had developed relationships with teacher associations in virtually every state and multiple statewide chambers of commerce joined our movement, in addition to hundreds of local businesses across America. The crowning accomplishment was the decision by the national PTA, along with their 40 million members nationwide, to join our Army of Advocates. This incredible collaboration of state and national organizations around a common cause had never been accomplished and has not happend since.

Within 12 months, we had built the NSBA Army of Advocates from the ground up to 50 million. It was absolutely mind-boggling what we accomplished as we engaged millions in our fight for public schools. It was truly a display of a deep commitment to advocacy and partnership. These partnerships established a foundation for public education advocacy and formed the framework for the creation of our American Public Education Foundation.

The Power of Advocacy

Whenever I contemplate the power of advocacy, I can't help but think of a movie I saw years ago, "Lorenzo's Oil," starring Susan Sarandon and Nick Nolte. This true-life drama tells the story of Michaela and Augusto Odone, who battled against all odds to save their son's life when he was diagnosed with adrenoleukodystrophy (ALD). This rare, incurable disease affects only about one in every 20,000 people. It causes loss of vision and hearing and learning disabilities, among other symptoms, and it significantly shortens the lifespan of those affected.

When doctors told these parents there was no cure for this horrible disease, they weren't willing to accept the dire diagnosis for their son. Setting up camp in medical libraries, they studied everything they could find about the disease. Badgering researchers and questioning top doctors all over the world, they organized an international meeting of scientists who were researching ALD. Armed with the knowledge they had gained, their only stipulation was that they, as non-scientists, could attend and participate in the meeting.

Pillars of Purpose

At the event, scientists united around a possible cure. But later, when more than 100 firms around the world refused to produce the promising treatment, the Odones personally engaged an elderly British chemist, Don Suddaby, who was willing to take on the challenge. The oil he produced, appropriately called Lorenzo's Oil after their son, proved successful in slowing the progression of the disease.

Although their son's symptoms had progressed to a point that the damage already done was irreversible, their efforts took on a much larger meaning when, in the movie, Augusto asks his wife, "Do you ever think that, maybe, all this struggle—it may have been for somebody else's kid?"

This profound statement shows the true meaning of advocacy. As Samantha Power, U.S. Ambassador to the United Nations from 2013-2017, once said, *"All advocacy is, at its core, an exercise in empathy."*

Partners in Problem Solving

The Odones achieved their positive results by engaging a group of advocates to support and participate in their cause. While one person, individually, can accomplish much, a group of people, committed to a common cause, can change the world significantly. Ultimately, that is *Power of the Possible*.

In the previous chapter (8), we talked about helping others solve problems and overcome challenges. When you personally cannot provide a solution, you'll need to find the people who can. The essence of partnership is understanding the need for and building a network of people who can help you get the job done.

Henry Ford, the founder of Ford Motor Company, once said, *"If everyone is moving forward together, then success takes care of itself."*

As the Odones surrounded themselves with the absolute best people in their respective fields, they organized a group of advocates who shared their values and enthusiasm for finding a cure, resulting in a miracle.

Partnership for Music Excellence

Another story illustrating the power of partnerships arose from a challenge I encountered in 2004, when my cousin, Robin Yates, called asking for help

9. Advocate & Partner

raising money for the Arkansas State University (ASU) music department.

I had grown up in a house brimming with music. My mother was a music major with an exquisite performance voice. She regularly performed impromptu concerts on her beautiful grand piano and was often hired by churches and groups to sing at their special events. Thanks to my mother, I developed a deep love for music early in life. So, when Robin called, I wholeheartedly agreed to help out my alma mater.

The music department at that time needed a serious upgrade, starting with the pianos. They were uninspiring, hopelessly worn-out remnants from the 1960s that included one broken-down piano in the concert area as well as declining uprights in the rehearsal rooms. The poor status of the equipment made it difficult to recruit quality students into the Arkansas State music program, and thus far the fundraising efforts had not made much headway for improvements.

As I had learned from previous experiences with raising capital for not-for-profit organizations, the right partnerships can move mountains. I quickly formed a plan. One of my clients was piano sales director at Amro, a musical instrument store in Memphis that served more than 600 school bands and orchestras in a four-state region. My client, Rick Jefferies, helped institutions work toward becoming All-Steinway programs with rent-to-own pricing and incentives that gave donors reasons to donate now and in the future. With Rick's and my help, and after three years of successfully soliciting donors in a capital-raising campaign, the University acquired 27 Steinway pianos, with a goal to eventually purchase a total of 42.[1]

Without Rick's connections in the music world, the University's "All-Steinway Initiative" would never have happened. This initiative continues today and has lent immense credibility and pride to the music department, giving donors an extra reason to support the school. Partnering with the right person and the right company at the right time paved the way for this successful program.

---

1 For more than 160 years Steinway & Sons, a pioneering American company, has been known for artisanship, quality, and attention to detail. The Steinway piano remains the peerless instrument of uncompromising musicians and institutions.

Pillars of Purpose

The Far-Reaching Effects of Partnering

While passion motivates us, fulfills us and makes us happy, partnering with others magnifies our capacity to make things happen and to make dreams come true.

Shortly after beginning the promising capital-funding campaign at Arkansas State, I received a call from Steinway asking if a group of us would like to tour their facility in Queens, New York. Along with my cousin and three other people from the Arkansas State music department, we witnessed the awe-inspiring process of creating a Steinway piano from the frame up.

As I watched the meticulous process, in which craftsmen used 27 different layers of wood, I couldn't help envisioning an earlier era when dedicated workers built everything from scratch. Constructing these world-famous instruments required an unrelenting focus on detail, as well as commitment by each team member to work toward a common goal. Today, more than 90 percent of concert pianists throughout the world perform on Steinway pianos—the gold standard of piano performance.

When I walked out of that facility in New York, I set a new life goal of owning a Steinway piano someday. A few years later, I received a call from Rick shortly before his planned retirement from Amro. "I've got unfinished business," he said. "We've got to get you a Steinway."

He made me an offer I couldn't refuse. And now, a Steinway baby grand piano graces our firm's Event Centre where we have hosted several concerts with local pianists over the years.

In 2016, our friends at Steinway once again helped us fulfill a dream. Our foundation, the American Public Education Foundation, was asked to organize a national campaign to commemorate the events of 9/11 through a national anthem sing-a-long, incorporating schools all across America. This effort culminated with a national broadcast in partnership with Fox News anchor Harris Faulkner. The sing-a-long was streamed from P.S. 174, a public school in Queens, New York, and broadcast across America. Over five million students across the country participated in thousands of local schools as we collectively stood up for America and recited our National Anthem. It often takes an army to fulfill your purpose—your passion.

9. Advocate & Partner

For the event, Steinway generously provided the use of a grand piano for P.S. 174, not far from their headquarters. They even brought in a Broadway concert pianist for the online streaming broadcast. It was truly a heartfelt and much needed unifying moment.

As President Ronald Reagan once said, *"By working together, pooling our resources and building on our strengths, we can accomplish great things."*

Years later, we once again reached out to our local Steinway partner, Amro Music. By this time, Rick had retired and his position was assumed by Gabe Staton. We asked if Amro and Steinway would partner with us to build a music program that included several small practice pianos and a concert grand piano for the new Collierville High School auditorium. It was a done deal, and the addition of these pianos made the school the first "All Steinway High School" in the Southeastern United States. For the dedication ceremony, Amro Music brought in an acclaimed pianist to perform a concert on their new piano. I will forever be grateful to Rick, Gabe, the Steinway people and everyone else who advocated for this cause and helped to make a musical dream come true.

The power of this partnership was personally significant when, a few years later, Steinway and Amro agreed to donate the use of a Steinway Grand Piano for my daughter's wedding at the historic Orpheum Theatre in Memphis. Our friend Gabe entertained guests by playing beautiful music on the piano.

Walking the Talk

I mentioned early on in this chapter, that many people don't feel confident serving in an advocate role. Advocacy requires taking a risk, putting yourself out there for someone else or for a cause. I've learned to shake off external criticism and focus only on my objectives for the person or group I'm serving. And that ultimately wins respect. While people may not always agree with me, they do know where my heart is. They know I will serve as an advocate for those I represent. I believe others can grow into that role as well. Over the years I've built a team of people who are prepared to fight just as hard as I do for our clients. They're prepared to do what is right.

Part of advocacy simply means being true to the commitments you make. We pride ourselves in making sure we manage the issues our clients care about—small and large. We strive to be present when talking to them. We know that by listening intently to their concerns, we can better advocate for them.

The role of an advocate is to:

- *Listen carefully* to better comprehend their clients' concerns and learn their significant issues. Then dig deeper to understand the underlying messages that sometimes clients aren't easily able to vocalize.
- *Explore options and viable solutions* empowering clients to make informed decisions that will help them and their families.
- *Connect clients with problem solvers* or influential decision makers if the advocate is unable to provide the solution.
- *Provide support* by partnering with clients to implement the plan.

A trusted advocate is responsible for:

- *Identifying challenges* and helping clients stay focused on the solutions.
- *Clarifying the process* while eliminating industry jargon other advisors spew at them.
- *Promptly responding* to any questions and concerns clients may have.
- *Setting realistic and meaningful goals* that will help clients reach their long- and short-term objectives.

Additionally, and most importantly, advocates should strive to under-promise and over-deliver, and always place the needs of their clients before their own. In all ways, they should position themselves as fiduciaries do for their clients and hold this to be a sacred trust. This commitment to acting in their clients' best interest at all time is the basis for calling themselves true advocates.

Advocacy Based on Love

I honestly believe that "love" is the greatest driving force for advocacy. As an advocate, you undoubtedly would do anything you could for a parent, spouse, child or other family member. When you love someone, you feel it more deeply than if it happened to you. When you believe strongly in

9. Advocate & Partner

an issue that can affect those you love, you're willing to defend that cause.

Advocacy springs from love, passion and a deep commitment to act in the interest of others. We all have the ability to be an advocate. As an advocate, I encourage you to:

- Listen deeply to the concerns of others.
- Be ready to assist with the challenges they face.
- Bravely step forward to fight for the causes you believe in.
- Act out of love. While you may feel a powerful sense of responsibility to a person or cause, love needs to be the driving force behind your actions.

Well-known author William Faulkner once wisely said, *"Never be afraid to raise your voice for honesty and truth and compassion against injustice and lying and greed. If people all over the world ... would do this, it would change the earth."*

To me, advocacy is an assertive and collaborative approach to problem solving. I've identified four virtues, or the "Four Ps" for advocacy:

1. **Patience.** Things can't always be achieved overnight. Instead, establish your goals and develop a plan, always keeping in mind: if it's worth committing to, it's worth committing to for the long haul—sometimes without remuneration. The Chinese philosopher Confucious said: *"It does not matter how slowly you go as long as you do not stop."* Everything takes *time*.

2. **Perseverance.** In many cases, you'll have to overcome adversity to reach your advocacy goals. Achieving something great requires great effort. Don't be afraid to ruffle feathers or upend the status quo to get things done. In my role on the school board, I had to be willing to break a few eggs. But as Steven Colbert once famously said: *"You can make an omelet without breaking eggs. It's just a really bad omelet."* Don't make a bad omelet!

3. **Persuasion.** Articulate your case to convince people the course you're pursuing will benefit everyone involved. Even if they don't necessarily agree with you, they'll admire your commitment and tenacity, and they'll understand your sense of urgency.

Pillars of Purpose

4. **Partnership.** Bring people together in the spirit of cooperation. Build a strong stakeholder base. Remember, if no one's following you, you're just taking a walk. As Helen Keller put it: *"Alone we can do so little. Together we can do so much."*

Whether you're an advocate for one person, a group, or a supporter of a cause or policy, advocacy is all about helping them find their voice and engaging others in the cause.

Considered one of the 20th Century's greatest humanitarians, Mother Teresa is proof that even one person can make a difference. As an advocate for the poor, she devoted her life to serving the destitute around the world. As the founder of Missionaries of Charity, a religious congregation devoted to helping those in need, she engaged more than 4,000 sisters to serve in 610 missions in 123 countries by the time of her death in 1997. Despite the obstacles she faced, she tirelessly served others with everlasting compassion and by engaging others in her cause. Most importantly, she acted in the spirit of pure love.

> *"It's not how much we do, but how much love we put in the doing. It is not how much we give, but how much love we put in the giving."*
>
> – Mother Teresa

Mother Teresa was awarded the Nobel Prize for Peace in 1979 for her work in bringing help to suffering humanity. However, she wisely counseled that advocacy must first start in our own homes: *"We think sometimes that poverty is only being hungry, naked and homeless. The poverty of being unwanted, unloved and uncared for is the greatest poverty. We must start in our own homes to remedy this kind of poverty."*

Join with me today in advocating for the rights of our loved ones. Then extend that love to making your community, our country, and our world a better place for all humanity.

Chapter 10
ORDER & CONTROL

"Order and simplification are the first steps toward the mastery of a subject."
– Thomas Mann, 1929 Nobel Prize for Literature

In the 2008 Wimbledon Final, two legendary tennis players, Rafael Nadal and Roger Federer, faced each other in what is widely regarded as one of the most thrilling, unpredictable tennis matches in history.

Nadal jumped out to an early two-set lead. But Federer stormed back to tie the match in close games. Many expected Nadal to fold in that moment of pressure in the final set. However, during the break, Nadal told his coach and uncle, *"Relax, I'm not going to lose this match. Maybe Federer will win, but I'm not going to lose it."*

Nadal knew there was one aspect of the match he could control—his effort and determination. He maintained his poise to defeat Federer 6–4, 6–4, 6–7, 6–7 and 9–7, prevailing in a quadruple tie breaker in the final set and winning what is considered one of the greatest tennis matches of all time.

Pillars of Purpose

In these foundational pillars I'm sharing with you, I hope you're discovering similarly powerful mental tools for overcoming pressure and achieving victory in your own life. Just as Nadal knew he had to find control within himself to win the match, we need to find *Order and Control* in our lives. That is the essence of Pillar No. 5.

Finding order and control requires understanding how opposing yet complimentary forces work to create stability.

A Blend of Forces

You've probably seen the yin/yang symbol—two teardrop shapes that fuse to form a circle referred to as Qi. This symbol represents the power of contrasting forces, e.g., light/dark, spiritual/physical, summer/winter, female/male. The yin and yang continuously transform into one another. Though opposites, they complement one another and are interconnected and interdependent in the natural world.

In this chapter, we'll use the concept of yin and yang to explore the natural juxtaposition of *internal order* and *external control* and how they contribute to a life of *order*. To understand how these two concepts, order and control, work in our lives, you need to understand their differences:

- *Order* comes from within. It is the natural result of a well-planned life. We can think of it as self-governance, achieved with deliberate effort, and *by design*.

- *Control* is placed on us from external sources, and often takes the shape of rules enforced by those in power, such as the rules parents set for their children or the laws politicians pass ostensibly to protect the people.

Both order and control help us create organization out of chaos and confusion, but they do so in completely different ways. Order requires a much higher level of thinking and flows from the ground up, i.e. self-control, discipline, will power from within. Control, on the other hand, is exemplified by top-down management systems where rules are paramount and decisions are predetermined at the top and cascade downward like an avalanche of bureaucracy.

10. Order & Control

At our firm, even though we function in a highly regulated field, we adhere to an "order-based" system. We rely on our internal structures and design to govern our organization, and we operate with a high degree of trust. This system, based on order, gives us more flexibility, and less red tape.

In contrast, the leader in a "control-dominant" organization must constantly recite and memorize rules, and when under pressure, often defaults to positional authority—*"I'm the boss, do what I say."* Feeling there is a lack of trust, individuals in this setting depend on *external control* for their marching orders. But a system dependent on external control makes people even less capable of exerting their own internal control. It can encourage weakness and irresponsibility, and sometimes even resentment.

Loss of Control

Obviously, there would be less need for external control in any organization or system if we all exerted greater internal control over our own lives. Think of all the laws passed because individuals could not or would not control themselves, including burdensome rules resulting from frivolous litigation.

We all recall the infamous 1994 product-liability case involving McDonald's "hot coffee" that resulted in a $2.7 million punitive damages award. (It was later appealed and reduced.) But the case became the poster child for excessive litigation and resulted in labeling rules that seem ridiculous to most people.

More recently, we've seen the loss of freedoms after the tragic events of 9/11. When terrorists flew planes into the twin towers of the World Trade Center in New York City, the Pentagon in Washington D.C. and a field in rural Pennsylvania, as a nation we became acutely aware of our security weaknesses. As a result, military bases restricted civilian access, and airports required passengers to pass through security checkpoints before being allowed in the terminals.

Later that year when a terrorist on a plane attempted to detonate an explosive device hidden in the sole of his shoe, airports began requiring passengers to remove their shoes and pass them through x-ray machines when going through airport security.

Pillars of Purpose

Additional examples of how losing internal control results in more external control, include:

- The great financial crisis in 2008-2009. It occurred because individuals failed to pay their mortgages. Of course, many of them shouldn't have qualified for mortgages to begin with, but received them due to the mortgage lenders, government agencies and the Wall Street firms that financed and profited from these "mortgage schemes." As a consequence of increased regulation, the process of qualifying for a home loan became much more burdensome, and regulations trickled down to every aspect of home construction and purchase.

- Frauds perpetrated by individuals like Bernie Madoff, Sam Bankman-Fried and Michael Milken, as well as the Enron abuses. As a result, our financial services industry has become more heavily regulated and burdened with excessive paperwork. Firms spend an inordinate amount of time and money trying to satisfy regulators, but are their clients really benefiting? Are clients safer nowadays? Wouldn't it be simpler and work better to always put clients' interests first?

Most of these external controls wouldn't be needed if we could self-govern. But if we fail to control ourselves, we lose control.

Holding Others Accountable

While we might not like following rules, they hold our society together in times of crisis. In 2002, a Gallup Organization survey found that nearly four in five (78%) of Americans were willing to give up certain freedoms to gain security. While it's hard to understand how people could so easily agree to forfeiting their freedoms, the fact that 42% of the respondents said they were "personally more afraid to fly" after September 11, and 31% reported having "no confidence at all" or "not much" confidence that the airlines in this country are adequately protected from terrorist attacks,[1] explains their need to feel secure in spite of the sacrifices.

Still, we often associate negative emotions with the word "control" because

---

[1] *Which Freedoms Will Americans Trade for Security*; Gallup; June 11, 2002; https://news.gallup.com/poll/6196/which-freedoms-will-americans-trade-security.aspx

10. Order & Control

it feels restrictive. Some people resent having their freedom curtailed by laws and rules. Many of these "external controls" come about only because people abuse their freedom and can't control themselves internally. Instead of empowering us, they often limit what we can do in order to protect us from outside threats and sometimes even from ourselves.

For example, the law requiring children to be strapped into car seats that meet or exceed federal standards when in a moving car was established when statistics revealed car crashes were one of the leading causes of death and injury for children. This law was the only way to ensure "all parents" would provide this protection for their young children.

The law requiring a person to not "drink and drive" was passed when thousands of people were dying because of alcohol-impaired car crashes —11,654 died in 2020 alone.[1]

I think most everyone can agree that these laws make sense. We need these external controls to protect us and ensure our rights as citizens against abuses by other people. However, if everyone practiced internal control, would they be necessary?

A Need for Balance

In considering how we can combine internal and external controls, I can't help but reflect on the reported work habits of Al Pacino, one of the greatest actors of all time. An Academy Award-winning force of nature, Pacino puts his whole heart into every role. In fact, at times his acting feels so intense, so memorable, it can eclipse everything and everyone else in the movie. Occasionally that works, but most of the time, it's not ideal for the film.

Wisely, Pacino knows his strengths and weaknesses (and excesses). He knows he needs a strong director to help channel his natural talent in the most effective way for the story. He knows that to do his best work he must connect with a director who can help him portray his role within the confines of the larger ensemble (and he's collaborated with some great directors, Martin Scorsese and Francis Ford Coppola to name a few).

---

[1] NHTDS; *Drunk Driving; How Alcohol Affects Driving Ability*; https://www.nhtsa.gov/risky-driving/drunk-driving#:~:text=Overview,These%20deaths%20were%20all%20preventable.

Pillars of Purpose

Self-development author Brian Tracey provides this example: *"Just as your car runs more smoothly and requires less energy to go faster and farther when the wheels are in perfect alignment, you perform better when your thoughts, feelings, emotions, goals and values are in balance."*

So it is with each of us. Our lives can be "Oscar worthy" if we know when we need to exert "internal control" or when we're better served by giving control to an "external" resource. As with Pacino, sometimes you will need to surrender some freedom to achieve a better outcome.

As financial advisors, we ask clients to trust us to build a financial plan that provides the structure to help them reach their short- and long-term goals. We help them navigate their own emotions and fears when short-term market fluctuations occur and global disturbances hit the headlines. We discourage them from making short-term decisions and encourage them to stay focused on long-term goals.

This process resembles hiring a personal trainer. When people know they lack the self-discipline to achieve their physical fitness goals, they hire a trainer to provide a system of accountability. Along with providing instruction and feedback, a trainer creates a daily regimen of exercises targeting the individual's specific needs and then helps them reach their goals.

Achieving your individual fitness goals requires internal focus, commitment and hard work. A trainer provides the external action—education, encouragement and a well-defined process—to keep you on track.

Internal Controls

Now that we've defined the differences between external and internal control, and the benefits and pitfalls of each, let's further explore the value of internal order. When we adopt our own controls or limitations, we're using self-control or "internal control." When we are self-disciplined enough to design and follow a structure that empowers us to be the best we can be, we're more likely to reach our goals and dreams.

As the ancient Chinese philosopher and writer Lao Tzu wisely said, *"He who controls others may be powerful, but he who has mastered himself is mightier still."*

10. Order & Control

On any given day, I find at least 40 to 50 items requiring my attention. I've learned that I must either delegate the responsibility to others, address the issue or add it to my schedule. Previously I mentioned how I list my "to do's" on yellow legal pads kept at my desk, on my nightstand or in my car. These lists keep my obligations visible, top-of-mind and help create order in my life. When something needs immediate attention, I schedule it on my iPhone and iPad calendars.

While each of these tasks usually occupy just a single line on a yellow pad, the process helps me to not lose site of the forest for the trees. My internal controls reduce my mental workload, preventing me from being overwhelmed by minutiae of the day. When staying focused on the bigger picture, I can accomplish even more.

There is a fundamental difference between people who get things done and those who don't. People who struggle to accomplish their daily goals just let "life happen to them." Instead, they need to "happen to life." This requires taking control and then creating order in our lives. While we can never control everything in life, our lives feel in order when we maintain the appropriate control over the things we can.

I'm reminded of a time the local minister and his schoolteacher wife asked to meet with me. They wanted to invest the $10,000 they had managed to save. After a nice conversation and listening for underlying concerns, I learned they had $50,000 of credit card debt and were considering filing for bankruptcy.

I told the couple, "I'd love to work with you, but I can't until you address this debt." I explained that I was not a fan of bankruptcies as a Chapter 7 bankruptcy would remain on their credit report for 10 years from the date of filing, and a Chapter 13 reorganization would affect their credit score for seven years. And even after that, it would take years to begin to rebuild their financial life.

Not wanting to leave them with no plan of action, I suggested creating a budget plan for them and strongly recommended they commit to this budget in their everyday life. I ensured them that, while it would require significant sacrifices, such a plan would get them to where they wanted to be financially in fewer years than declaring bankruptcy. They both agreed.

Pillars of Purpose

The plan we put in place was draconian. They would have to cut up their credit cards and cut back significantly on their spending, all of which would require a drastic change in their lifestyle.

However, in spite of the discomforts they endured, they followed the plan religiously (pun intended) exhibiting internal control. In just three years, they had clawed their way completely out of debt.

Today this couple enjoys their happy and successful retirement. In addition to accomplishing their retirement and lifestyle goals, their committment to this plan empowered them to be in position to help their daughter when she went through a difficult divorce.

Our relationship worked because they willingly listened to and took my hard advice. They granted me permission to exert control, and I was able to develop an appropriate plan of action for them. Most importantly, they practiced self-discipline by faithfully adhering to that plan.

Harmony only exists when these two energies co-exist and are in balance. It's a great manifestation of yin and yang in action.

Dangers of an Unbalanced Life

The minister and his wife reached their goals by practicing a balance of internal and external control. However, should either of these attributes slip out of balance, more chaos and unhappiness can result. A prime example of this is the Apple TV+ real-life drama, *The Shrink Next Door*, a true story about billionaire Marty Markowitz (played by Will Ferrell) who gave control of his life to his psychiatrist Issac "Ike" Herschkopf (played by Paul Rudd).

Overwhelmed with responsibilities and still grieving the loss of his parents, Markowitz gradually over the years gave Herschkopf complete control over his life. Not only did he allow him to control his finances and family relationships, but Herschkopf also relegated him to the guest house so he, himself, could take possession of the family mansion. During this time, Herschkopf was paid millions of dollars for his so-called "psychiatric services" and bilked Markowitz out of millions more to pay for his lavish lifestyle.

10. Order & Control

Some have asked how this could happen. The reality is, life happens. It didn't happen in just one day, but over a long period of time. Because of Markowitz's mental state, he gradually relinquished control of his life to a person he thought he could trust. Letting someone else make the decisions for him was a far easier path to take. Gradually, the balance between external and internal controls disintegrated, leaving him with an unhappy and chaotic existence.

Taking the path of least resistance requires no plan and no output of effort. Instead, it's just going with the flow to wherever the current may take you. Markowitz found it comforting to do nothing. Kind of like a child being coddled (and cuddled) by his mother, he felt satisfied his basic needs were being met. However, eventually he realized he had lost total control of his life.

SPOILER ALERT: Fortunately, after 30 years of living this way and losing millions of dollars, Markowitz took control of his life again.

A Universal Plan

During each day of our lives, we deal with disruptions that can pull us in many directions. If we choose to just "go with the flow" and surrender completely to the chaos, it's hard to see how anything of importance can be accomplished at the end of the day. That's why I'm such a big believer in planning. To make the most of our *entire* lives, we must create order in our *daily* lives. This means gaining order within our family, work and communities. Too often people think creating order means living in a prison camp of constant painful obligations. But as American monk and theologian Thomas Merton once said, *"Happiness is not a matter of intensity, but of balance, order, rhythm and harmony."*

Order is a universal concept. The Good Lord created our universe by design and in an orderly fashion. He gave us the resources and opportunity to do great things. He created us with innate determination and the ability to make decisions. Every day is a gift from God, and it's up to us how we use that day.

Without a plan, each day can be frittered away. Do you organize your day to include activities that truly matter? Do you set goals and then diligently strive to reach them? We can either see each new day as a valuable gift to be spent wisely, or we can slink into the corner of a dark closet and accomplish nothing. Having a plan helps us seize control of each day.

Order and Balance = Happiness

I have identified seven components of life that require balance and order to help us achieve peace of mind and ultimate happiness. While each plays a vital role, too much attention paid to any one area can become debilitating or dangerous.

- Spirituality
- Physical health
- Emotional wellbeing
- Financial stability
- Career contentment
- Relationships
- Sexual health

As you review this list, people you may know or have heard of may come to mind, people who became obsessed or "unbalanced" in one or more of these areas. Here are five examples of the dangers of these kinds of extreme behavior:

1. In one of the most horrific examples of religious fanaticism in history, more than 900 members of The People's Temple, a San Francisco-based religious group, died in 1978 after drinking poisoned punch at the urging of their leader, Reverend Jim Jones. They had surrendered total control of their lives to an obsessive and paranoid extremist.

2. Addiction to exercise is a real thing for some individuals. Over-exercise can result in tiredness, depression and trouble sleeping, but in the extreme it can cause Rhabdomyolysis, a syndrome involving muscle breakdown and damage. In 40% of these cases, kidney damage occurs.

3. Chronic self-sacrifice—sometimes referred to as co-dependency—can cause individuals to behave contrary to their own values as

10. Order & Control

they overindulge and coddle people who should be doing more for themselves. Constantly putting others ahead of ourselves and never establishing appropriate boundaries can be detrimental to our emotional and physical well-being.

4. Workaholics spend an exorbitant number of hours at work, compromising their relationships with others and their health in the process.
5. Sex addiction in all its forms can interfere with a person's daily life, create relationship issues and cause harm to others. It's estimated that between 3-5% of the adult population suffers from some form of addictive sexual behavior.[1]

While the seven attributes I listed are necessary for a healthy and happy life, prioritizing just one over all the others leads to excessive behavior and unhappiness.

Jules Henri Poincaré, French mathematician and philosopher of science, once said: *"It is the harmony of the diverse parts, their symmetry, their happy balance; in a word it is all that introduces order, all that gives unity, that pessimism in us to see clearly and to comprehend at once both the ensemble and the details."*

Creating Order from Chaos

Where you are today is because of the decisions you have made. While some things were not entirely in your control and will not be in your control going forward, you still have the choice to overcome obstacles and to again take control of your life. Following are 10 steps for doing that:

- **Realize.** Start by acknowledging that your life is not where you want it to be right now. Is an area of your life off balance, e.g., spirituality, physical health, emotional well-being, financial stability, career contentment, relationships or sexual health?
- **Responsibility.** Admit that where you are right now is because of the choices you have made. When doing this, you will immediately gain the power to achieve your greatest potential.
- **Reverse.** Reverse the direction you are going and commit to mak-

---

[1] Megan Hull; *Sex Addiction Facts and Statistics*; The Recovery Village; https://www.therecoveryvillage.com/process-addiction/sex-addiction/sexual-addiction-statistics/

ing changes. This is the most difficult step, but also the most important. Until you make up your mind to change, change will not happen. You must exercise your will.

- **Remember.** What is most important to you in life, most significant? How have your unbalanced actions affected what you value most? Identifying the people or things in your life that are important to you will give you the motivation to change.

- **Reflect.** Find a quiet spot and determine your top priorities. These are not your goals, dreams or desires. Instead, they are the fundamental areas of importance to being who you are and who you want to be. They are the immovable building blocks of your life.

- **Visualize.** Write down your priorities, so they become a constant reminder. Put them in a visible place to see them every day. Gain control and restore order to your life.

- **Prioritize.** Keep your priorities front and center in every decision you make throughout the day. Commit to them. They are your Bedrock Principles and will keep you steady, bring order and control to your life and peace to your existence.

- **Consistency.** Bring order to your life. Create habits that will keep you focused and disciplined. Commit to a goal for 21 straight days, and after three weeks it will become a habit. Continue to do it another 90 days and it will become part of your character.[1]

- **Learn.** Sharpen your saw! Committing to continual life-long learning will help you break old habits and adopt new ones. *"Live as if you were to die tomorrow. Learn as if you were to live forever."* – Mahatma Gandhi

- **Implement.** Just as it takes time to build bad habits, it will take time to break them. With patience, perseverance, and discipline you can do anything. As Helen Keller once said, *"A bend in the road is not the end of the road… unless you fail to make the turn."* Be patient with yourself and eventually you'll have control of your life.

---

1 *How the 21/90 rule helps you build good habits and a better life;* CapeSpace; https://capespace.com/how-the-21-90-rule-helps-you-build-good-habits-and-a-better-life/

10. Order & Control

Bringing order to your life will reduce your anxiety and bring you peace of mind.

Order Eliminates Stress

I often think of life as being divided into two parts, the things we can control and the things we can't. At one time or another, all of us face challenges that can throw us off track and cause considerable stress. However, if we focus on the things we *can* control and quit obsessing about the thing we can't, our lives will be much easier and we'll gain peace of mind.

Remember in the Intro to the Bedrock Principles when we talked about the fortitude of Viktor E. Frankl, Holocaust survivor and author of "Man's Search for Meaning?" While Frankl had no control over his situation, he knew he had a choice in how he reacted to it. He could turn bitter and hateful, or he could strive to have a positive attitude in spite of the horrific conditions.

He wisely said, *"Everything can be taken from a man but one thing: the last of the human freedoms—to choose one's attitude in any given set of circumstances, to choose one's own way. When we are no longer able to change a situation, we are challenged to change ourselves."*

I opened the chapter talking about a classic tennis match between Swiss-player Roger Federer and Spaniard, Rafael Nadal. I've always admired the resilience of Nadal, who won 14 French Opens, 22 Grand Slam men's singles titles and 36 Masters titles, as well as his ability to endure and overcome great physical pain caused by multiple injuries. His positive attitude transcended many of his peers, some of the best athletes in the world.

As I alluded to in describing his poised victory over Federer in 2008, Nadal maintained a deep belief that a person can only control what they can. While he approached his matches stoically, he knew he could not control the outcome of the match, as each depended on many variables, including luck and the opponent's performance.

As you begin to bring order to your life, be astutely aware of what you can control and what you can't. Pursue your goals with vigor and persistence.

Pillars of Purpose

As Nadal once said, *"When one player is better than you, at this moment, the only thing you can do is work, try to find solutions and try to wait a little bit for your time. I'm going to wait and I'm going to try a sixth time. And if the sixth doesn't happen, a seventh. It's going to be like this. That's the spirit of sport."*

Nadal always had a goal he was working toward. He said, *"The goal is to improve as a player and a person. That, finally, is the most important thing of all."*

Like Nadal, I encourage you to write down your goals and commit to doing your absolute best to achieve them. Crossing completed goals off your list will help acknowledge the effort you've put forth. The following three tips can help you bring order to your life.

- **Organize your thoughts.** "Mind mapping" provides a simple way to visualize your thoughts and explore solutions. From as early the 13th Century, people such as Leonardo da Vinci, and Michelangelo, and later Albert Einstein, Marie Curie and Thomas Edison from the last century, were known for creating organic notes filled with curling words, drawings and doodles. Follow their example by writing down your thoughts organically. Include all the crazy ideas that are cluttering your mind without worrying about any particular order. As you clear the brain, you'll be able to identify which thoughts are important or have potential and which can be discarded. And some thoughts may just be a nice surprise.

- **Declutter.** Removing the clutter from your surroundings can have a positive effect. I have a friend who, when overwhelmed by the demands put on her at work, finds decluttering and organizing her workspace eliminates stresses from her life by making her feel more in control. Removing clutter from your home, keeping only items you really want, will help you feel calm. You'll feel less pressure as you conquer this seemingly insurmountable task.

- **Organize your day.** There are many applications available on our computers, smart phones and tablets to help us organize our days, files, pictures and life in general. My team and I keep track of all our meetings on our shared iPhone calendars. At the beginning of each day, we each can easily see whom we are going to meet with

10. Order & Control

and at what time. Equally important, we're able to organize all our files so we can access them in an instant. As you go through your day, be intentional. Know what you are doing that day, and always keep focused on the big picture—WHY you are doing it! Then be consistent.

Organization isn't about perfection. It's about efficiency, reducing stress and clutter, saving time and money and improving your overall quality of life."

– Christina Scalise, professional organizer
and author of *Organize Your Finances, Your Kids, Your Life!*

While planning and organizing will help bring order and control to your life, there will still be days when you feel completely overwhelmed. That's when it's time to take a break. Studies have found that taking a break (detaching from work) increases energy and can reset your mood.

I always tell my team, "I really don't care how hard you work. I assume you are diligent workers. I'm more concerned with how smart and efficiently you work."

They govern themselves because we have a strong culture and work ethic. If they can finish a job more quickly by working smarter, I'm impressed. Then, if they need to take a break to refresh their mind and replenish their energy, I encourage them to do it. I know that by taking periodic breaks, they will be better equipped to finish the project. I trust them to make those basic decisions. Likewise, I encourage you to take regular breaks to do something you enjoy and can look forward to when things are overwhelming.

A Balanced Life

As a wealth manager, a husband and father, I have a clear vision of where I want to go and what I need to do to get there. I've shared that vision with my family and with my team at work. While there are multiple avenues available to get us there, we have a clear sense of the direction and a defined road map that we follow. We try to avoid chaos and confusion at all costs, and instead create an organization (and a family life) that generates peace of mind.

Pillars of Purpose

The complementary forces of yin and yang remind us that to bring balance to our lives we must learn to embrace its dualities—the ups and downs, good times and bad, joy and challenges, internal and external controls.

I encourage you to carefully examine your life to see if your life is in balance. Are you where you want to be? If not, create a plan that brings order to your life, and ultimately peace of mind.

Chapter 11
OBJECTIVITY

*"What objectivity requires is not an 'open mind,'
but an active mind."*
— Ayn Rand, writer and philosopher (1905-1982)

In the previous chapter, Order and Control, we discussed the value of two contrasting forces—internal self-control and external structure—and how pursuing a balance between the two helps us create lives of significance. The same holds true for *objectivity* and s*ubjectivity*. Two seemingly conflicting values, they work beautifully together much like the yin and yang we referred to in our last chapter.

Let's start with *objectivity*.

When we think of objectivity, we might picture Sergeant Joe Friday of the famed 1950s TV show, *Dragnet*, credited for the popular phrase: "Just the facts, ma'am." Or we might think of our family doctor, asking questions about our symptoms, looking over our blood-work analysis and medical charts in an attempt to objectively diagnose us. Objectivity seeks facts. An objective person is impartial, dispassionate and gathers the most relevant details, leaving out the so-called fluff. Objectivity is essential in any truth-seeking endeavor. Facts, after all, don't care about our feelings.

Subjectivity, on the other hand, includes emotions, opinions and experiences—all of our personal perspectives that, admittedly, can make for a more entertaining story! These days we're surrounded by opinions and hard-pressed to find straight facts anywhere even if we wanted to.

When younger, I watched Walter Cronkite (CBS), Chet Huntley and David Brinkley (NBC) and Peter Jennings (ABC) as they delivered the news. In my adolescent mind, I thought they were delivering the facts. But were they? Did they have biases? A point of view? Absolutely. Being newscasters didn't stop them from having human emotions and biases.

When President John F. Kennedy was assassinated, I watched as Cronkite wiped away a tear while reporting the horrific news. It was the first time I'd seen him express his feelings. It was both emotional and human. When Richard Nixon resigned, I was stunned by the way Cronkite's voice changed to disgust when he said the name, "Richard Milhous Nixon." While I didn't know whether he was a liberal or conservative, I realized he had an emotional reaction to the news he reported.

Can we even escape our own subjective reality? Charlie Kaufman, acclaimed American screenwriter and producer suggests: *There's no way to approach anything in an objective way. We're completely subjective; our view of the world is completely controlled by who we are as human beings, as men or women, by our age, our history, our profession, by the state of the world."*

While it's true that our feelings strongly influence the decisions we make and how we see the world, we can develop a balance between facts and feelings by tapping into the right resources. We can draw information from the wider world around us to shape our internal preconceptions. We need a balance between objectivity and subjectivity to make good choices and to counsel others. And this process is an important pillar for creating a life of significance.

Striving for Objectivity and Balance

If you've ever had the experience of serving on a jury, you understand the

11. Objectivity

difficulty of setting aside judgment and focusing only on facts. A recent study, for example, found that although jurors were instructed to reach a verdict based on proven evidence and reasonable doubt, a substantial proportion of them reported relying on additional subjective factors to arrive at a decision.[1]

We all like to think we can be "objective" when forming an opinion or making an important decision, but we constantly trip over our own experiences, feelings and even unconscious biases. Sometimes people become so deeply enmeshed in their own subjective reality they can't see the forest for the proverbial trees. In these situations, they often make poor choices based on limited information, and they are unwilling or unable to entertain a broader set of facts. It's vital in these cases for them to turn to people they trust for unbiased advice and fresh perspective on what may be a difficult path ahead.

Barton Goldsmith, Ph.D., a relationship counselor who wisely advises, *"Look for truth and be open to see how it's possible that your feelings may not be accurate. It also can be helpful to get an outside perspective from someone you trust."*

Gaining objectivity will help you:

- Acknowledge and compensate for your own biases.
- Develop the capacity to identify the critical facts in complicated and confusing scenarios.
- Create separation from the heat of your own emotions or the emotions of others.
- Develop the skills and analyses necessary to convince someone who tends to operate in an subjective manner.
- Gain insight into subjects that create strong emotional reactions and responses.
- Declutter your decision-making factors by focusing only on primary considerations.

---

[1] Blake M. McKimmie, et al; *Objective and Subjective Comprehension of Jury Instructions in Criminal Trials*; https://www.researchgate.net/publication/271788557_Objective_and_Subjective_Comprehension_of_Jury_Instructions_in_Criminal_Trials

It's useful to create your own customized scoring system by listing the pros and cons of a situation. Doing this, you'll be better able to evaluate the impact your decision will have on yourself and others, e.g., risks versus rewards, costs versus benefits.

Engaging an outside advisor, educator, consultant, mediator or therapist who has "no skin in the game," also can provide an unbiased view beyond our emotional flash points. An outside opinion often gives us a satellite perspective of our problem or issue, bringing wider vision, greater expertise, as well as more refined solutions.

However, unbiased advice that ignores our feelings and emotions can cause internal turmoil and stress. While that birds-eye view can be helpful in identifying previously unknown solutions, it might miss key emotional concerns that would render the solution useless.

That's why it's important to look at all aspects of a solution to create a healthy balance.

Remember the story I told you about the woman who was initially happy with the retirement portfolio we created for her. However, when the stock market experienced significant volatility, she realized she wasn't equipped emotionally to deal with the turbulence. Although the initial portfolio would help her reach her long-term goals sooner, actually living with that decision affected her ability to sleep at night; it didn't match her internal disposition. After learning of her discomfort, we created an alternative plan that would not only allow her to reach her retirement goals but would afford her peace of mind.

Again, that's why it is so critical to create balance between *subjective and objective* perspectives—so we don't miss anything vital!

A "Do it Yourself" Approach

As financial advisors, we understand the importance of gathering sufficient information about our clients' assets, liabilities, income and expenses in order to make appropriate recommendations. But we also know the world can't be viewed as being black and white. Everyone we meet has a life spattered with various shades of red, orange or purple—their dreams, fears, emotions and aspirations. All of these things contribute

11. Objectivity

to their *why*—why they do what they do, why they make the decisions they make.

As we dig deep to understand our clients' needs and desires, we provide them with our best analysis, and sometimes these are hard pills for them to swallow. In devising solutions, we strive to consider a client's feelings and emotional state, and then to find an approach that reflects a full understanding of each person as an individual.

I always chuckle to myself when someone tells me they can manage their own investments using an online trading platform. They don't realize that self-service investing won't save them from their own emotions. Too many do-it-yourself investors rely on gut intuition as they jump into the "hot stock" of the moment and cross their fingers. But counting on luck and bailing at the first sign of volatility is not a sound investment strategy for a secure retirement.

Now I'm not saying that all people who do their own investing and due diligence lack the discipline to succeed. There are those who use their own platforms and research, and they do it well. However, some of the greatest mistakes are made when investors react to their emotions. While we all know the best strategy is to "buy low, sell high," it's human nature to want to sell as soon as the stock market drops and buy even more as it goes up and up. Timing the stock market is, of course, rarely successful.

Investment guru Peter Lynch further proved the futility of trying to time the market as manager of Fidelity's extraordinarily successful Magellan Fund from 1977 to 1990. Fund assets grew nearly 700-fold (69,990%)—from $20 million to $14 billion.[1]

Retiring from Fidelity in 1990, at the age of 46, he began to compare the fund's average growth of 29.2% per year to that of the individual investor. He was frustrated when he found their returns only increased an averaged 7.3% per year over the same period. Why the gap? Because the average investor lacks the discipline to stay invested over the long haul. Another reason for the gap would be the tendency for investors to get caught up in the euphoria of rising prices to buy high then panic in times of market downturn to sell low.

---

[1] *Peter Lynch Strategy and Portfolio*; Quantified Strategies; April 18, 2023; https://www.quantifiedstrategies.com/peter-lynch-strategy/

Pillars of Purpose

Upon further comparison, he found that people who stayed in the stock market from 1965 to 1995 earned similar returns to those who tried to time the market. He used an example of three investors investing in the market at different times over the 30-year period[1]:

- Investor 1 invested $1,000 each year on the lowest day in the market.
- Investor 2 invested $1,000 each year on the highest day in the market.
- Investor 3 invested $1,000 each year on the first day of year.

The results showed:

- Investor 1 (perfect market timing) gained an average annual return of 11.7%.
- Investor 2 (worst market timing) gained an average annual return of 10.6%.
- Investor 3 (no market timing) gained an average annual return of 11.0%.

Thus, there was only a 1.1% difference between the earnings of the three investors. Lynch advised: *"The trick is not to learn to trust your gut feelings, but rather to discipline yourself to ignore them. Stand by your stocks as long as the fundamental story of the company hasn't changed."*

As an investment advisor, I follow five rules to help me stay objective when creating a client's portfolio or managing my own investments. I encourage you to embrace these guidelines, too.

1. **Turn off the noise.** In this day and age, we face an endless barrage of commotion. As an investor, you'll find hundreds of opinions on the latest "hot stock" and where you need to put your money *today*. Tune out the noise to avoid information overload.
2. **Create a long-term plan.** Don't be a "day trader" going in and out of the market. Instead, hold steady to the course. As the late economist Paul Samuelson says, *"Investing should be more like watching paint dry or watching grass grow. If you want excitement, take $800 and go*

---

[1] *Time Factors n the Stock Market*; Plancorp®; https://www.plancorp.com/blog/time-beats-timing

11. Objectivity

to Las Vegas."

3. **Buy quality.** Invest with great companies. Billionaire investor Charlie Munger suggests, *"All intelligent investing is value investing—acquiring more than you are paying for. You must value the business in order to value the stock."* Invest in solid and trustworthy companies.

4. **Manage expenses.** As an advisor, I pay attention to expense ratios in my investment recommendations. You, too, should know the cost of investing. Know how your financial advisor makes their money. Do they make a commission? Are they fee-based? When investing in mutual funds, insurance policies or annuities, know how and what fees are being charged. These are important considerations when investing your money.

5. **Keep calm and stay the course.** Don't become obsessed with checking your investments every day. They will go up and down, and it can drive you crazy watching the roller-coaster effect. Instead, stick to your plan and keep your end goals in mind.

No matter what decisions you are making—buying insurance, saving for retirement, writing a will or buying a home, you should strongly consider hiring a professional who can see the entire picture and can help you avoid making big mistakes that can jeopardize your future goals. They'll help you create a logical plan of action and avoid emotional blind spots. However, I do caution you that if the advisor doesn't take the time to really understand your situation and your internal makeup, run for the door!

Understanding Decisions Based on Emotions

As a wealth advisor, I like to spend time upfront to connect with clients on an emotional level and to listen to their concerns. When exploring their life history, I'm able to gain a better understanding of the experiences that influence their investment decisions, behaviors and goals. The resulting portfolio takes into consideration those subjective influences.

While my team and I do our best to create the best path toward client goals, we sometimes encounter roadblocks along the way.

I'm reminded of a client who has been a dear friend for a long time. We were going through a planning analysis several years ago when I learned part of her plan for creating financial security was acquiring real estate properties throughout the community. She was using the rent to pay down the debt with a goal of paying off the properties over the next few years. Then she and her husband could use the income to sustain them once they retired.

As I further questioned her about the viability of her plan, I discovered her adult son had moved into one of the rentals, but he wasn't paying any rent. Of course, that put a glitch in her entire plan. I explained that she would either need to sell the property or find a renter who could pay if she wanted to reach her goals.

Giving me an intense look, she said directly, "David, don't go there. I'm not moving my son out. If that means I won't accomplish my goals, so be it. But don't go there!"

I had unknowingly stepped into "no man's land." While I could have pressed the point and potentially lost her as a client and as a friend, I had to tell myself that everything is not based on logic and reason. Instead, their family situation had to be taken into consideration, and most importantly, her feelings as a mother.

After a lengthy discussion, we created an alternate plan based on her strongly held belief that her first priority was to take care of her son. While it wasn't exactly the best use of their money, it was important to her. Of course, her husband wisely went along with her wishes.

Our job as financial advisors is to assess the situation, analyze the emotions tied to the prospect's decision-making process and produce a solution that will allow them to reach their goals.

After doing our research, we then commit to presenting clients with a fact-based and balanced analysis. And, while it's never pleasant, we are committed to "calling it as we see it," delivering brutal honesty when needed.

To further live up to my commitment to clients, in 2021 I became certified in the state of Tennessee as a Rule 31 Mediator. This is someone who serves as a neutral party in trying to achieve a negotiated settlement of a legal matter. I've been privileged over the years to have counseled many clients on pending divorce matters and have even helped several cou-

11. Objectivity

ples achieve an amicable settlement on the dissolution of their marriage, avoiding enormous legal expenses and court costs. In these matters, I'm often wading through a lot of subjective client emotions.

The important distinction here is that as a "mediator" or "legal neutral," I take NO position on the issues. I simply serve as a facilitator who tries to help both parties achieve an equitable resolution. When acting as "objective advisors," we're able to review the evidence and engage in a fact-based analysis to reach a verifiable and defensible conclusion. As advisors, we empower our clients to make great decisions by providing objective recommendations.

Overcoming Interpersonal Obstacles Without Second Guessing

Just as with my client who didn't want to evict her own son (and I learned it was pointless to ask her to try), it's important to always be cognizant of how emotions impact a person's decisions. Our emotional response to other people's emotional decisions can further exacerbate the problem!

My team and I are keenly aware of how potential clients' experiences impact them. We listen to the way people respond to our questions and we watch their body language. Then we strive to deliver a plan that takes into consideration both the *objective and subjective* elements in their lives. However, no matter how closely we watch and listen, it's sometimes impossible to get to the heart of a situation.

For example, recently a client referred her in-laws to me. I spent more than an hour asking questions as I tried to get to know them. Despite my best efforts, we never quite connected. It was very frustrating because all the things we talked about were important, and I just wanted to provide them with sound advice. I didn't understand why they seemed so disinterested in what I was saying. I felt I must have dropped the ball somehow in failing to win them over or to capture their attention.

Two days later, I learned that 15 minutes prior to our meeting, they had just received a call from their son telling them he had been diagnosed with an aggressive form of cancer. Obviously, that information was not shared during our meeting. If I had only known, we could have rescheduled. I felt horrible.

The point is, despite our best efforts, we never know everything that is going on in a person's head. While it's important to connect, to be present, sometimes there are interpersonal barriers that won't allow us in.

So how do you break those barriers?

First off, don't beat yourself up or bring in your own insecurities. Don't make things worse by reacting emotionally and losing your own objectivity. When communicating with someone and getting the feeling that things are "off" or just not lining up, we often assume we're at fault. In fact there could be extenuating circumstances—as with my clients' in-laws.

According to Barton Goldsmith, therapist and author, the initial read of a situation is often completely wrong: "*Upon occasion, every now and then, some people get a feeling (of self-recrimination) that isn't real. They may think that it's real, it may feel very real, and they may truly believe it's real, but it's just a feeling. It is wise to remember that, as important as emotions are, feelings aren't facts.*"

He advises us to never assume to know why a person reacts to us the way they do. "*The best thing to do when you are feeling like something isn't right is to check it out. Don't sit on it, push it down, or try to ignore it.*" Ask the person directly and try to understand why your feelings may not be accurate. It's also helpful to get an outside perspective from someone you trust.[1]

In the case of my client's in-laws, as a consultant, I shouldn't have assumed I caused the lack of connection. Instead, I should have asked them directly, "Are you okay?" or "Is there a problem I'm not aware of?" A straightforward approach is usually the best policy. This also was an example that even though at this point I had been an advisor for 40 years, I still needed to grow, sharpen my saw, and improve my skills.

Breaking Barriers Through Objectivity

Being objective can help in other areas of your life—including when

---

1 Barton Goldsmith Ph.D.; *Feelings Aren't Facts*; Psychology Today, https://www.psychologytoday.com/us/blog/emotional-fitness/201310/feelings-aren-t-facts

11. Objectivity

making decisions about the trustworthiness or competence of individuals you meet. For instance, have you ever met someone for the first time and felt immediate rapport with him or her? On the other hand, have you met someone for whom you felt an immediate dislike? Did those instincts turn out to be right or wrong? We're all governed by our beliefs, our ideas and biases, hopes and fears, and past and present experiences.

You've probably heard the adage, "Don't judge a book by its cover." A good example of casting premature judgment is society's feelings about tattoos. A study conducted by researchers Kristin Broussard and Helen Harton found an estimated 47% of Millennials (born 1981-1996) and 36% of Generation Xers (born 1965-1980) have tattoos. While the numbers are increasing daily, many of these tattoo-bearing individuals suffer from perceptions of being socially undesirable and labeled as having negative personality characteristics, such as lower levels of inhibition and a higher level of promiscuity. Interesting enough, the study found that people judged tattooed women even more harshly than their male counterparts.[1]

You might examine your own feelings about this issue. For example, if you interviewed a woman for a job who has tattoos on her arms and multiple piercings, would you have negative feelings about her capabilities?

I'm reminded of a good friend, Jan Wilson. Her husband, Michael, was the assistant band director when my daughter, Katie, was in the high school marching band. We had worked closely with him and his father, who owned a trucking company, to procure an 18-wheeler to haul the band instruments to and from various events.

We were devastated when we learned that Michael had been diagnosed with leukemia. Stoically fighting the disease, he went through five remissions. During those times, we helped Jan and him buy their first house, sign up for Social Security Disability, and complete their estate plan. Unfortunately, in 2021 the disease won the war for Michael's life.

Shortly after the memorial service, Jan found a note Michael had written expressing his love for her. Clinging to memories of their life together,

---

1 Kasasa; *Boomers, Gen X, Gen Y, Gen Z and Gen A Explained*; 07/06/2021; https://www.kasasa.com/exchange/articles/generations/gen-x-gen-y-gen-z#:~:text=Gen%20Y%3A%20Gen%20Y%2C%20or,million%20people%20in%20the%20U.S.)

she had a tattoo artist convert the note into a tattoo on her arm. Replicated in his handwriting, Jan will tell you it's the most meaningful thing on her body.

Knowing there is a powerful story behind a person's tattoos might make you more accepting of them. Often tattoos represent a personal expression of love, a memorable experience or deeply held belief that is transferred into "body art."

If you saw a group of Harley motorcyclists, dressed in leather and hanging out in front of a restaurant, would you feel uncomfortable approaching them?

If your sole image of motorcycle riders involves the Hell's Angels biker gang, you might walk on the other side of the street to avoid them. However, if you had a successful relative or a neighbor who enjoys motorcycles, you would probably be more comfortable striking up a conversation, knowing that people from all walks of life ride Harley-Davidsons.

The late British author Elizabeth Thornton wisely suggested, *"To increase our objectivity, we must learn to switch off the mini movies. Objectivity requires us to be mindful, present in the moment, and experiencing what is happening without judgment."*

Unfortunately, like others, I'm not immune to being biased. For example, after pre-screening the application of a candidate for a job at our firm, I was put off when, in person, I discovered some language barriers and cultural differences existed. However, as I delved deeper during the interview process, I got to know her better. As I peeled the layers off the onion, so to speak, I really liked her and found she had a lot to offer our firm.

If I had stuck to my first impression and had never given her the respect and opportunity she deserved, it would have been a great disservice not only to her, but to our firm. True objectivity is based on giving people equal access within your head … and reserving judgment. It's about judging them on their character, the quality of the work they produce and the true nature of who they are.

To become truly objective, you need to:

- **Realize objectivity has its limits.** Each of us is inherently not

11. Objectivity

objective.

- **Identify your own weak spots.** What are your pet peeves? What can cause you to overreact?

- **Assemble your personal advisory council.** Expand your network to include people whom you respect and whose viewpoints often vary from your own.

- **Understand your own personality type.** Do you see the glass as half full or half empty? Does your perspective have a negative or positive influence on your opinions?

- **Solicit alternative points of view.** Understand that no person has a monopoly on great ideas or solutions.

As Thornton advised, *"switch off the mini movies"* in your head.

Left Brain Vs. Right Brain

In our society, people too often get labeled early on as being left- or right-brained. A left-brained individual is thought to be more analytical, methodical and objective, while a right-brained person is said to be more intuitive, creative, emotional, thoughtful and subjective. However, while each of us has a dominant side, understanding the characteristics of both sides helps us to form a bigger and more accurate picture of an individual.

A world based on a purely robotic and analytical approach would be totally void of empathy and understanding. On the other hand, a world ruled purely by emotions would be disastrous.

You might remember the time an international airline took an analytical approach to customer service. Putting a single-minded focus on "on-time departures," it would literally back the planes away from the gate on time, even if they were only moved three feet. This way the company could claim a plane had departed on time.

While they accomplished their goal, the cost was high. Customers were unhappy when their bags didn't make it on the plane and when they were without necessary items upon reaching their destinations. Was this a win? I think not.

Pillars of Purpose

Again, author Elizabeth Thornton suggests, *"Complete objectivity is not an option. We are all subjective about the way we respond to 'what is' whether it's the people we encounter, the circumstances in our lives, or ourselves."*

A business that runs purely on data, metrics and profits, ignores its most valuable asset—its customers. However, if a company fails to measure the data and never tracks its inventory or the inflow and outflow of cash, it will soon be out of business. Instead, every company needs to have a system that creates balance and harmony between the right and left sides of the brain.

This harmony can be hard to come by in corporate America. While spending 20 years working at a major Wall Street firm, I became distressed at how advisors were treated, not as individuals who were contributing to the success of the business, but as distribution channels for the firm's products. Even more upsetting was the lack of value put on the individual client. Instead, advisors and clients were just cogs in the moneymaking process. The company's systems were completely out of sync with how I believed a firm should be run.

What Happens if ...?

When I made the decision in 1999 to start my own firm, it took significant preparation and hard work. My main goal was to establish a firm where the values aligned with my core belief ... *it's ALL about the client.*

Our twin pillars are: 1) advisory excellence with a focus on investment excellence and exemplary service, and 2) community engagement. These haven't changed over the years, even though we continue to evolve as professionals as we grow and learn from our experiences.

When we first meet with prospects, we ask them three particularly important questions, ones that dig deep into their feelings and emotions:

1. What happens if you were told you have five years to live?
2. What happens if you were told you have one year to live?
3. What happens if you were told you have one day to live?

These are hard questions to consider, yet I'm now asking you: "What happens if ...?"

11. Objectivity

Are you living each day to the fullest? Like the lyrics to Tim McGraw's song, do you "Live Like You Were Dying"?

In this song about a man who finds out his father is battling a terminal illness, he sings: *"And all of the sudden, goin' fishing wasn't such an imposition, and I went three times that year I lost my dad."* The lyrics were particularly meaningful to McGraw because the same month he recorded it, his father, Tug McGraw, passed away from cancer.

The song won every major award after it was released in 2004, including ACM and CMA trophies for Single of the Year and Song of the Year, as well as two Grammy awards. Landing at No. 1 on the U.S. Billboard 200 chart, the song inspired people to make positive changes in their lives and make the most of the time they had. On YouTube, one fan shared the impact McGraw's song/message had on her marriage during her husband's lengthy health challenges:

> "When my husband and I married, the doctor had told him he would probably only live five years because of his heart. I told him that we'd have five good years together. We lived our lives as full as we could: motorcycle riding, raising Great Danes, camping and finally building a 'trike' for him. My husband lived seven years beyond what the doctor had predicted. He took his ride with God in 2016."

This fan and her husband decided to live life to the fullest. Even through an uncertain future, they seized every moment they had. The memories they made will last forever.

While considering the three penetrating questions listed on page 182, continue by asking yourself:

- What are my hopes and dreams for the future?
- What keeps me up at night or has been left undone?
- What do I still want to accomplish?
- What do I still want to experience?
- What can I do differently from this day forward?
- Who do I really want to be?

Pillars of Purpose

Your answers to these questions will reveal relevant pieces of your experiences, emotions, fears, dreams and goals—some of which you may not have consciously recognized.

As financial advisors, we believe it's important to probe these deeper questions before crafting a financial plan for our clients. Admittedly, some people will find they are not on track to reach their goals. By encouraging them to provide these additional layers of information, we can artfully create a comfortable path to their desired destination.

According to Leo Tolstoy, renowned author of *War and Peace*: *"Art is the uniting of the subjective with the objective of nature with reason, of the unconscious with the conscious, and therefore art is the highest means of knowledge."*

We think of our business as a combination of art and science. Maybe the most important part is the art of listening, understanding and being present.

You are the artist painting your own life. I encourage you to live it in full color. You are one of a kind. Your experiences, feelings and emotions are unique. While others may claim they know what's best for you, you alone know honestly what you can live with and what you can't. While it's important for you to be objective when making decisions and to seek the unbiased advice of a professional when needed, make sure you take into consideration the things that are important to you. Strive to create this important balance in your life.

Chapter 12

NAVIGATE LIFE

"It is not the strongest of the species that survives, not the most intelligent that survives. It is the one that is the most adaptable to change."
– Charles Darwin

Mike Tyson, one of the greatest heavyweight boxers of all time, was known for his ferocious punches and intimidating fighting style. Like a proverbial "bull in a China shop," Tyson charged through his first 29 opponents in the 1980s and 90s—going undefeated with 25 knockouts.

Before each bout, reporters huddled around the next challenger asking what strategy they intended to use to outsmart the champ. Some of those boxers talked about their ability to use lateral movement, some thought they would try quickness to elude Tyson's gloves, and some intended to simply "dance around."

However, none succeeded. As Tyson famously and succinctly put it before one of his fights: *"Everybody has a plan until they get punched in the mouth."* No matter what his opponents hoped to do, so much of their strategy went out the window after absorbing one of Iron Mike's devastating left hooks.

Pillars of Purpose

Navigating life can feel like getting hit in the face, too. You might start out with a great game plan for a great life—but the punches catch you off guard. It may be in the form of a sudden job loss, an unexpected illness, the death of a loved one or a devastating divorce.

In fact, few people can say life went according to "plan." The key is to not get knocked out but keep fighting and trying to re-establish a winning game plan. Our strategy may need to change, but we can update our approach and change right along with life. It amounts to getting back into the ring and continuing to battle, bruises and all, no matter how often we may get knocked down by life.

Navigating Through Tough Times

As articulated in the Darwin quote at the beginning of this chapter, it's the ability to adapt to change that gives any species an evolutionary edge. We see so many examples of adapting in the world of sports. And you might have noticed by now, I'm a pretty big sports fan—especially football.

In the classic 1971 ABC TV movie *Brian's Song*, one of my favorite sports movies, we see the poignant journey of football players Brian Piccolo and Gale Sayers through career setbacks, cultural tension and ultimate tragedy. At each turn, these two men demonstrated the ability to adapt to whatever life handed them. They set a good example for all of us to follow.

Sayers rose to fame as a football star during his college days. Nicknamed the "Kansas Comet" for his elusiveness and agility on the field, he compiled 4,020 all-purpose yards over three seasons and was twice recognized as a consensus All-American. Piccolo, too, won accolades in college, leading the nation in rushing and scoring during his senior season.

However, while Sayers became the top draft pick for the Chicago Bears in 1965, Piccolo went unselected in both the AFL and NFL drafts. Not willing to give up his dream of playing professionally, he tried out for the Chicago Bears as a free agent and made the taxi squad (or practice team), meaning he could practice but not suit up for games.

Eventually, however, Piccolo's determination and positive attitude won him a job on the Bear's roster, his big break coming when starting tailback Sayers injured his knee in 1968. Even when Sayers returned as a

12. Navigate Life

halfback the following year, Piccolo remained a starter, but primarily in a blocking role.

I liked how the movie captured the inspiring friendship that developed between Sayers and Piccolo and their wives. Bear in mind, they were competing against one another in the backfield during this time. Adding to the mix, this took place in the tumultuous '60s when interracial friendships weren't as common. In fact, race riots divided the country. Piccolo (white) and Sayers (Black) became symbols of racial harmony at a time when professional football still practiced segregation in travel accommodations.

Brian's daughter, Lori Piccolo, later shared the depth of their relationship when she wrote:

> "Players (at that time) were still segregated by race for hotel room assignments. The Bears' players changed that, asking to be reassigned by position instead. Running back was the only position on the team at the time with one black and one white player: Gale Sayers, the first-round draft pick nicknamed the 'Kansas Comet,' and my father, the undrafted free agent from Wake Forest. They roomed and bonded together during the civil rights movement and so much social upheaval in the late 1960s. I look at their relationship now and think how much we could learn from them."[1]

On and off the field, the unbreakable bond these two former rivals forged helped change the status quo in professional football. Willing to stand up for their values, they bravely stood together to oppose discrimination.

As mentioned previously, during the 1968 season, Sayers suffered a significant knee injury that resulted in Piccolo taking over the starting running back role. Many thought Sayers would never recover his elite speed and agility. But with grueling effort and the help of Piccolo, who encouraged, motivated and supported him throughout the painful process, Sayers rehabbed his knee, returned to the field in 1969, and led the NFL in rushing yards.

---

[1] Bryan DeArdo; *Five things you may not know about Gale Sayers, the NFL legend who died at age 77*; 9/23/2020; https://www.cbssports.com/nfl/news/nfl-games-today-expert-picks-predictions-props-for-nfl-playoffs-divisional-round-schedule-2022/

Pillars of Purpose

In the midst of Sayers' comeback season, in November 1969, Piccolo was diagnosed (at age 26) with embryonal cell carcinoma—an aggressive and deadly cancer. The news shook his family and teammates to the core, but especially Sayers, who would go on to provide unconditional support to his friend during his cancer treatment. The emotional season culminated in a Pro Bowl appearance for Sayers, and he won the NFL's George S. Halas Most Courageous Player Award, a character award given for his return from an injury.

Flying into New York in May of 1970 to accept the award (after convincing organizers to move the date up four months), Sayers told the crowd at the Pro Football Writers Awards Dinner: *"You flatter me by giving me this award; but I tell you here and now that I accept it for Brian Piccolo. Brian Piccolo is the man of courage who should receive the award. It is mine tonight. It is Brian Piccolo's tomorrow."* Then, taping Piccolo's name over his own, he presented the trophy to his friend the next day in the hospital, an unselfish testament to their devotion.

Piccolo passed away just a month later, in June 1970. Though his career and life were cut tragically short, he is still remembered as a man of character who navigated life with determination and conviction. He demonstrated integrity throughout his life and was a true friend who inspired his one-time rival to become the best he could be while showing a nation the meaning of equality.

> *"When they think of him, it's not how he died that they remember, but rather how he lived, how he did live!"*
> – Chicago Bears' coach George Halas, from the movie *Brian's Song*

While Sayers played just two more seasons, he earned induction into the Pro Football Hall of Fame in 1977 at age 34, the youngest player to date to achieve such an honor. Sayers remained close to Piccolo's widow and family and helped to keep Piccolo's memory alive by sharing their story and championing the Brian Piccolo Cancer Research Fund until his own death in September 2020.

In navigating life through some brutal punches, Piccolo and Sayers counted on each other. They recognized that their personal goals could never preempt their selfless support for one another.

12. Navigate Life

Planning for the Future, Adjusting for the Present

Often the key to survival in life is flexibility. Piccolo showed flexibility when he accepted a role on the "taxi squad." It's the ability to change how we think, feel and act. Shedding the "I've always done it this way" attitude helps us adapt to the punches life throws at us. I like to think of flexibility as fitting into three distinct categories—cognitive, emotional and dispositional. Let's explore these concepts a little further.

Cognitive Flexibility is the ability to think differently or reframe your approach to a problem. Exploring different solutions and approaches or seeking professional feedback can be helpful when dealing with change.

Emotional Flexibility is being aware of your feelings, acknowledging them and guiding them in a constructive way. Research shows that being emotionally flexible or having the ability to adapt or change can have a positive effect on a person's physical and psychological well-being.

Dispositional Flexibility is the ability to remain optimistic and realistic at the same time. It's the ability to change a problem into an opportunity. It's important to keep an open mind when different views and opinions are shared. When faced with challenges, remember, "this too shall pass."

While planning ahead is an important part of life, it's equally important to know that when "life happens," staying flexible will allow you to rise to the challenge. As a business owner, I've had to be a chameleon, changing my business practices and philosophies as conditions in the market changed, new regulatory requirements evolved, technology became more advanced and communication systems were modernized. I practiced cognitive flexibility through constant change.

When I started in business, paperwork for client accounts was literally kept in a three-ring binder called our "book of business." Today, we track everything digitally and our "book" can be accessed on an iPhone. A paper trail is no longer required as this information is securely recorded in the "cloud."

As we adapted to these changes, we had to be flexible in our thinking. We no longer could look at problems from the usual stance (cognitive flexibility). More importantly, we couldn't be intimidated by these newer, more modern approaches to running a business. Instead, it was necessary to become the master of our emotions, not victims (emotional flexibility).

We also found that having a positive approach to changes helped us to weather some rather turbulent times (dispositional flexibility). We didn't buy into the common phrase, "can't teach an old dog new tricks." Instead, when help was needed, we turned to people who had more experience. Building a successful business depends on tapping into internal and external resources. It's about building a strong and diverse team.

Likewise, whether your challenges are personal, financial or business related, you need to have a trustworthy network of people who can assist you in navigating change. You might remember the famous "No Man is an Island" sermon written in 1642 by John Donne. In it he brilliantly conveys the interdependence of human beings and how important that connection is for the well-being and survival of mankind.

> No man is an island, entire of itself,
> Every man is a piece of the continent, a part of the main …
> … Any man's death diminishes me, because I am involved in Mankind,
> And therefore, never send to know for whom the bell tolls,
> It tolls for thee.

In navigating life and adapting, nothing can help you more than a trustworthy network of family members, friends, colleagues or professional resources, most of whom are eager to help in your time of need. Lean on them and be willing to be a resource for your friends as well.

Navigating Bad News and Hard Times

During my lengthy career in business, I've experienced good and bad investment cycles. I've experienced times when the market did nothing but rise and just the opposite when stocks fell like rocks. During these times of extreme stress and change, our clients know they can trust us to help them navigate. They know we embrace being a fiduciary, meaning we put the interests of our clients above our own. As we deal with the obstacles they face, we help them analyze and understand any adjustments needed to reach their desired destination.

12. Navigate Life

While we spend a significant amount of time talking about a client's plans for the future, such as retirement planning, education funding or business planning, we also recognize that the future can be uncertain. In other words, "Life happens!"

To give you a better perspective of what I'm talking about, let's review some unplanned events that have shaken the financial markets and explain how we have been flexible in our response, thus helping us to navigate proactively for the best interests of our clients.

Black Monday

On Monday, October 19, 1987, the Dow Jones Industrial Average plunged 508 points in just one day, a record 22.6% drop. Many in the investment industry feared this sell off could trigger a second Great Depression. As fate would have it, I had just joined a new firm, bringing my clients with me, when Black Monday hit.

That night, cable news talking heads squawked about the end of life as we knew it, predicting doom and gloom as far as the eye could see. The financial markets would never recover, they sternly warned. Naturally, my clients called me in a panic, fearing they might not have any money left if stocks continued falling Tuesday morning. My job was to exhibit calmness amidst the storm and to remain optimistic. Copious amounts of wine and M&Ms may have helped me retain that calm. However, I tapped into my dispositional flexibility and assured clients they would be okay.

The craziness continued the next day when the market opened down another 200 points. This created a perfect opportunity for panic, but again, I was determined to be the calm in the storm for them.

When the Federal Reserve chose to intervene by injecting liquidity into the market through Treasury purchases, it had a calming effect, thus preventing the crisis from widening. By the end of the second day, the market was up 100 points, and by the following Thursday, it had moved ahead another 186 points. Still, it took nearly two years for the markets to regain the values lost in that crash.

During that time, many investors panicked and converted paper losses into permanent ones, while those who stayed the course were able to recoup their losses, many within just six months. This experience represented a wonderful lesson about the value of long-term investing, staying true to your strategic plan, and avoiding the temptation to panic.

The Bursting of the Dotcom Bubble

In the late 1990s, technology stocks skyrocketed, fueled by the growth of the internet and the proliferation of companies with dotcom domains. This raging bull market was quickly dubbed the Dotcom Bubble. However, the bubble began to show signs of trouble by the end of 1999 as the economy slowed down. In March 2000, the dotcom bubble finally burst, creating a record-breaking bear market. Stellar companies such as Cisco, Intel and Oracle lost more than 80% of their stock valuations.

Again, some people thought it was the end of the world. While Black Monday had been painful, this bust was a slow death as the Dow Jones Industrial Average (DJIA) tumbled 76.81% from a peak of 5,048.62 on March 10, 2000, to 1,139.90 on October 4, 2002, culminating in the majority of dotcom stocks going bust and evaporating trillions of dollars of investment capital in its wake. It would take 15 years for the Nasdaq to regain its peak.[1] Our cognitive, emotional and dispositional flexibility were put to the test.

Early on in this business, I learned it was easy to have conversations with clients when everything is going great. However, clients really need you the most when the world is falling apart, when things are the darkest. Of course, it's never easy to have these conversations with clients, telling them their accounts are down 10%, 15% or even 20%.

While the misery created by the dotcom bust went on and on, we strived to be true fiduciaries by always operating in the best interests of our clients. It was 18 months of constant hand holding as investors continued to lose money. During this time, we increased client communication, explaining to them the need to think long term and encouraging them to stay invested in the market.

In the middle of that chaotic time, I made the decision to start my own

---

1 Diana Paluteder; *Dot-com Bubble Explained | The True Story of 1995-2000 Stock Market;* Finbold News; Aug 8, 2022; https://finbold.com/guide/dot-com-bubble/

12. Navigate Life

financial advisory practice. My clients' trust in me was manifested when virtually all of them followed me as I made the huge leap to open my own firm.

The Real Estate Bubble Crisis

While the stock market ebbed and flowed after the dotcom disaster, the real estate market heated up. People flocked to buy houses even if they didn't have a down payment or couldn't afford it. Real estate investors bought houses, made interest-only payments for a few years then sold the houses before the bills came due. They made lots of money.

Just as investors were just beginning to recoup their losses from the dotcom bust, the market came crashing down in 2008 with the sub-prime-mortgage crisis. The housing market collapsed, and homeowners began facing foreclosure in record numbers. The U.S. Treasury called the housing crisis, "the most significant risk to our economy" in decades.

By early 2010, approximately 1.65 million homes fell into foreclosure. The ensuing recession affected not only home valuations, but mortgage markets, home builders, real estate, home-supply retail outlets, as well as financial lenders and investors.

I thought I had seen the worst after Black Monday and the dotcom crisis, but they were child's play compared to this. Although the Fed stepped in to bail out the major banks, stocks plummeted. On September, 29, 2008, the Dow Jones Industrial fell 777.68 points. This was the largest single-day loss in its history up to this point. On October 9, 2007, the Dow hit its pre-recession high and closed at 14,164.53. By March 5, 2009, it had dropped more than 50% to 6,594.44. As an industry … as a nation … as a society, we were standing on the edge of the abyss and very nearly went over.[1]

I realized our firm had to do things differently for our clients. We needed to rethink how we could protect our clients' assets. This decision would set us apart from so many other firms over the course of the next few years.

---

1 Kimberly Amadeo; *The Stock Market Crash of 2008*; The Balance; May 25, 2022; https://www.thebalancemoney.com/stock-market-crash-of-2008-3305535

Pillars of Purpose

Reaction vs. Action

We have always been focused on having a systematic process. Previously we'd visited with all our clients at least once a year, sometimes every quarter or bi-annually. However, when things started going crazy, we knew we had to initiate cognitive, emotional and dispositional flexibility in order to meet the challenges we faced. While we already had a commitment to ongoing client review, we immediately resolved to meet with every one of them as soon as possible—nearly 400 of them. Over the next few weeks, we reached out to every client, doubling and sometimes tripling the number of appointments we had with them each year. Nearly every one of our clients had taken a huge beating financially, and we wanted to reassure them we were there for them. More importantly, we developed customized strategies to help them overcome this market challenge.

At that time, our clients were invested primarily in mutual funds and advisory accounts. But as the market kept imploding and we were moving deeper into a recession, it was time to change direction. After all, Darwin didn't say "survival of the fittest," he said, "survival of those who are most able to adapt." We had to create a tactical approach to reflect the challenges of this market.

In most market downturns, it's a natural instinct for people to sell. Then, as the market rebounds, they buy. It's a "buy high, sell low strategy" that, of course, doesn't work. I knew I had to talk my clients off the ledge to help them avoid making this terrible mistake. So, we began a campaign to explain our adaptation plan to clients.

We were determined to create opportunity out of chaos, and our ability to adjust to the situation helped our clients to traverse the rough waters.

Our conversations went something like this:

> "This has been horrible, and we've taken losses. What we are going to do is sell your mutual funds and advisory accounts. Your losses will allow you to take advantage of tax benefits. However, we're not going to cash out. Instead, we're seizing the opportunity to buy into some pretty amazing companies—reputable ones that we're confident will weather this storm."

12. Navigate Life

Stock valuations in these stellar companies had been greatly reduced. Some that had previously sold for $50 a share were now down to $20 a share. Instead of paying a 1% dividend, they were paying a 3% to 5% dividend.

I then told clients:

> "I don't know how long this market recovery is going to take, but you're going to earn decent interest on your money until it does. We're going to help you get through this."

Over the following months, we reallocated all of our clients' portfolios.

Our clients responded positively to the fact that we were taking the initiative. Instead of feeling helpless, they were relieved that we had a plan, a process that allowed us to adapt to market conditions. Over those difficult years, we almost never lost a client account unless a death occurred. And even if that happened, the heirs usually became our clients. When our clients' friends or family members expressed dismay at the lack of communication they were getting from their advisors, our clients would refer them to us.

During each of these dark periods in U.S. history, we learned valuable lessons about the power of communication, the importance of being there for our clients and of being sensitive to what they were going through. Again, we had to tap into our cognitive, emotional and dispositional flexibility. We learned the value of being a true friend to our clients, a confidante and trusted advisor. Of course, it was more than just talk, it was action and a commitment to doing the best we could for them.

Navigating an Unprecedented Pandemic

All my previous encounters with calamity could not have prepared me for the surprising shipwreck that was 2020. Interestingly enough, the year began with so much to smile about: near record-low unemployment rates and the Dow Jones Industrial Average soaring to 30,000. Everything looked positive until we suddenly began hearing about something called "the coronavirus," a deadly and highly contagious virus from China that was spreading to other parts of Asia. We started seeing people coming off of flights with masks on and thought, "How strange!"

Pillars of Purpose

The coronavirus, soon dubbed COVID-19, invaded our country in February 2020. In just over five weeks, the Dow experienced a 40% decline to 18,000. Due to government lockdown orders, schools closed. Many small businesses were forced to shut down, and where possible, send employees home to work. We'd never faced such uncertainty. No one had any idea what to expect next. It was time to step up our game. It was time to adapt to the new environment.

Several years prior to the pandemic, we had developed a contingency plan that included making a significant investment in technology so we could operate remotely if necessary. As COVID-19 raged, staff members were able to work from home if they or family members became ill or if they had young children who were unable to go to daycare or school.

For the next 30 days our team spent 18 to 20 hours a day, seven days a week talking individually with more than 600 clients. We increased the frequency of our market call, "BullTalk," from a quarterly event to a weekly communication to keep clients informed about the state of the economy, state of the financial markets and the pandemic. We made an extraordinary effort to get their portfolios back to where they were, with a goal to give them peace of mind and ease their concerns.

We were like steamboat captains trying to get our cargo safely down the Mississippi. There was no playbook telling us precisely how to navigate the challenges facing us. Just as the steamboat captain has to regularly assess weather conditions, the depth of the water and even river traffic, we had to assess each storm as it occurred and decide how best we could avoid the torrential rains. While it would have been easier to "stay the course," our approach evolved depending on circumstances. We regularly had to adjust.

Change is Inevitable

The reality is, economic and personal challenges can be caused by voluntary or involuntary acts. While goals, plans, dreams and aspirations are ingredients for a successful life, it's equally important to have a plan for adapting, altering and changing the plan as conditions change.

Change is not only inevitable, but it should be expected. Change should

12. Navigate Life

be built into any type of planning you do. Keep in mind that change brings lots of emotion. You must stand ready to channel those emotions into positive thinking.

I'm reminded of a client who was completely devastated when her husband asked for a divorce. After decades of marriage, her identity had revolved around their relationship. To transition to a "new normal," she had to progress through all the stages of grief, anger and betrayal. I felt my role was to listen and empathize with her, yet not let her wallow in her misery. As we talked about the options available, she was able to come to terms with her new situation. Over the past several years she has built a new life and has never been happier. She's now in a better relationship, has a beautiful home, a great business, and is completely independent and self-assured.

Your Role as a Friend, Companion, Advisor

Throughout your life, there will be times that people come to you with problems.

Below are some important skills our team practices that you can use when helping others through trying times:

- **Be Authentic.** It's important for people to feel they can trust you. Without trust, there is no depth to a relationship.

- **Be Trustworthy.** Whether it's a spouse, partner, child or neighbor, know that they wouldn't talk with you if they didn't trust you to keep a confidence. Don't break that trust.

- **Be Altruistic.** Just as we strive to put our clients' interests ahead of our own, it's important for you to put the interests of others ahead of your own. When giving advice, make sure you are doing it for the right reason. Are you doing what is best for them, or are you only focused on your own needs and desires?

- **Be Present.** When you are fully engaged with family members, friends, clients and business associates, they feel you genuinely care about them and will be there for them no matter the challenges they may face. Reinforce with them that challenges are part of life's journey—those things that don't kill you will make you stronger.

- **Accept Transitions.** Everyone goes through transitions in their life, i.e., moving, getting married, getting divorced, starting a new job, leaving a job, getting fired, getting promoted, having a child, heaven forbid losing a loved one, illnesses, injuries, medical concerns, losing a pet. During transitions, encourage them to adopt an "I can do this" attitude. Be there to support them throughout the process.

How we navigate life and respond to its challenges is a very personal thing. While some people charge headfirst into any "life quake," others need more time to adjust. There is no set process for dealing with changes, nor is there a set timeframe for when it needs to be accomplished. Change comes from within, and every person has to proceed at their own speed and only when they feel they are ready.

This well-known verse found in Ecclesiastes in the King James' version of the Bible expresses this sentiment clearly and simply:

> To every thing there is a season, and a time to every purpose under the heaven:
> A time to be born, and a time to die; a time to plant, a time to reap that which is planted;
> A time to kill, and a time to heal; a time to break down, and a time to build up;
> A time to weep, and a time to laugh; a time to mourn, and a time to dance;
> A time to cast away stones, and a time to gather stones together;
> A time to embrace, and a time to refrain from embracing;
> A time to gain that which is to get, and a time to lose; a time to keep, and a time to cast away;
> A time to rend, and a time to sew; a time to keep silence, and a time to speak;
> A time of love, and a time of hate; a time of war, and a time of peace.

You might also recognize these words from the song, "Turn! Turn! Turn!" written by Peter Seeger and performed by The Byrds in the 1960s, a testament to the fact that its applicability to life has endured

12. Navigate Life

throughout the ages.

Navigating a Personal Tragedy

Transitions in life bring emotions to the surface: fear, anxiety, sadness, stress, loneliness, feelings of fatigue, sleeplessness or longing. At the other extreme: joy, excitement, pleasure and even relief. It's not always about dollars and cents; instead it's about being present, being authentic and helping a person embrace their emotions without being overwhelmed by them.

Just remember, there is a time for emotion, and a person needs to be given the time to grieve and react. And understand, you'll never truly know how they feel until "you've walked a mile in their shoes."

When my daughter Katie was in the high school marching band, I met a fellow student, Michael, who was a couple of years older than her. Michael was a fine young man, and after graduating from college, he joined the military.

After serving, he returned home to become a state trooper, his dream job. One day, as Michael was directing traffic away from an accident, he was hit by an RV driven by a man who recklessly drove down the emergency lane to get past the accident. This thoughtless action caused him to hit Michael, killing him instantly. It was devastating to Michael's family and everyone who knew him. This was a 28-year-old man who had his entire life ahead of him.

Our team wrapped our arms around this family to help them get through the funeral and the legalities that had to be taken care of. We helped them file a wrongful death lawsuit as well. With the proceeds, memorials were established in remembrance of Michael. We collaborated with the family and many of my friends in the state legislature to get the "Move Over Law" passed in Tennessee. This would ensure something like this would never happen to another family. While this tragedy will forever live on in the minds of Michael's family and friends, their transition was easier when they focused on making positive changes in memory of Michael.

While all of us will experience upheavals in our lives, not all will be as painful as the one Michael's family had to endure. Nevertheless, they can

Pillars of Purpose

seem daunting.

Following are eight suggestions for navigating life's challenges:

1. **Draw strength from your personal network.** Seek the support of friends and family members. If you still feel you have hit a roadblock when dealing with your emotions, seek professional help.

2. **Focus on transitioning.** Just as Michael's family funneled their energy into taking positive actions, find activities and explore options that will help you better adjust to the changes you face.

3. **Develop healthy habits.** It's important to invest time in your personal health, whether it's getting more exercise or developing better eating habits. Remember life is a marathon, not a sprint, so you need to take care of the equipment (your body). Go to the gym, get a workout buddy, track your progress and give yourself a pat on the back when you achieve your goal.

4. **Avoid the desire to self-medicate.** When we think of over medicating, it's usually associated with drugs or alcohol. However, some people tend to over-exercise, becoming workout warriors. Others overeat or undereat. In everything, it's important to achieve balance in life.

5. **Practice mindfulness and gratitude.** Be grateful for the gift of each day. When people ask me "How are you doing?" I say, "Every day above ground is a good day." When you go through rough times, find something to love. It doesn't matter if it's the sunset, the smell of really good food cooking, or taking time to pet a cat or dog. It doesn't matter if it is walking outside just to breath some fresh air, watching an amazing movie or reading a good book. Just do something that you enjoy, something that inspires love.

6. **Listen to and learn from others.** There's always someone who has gone through something similar to what you are experiencing. Listen to their stories about how they were able to complete the journey. Share your own experiences and listen to the advice they give you.

7. **Be curious.** Follow a path of curiosity and creativity. So many people live a life controlled by fear. They're afraid of failure, afraid of screwing up. They're afraid of doing something that is wrong or

12. Navigate Life

doesn't work out well. Ultimately, they're afraid of the unknown and of change. By following that pattern of fear, they never really find out what they are capable of. Shed your fears and live.

8. **Be Resilient.** Life is a marathon. Always be prepared and know that challenges can occur. Bad things can happen; failure is rarely fatal. However, failing to make the effort can be. It's not about the fall, it's about pulling yourself up by your bootstraps and trying again, and again, and again. Overcome your challenges—endure.

Diagnosed with attention deficit disorder as a child, Ryder Carroll, digital product designer and author, devised the Bullet Journal system to help move past his learning disabilities. Facing life's challenges with strength, he said, *"No matter how bleak or menacing a situation may appear, it does not entirely own us. It can't take away our freedom to respond, our power to take action."* You have the power to overcome your challenges. Be resilient.

Just Keep Breathing

The movie *Castaway*, starring Tom Hanks, tells the story of a FedEx executive whose plane crashes over the Pacific Ocean. After washing ashore on a deserted island, Hanks' character "Chuck" is tested mentally, physically and emotionally for years as the lone survivor with only a volleyball, "Wilson," for company.

Then one day, a piece of a door washes ashore. Building a raft from that "sail," he is able to leave the island. After suffering intense heat and having little water to drink, he finally arrives back home only to find the love of his life is married and has kids. Disheartened and knowing they can never be together, he stays resilient, as he had all those years, saying:

"I know what I have to do now. I got to keep breathing, because tomorrow the sun will rise. Who knows what the tide could bring?"

During all of life's transitions, I exhort you to "keep breathing."

It's the gift of gratitude, the gift of life that keeps us all moving forward. It's about being present, being in the moment. The gift of enjoying life as each day comes.

Each night, before you go to bed, ask yourself:

Pillars of Purpose

- Have I practiced cognitive flexibility by reframing my approach to a problem and exploring different solutions?
- Was I emotionally flexible by being aware of my feelings, acknowledging them and guiding them in a constructive way?
- Did I remain optimistic yet realistic when faced with challenges (dispositional flexibility)?
- Am I the best partner, spouse, friend or advisor I can be? Do I get outside my own head and focus on the needs of others?
- Am I gracious, and have I developed a spirit of gratitude?
- Am I honest? When I make a mistake do I admit it, ask for forgiveness and then move forward?
- Do I seek the wisdom and counsel of others?
- Do I strive to maintain human connections? Do I put myself out there and engage with other people?
- Do I listen to different opinions and participate in healthy debates in a civil fashion?
- Am I continually learning new things? Am I committed to sharpening my saw? Do I take classes, read books and magazines, watch documentaries or attend a lecture? Is there a hobby I'd like to pursue? Am I actively trying to expand my knowledge and/or step out of my comfort zone? Did I learn something new today?
- Do I learn from my mistakes? Do I keep trying?

While it's important to have a life plan, allow yourself to be flexible as circumstances change. By doing this, you'll be more capable of navigating the obstacles in your path. As you learn to adapt and change, those seemingly large mountains will look more like molehills. Just *"keep breathing."*

Chapter 13
EDUCATE & COUNSEL

*"Tell me and I forget. Teach me and I remember.
Involve me and I learn."*
– Benjamin Franklin

At this point, I'm sure you've noticed how deeply I care about education. It's one of my favorite topics and truly a passion of mine. Supporting education has become a way of life, not just for me, but for my family and members of my firm. It's engrained in our psyches. I come from a family of teachers. My parents were teachers, and all my aunts and uncles were teachers. My wife was a special education teacher. Her mother was a teacher. Her sister and grandmother were both special education teachers. Education is in our family's DNA.

My love for education dovetails with my role as a wealth advisor. I consider client education to be one of the most important aspects of my job—and I've instilled that into my team. Along with helping clients understand the details of the financial plans we design for them, we want them to understand why we make certain recommendations, how financial markets work and how changing conditions might affect their future goals.

Ultimately, however, our client education goes well beyond helping them to understand their investments. It's all about empowering clients to make wise choices that will enrich their lives. After all, what good is all the knowledge we have gained if we fail to share it in a way that will benefit others? Margaret Fuller, a 19th Century author and philosopher, once said, *"If you have knowledge, let others light their candles in it."*

To do this, my team and I strive to understand our clients' needs and help them better understand their own situations by reflecting it back to them. Socrates candidly admitted: *"I can't show anyone anything. I can just make them think."* We designed our process to help our clients think about their goals and objectives, to understand their options and to help them make the best possible choices.

Sound financial planning starts with an advisor who:

1. **Understands the client's unique passions and goals.** They develop a clear understanding of their client's family, their interests and passions. This helps the advisor create a customized plan that will help the client reach their life goals.

2. **Analyzes the client's current and future circumstances.** They assess where their clients are financially and identify long-term goals, including in the areas of retirement, education funding, tax planning and their personal bucket list.

3. **Creates a customized plan to reach goals and objectives.** Once they understand the client's goals, they design a plan in multiple areas. This includes estate and succession planning, life insurance needs analysis, tax planning, charitable giving, and in some cases the creation of family trusts to transfer assets. These plans are customized based on a client's goals and objectives.

4. **Implements the plan.** Each plan requires action and specific strategies. Using many different vehicles to implement the plan, they make the client's money work for them.

5. **Provides ongoing monitoring and review.** This is perhaps the most important part of their process—ongoing monitoring, review and communication. As the client's life changes, so must their plan. No matter what happens in the financial markets, the advisor needs

13. Educate & Counsel

to be aware and to have a plan to address these issues and any personal ones that arise.

This five-step process ensures nothing falls through the cracks, and most importantly, it's client-centric. Additionally, we believe the role of the advisor is to advise clients using the knowledge they've gained through a commitment to life-long learning and by applying the wisdom gained from their personal and professional application of that knowledge.

Education is an ongoing process, and clients need to know the advisor has "invested his or her time before investing the client's money." This is an exhaustive process whereby advisors really get to know their clients and identify their plans and goals for the future. As they uncover the factors that influence their clients' decision-making process, their knowledge and wisdom positions them to assume the role of "trusted advisor" and "dedicated counselor."

Of course, an important part of our process is the continual monitoring of a client's account. As life happens, changes are bound to occur. As President John F. Kennedy once said, *"Change is the law of life. And those who look only to the past and present are certain to miss the future."*

To ensure our clients stay focused on their goals and are prepared to meet the future, we have developed a system of monitoring and review that includes meeting with clients regularly. At these meetings we educate them on how we're on the right path to reach their short- and long-term objectives or whether a new course of action is more appropriate.

As trusted advisors, we respond quickly and purposefully to changes in their lives. We make sure their financial plan matches the moment, whether it be a death of a spouse, birth of a child, change in job or retirement. We want them to share their concerns, fears and angst with us as we help them navigate each new life event and changing market environment.

Over the years, I've had the privilege of counseling clients on issues beyond their usual financial concerns. I've been honored to attend family celebrations and even speak at funerals. Our clients have become our friends—our extended family. They know they can call any time of the day and can count on us to be there for them during good or bad times. We want to be their Rock of Gibraltar, someone they can rely on to provide strength and assurance through life's many challenges.

Clarity in Communication

In our role as advisors, we understand the importance of communicating in the clearest way possible. Too often professionals fail to counsel clients using a simple yet well-defined message. Instead, they overuse jargon hoping to sound smarter. It's like the old colloquialism, "if you can't dazzle them with brilliance, baffle them with B.S." While they think it conveys sophistication, it actually has the opposite effect. As they ramble on and on, they confuse clients, leaving them feeling more anxious about their future, unsure about the "real" plan for managing their wealth, and not knowing whether they should trust this person.

I believe the best form of education is a succinct and simple message. As Apple founder Steve Jobs once said, *"It takes a lot of hard work to make something simple, to truly understand the underlying challenges and come up with elegant solutions."* He sincerely believed simplicity to be the *"ultimate sophistication."*

Simplification is the key to powerful communication, and powerful communication is the driving force behind a superior education. A poorly conveyed message can undermine our credibility and effectiveness, much like adding water to a car's gas tank renders it useless. A well-constructed message helps us fire on all cylinders and powers real change in people's lives.

President Abraham Lincoln was known for the simplicity and clarity of his speeches. It's been said he would sometimes devote two weeks preparing for a brief talk. Lincoln delivered his famous two-minute Gettysburg address, one of the most revered speeches in history, right after the elegant orator Edward Everett had delivered a two-hour speech.

After the speech, Everett, a former dean of Harvard University, wrote to Lincoln stating, *"I wish that I could flatter myself that I had come as near to the central idea of the occasion in two hours as you did in two minutes."* It doesn't take a two-hour speech to get to the point, as Everett, to his credit, recognized.

Clarity in communication should underscore all our efforts to educate.

13. Educate & Counsel

One of the greatest compliments I receive is when a prospect tells me how clearly I've answered their questions and explained things. I actually love when my clients and prospects ask questions. It assures me they are actively listening and truly engaged in the learning process. The more questions they ask, the greater opportunity I have to address their concerns and to develop greater trust and rapport. Clients come to trust us when they fully understand the value we provide to them.

At the end of the day, you want to feel confident in your advisor. "Is this someone who is going to help you move forward and act in your best interest? Do they have the knowledge, capacity and capability to help you reach your goals?"

We want our clients to recognize our lifelong commitment to learning and realize its potential value to them. We want them to trust us as we provide them with the appropriate counsel and knowledge to help them make wise decisions.

Transformation Through Education

Taking a step back from the educational process we use at my firm, let's think about the value of education more broadly. While we often visualize education taking place in the classroom, there are many teachers in our lives beyond the classroom. Our parents were our first teachers. As toddlers, we eagerly absorbed the things they taught us, and we were profoundly influenced by the examples they set. In elementary school, teachers instructed us on the fundamentals of reading, writing and arithmetic. As our social circle expanded, the people who influenced us grew as well. We learned from friends (for better or worse) and from leaders of organizations we belonged to. Then, as adults, we expanded our education and sought out skills, experiences and relationships to better perform our jobs.

Our knowledge flows from the people in our lives: our family members, friends, boss, colleagues, instructors, mentors and counselors. The learning never ends. It's a lifelong process, and all the people we associate with are our teachers.

As Eric Allen, author of *The New Awakening*, explains, *"Everyone is my teacher. Some I seek. Some I subconsciously attract. Often, I learn simply by observing others. Some may be completely unaware that I'm learning from them, yet I bow deeply in gratitude."*

Our lives represent the sum of all the knowledge and experiences we've gained and the lessons we've learned. More importantly, the application of that knowledge and experience can evolve into wisdom.

Just as we learn from those with whom we associate, we're all teachers as well. I'm a strong believer that to become genuinely great, and to lead a life of significance, a person must involve others. If each of us can educate and inspire others, if we can keep the light of knowledge burning brightly, we can light up the entire world.

As an educator, whether your role includes being a parent, business owner, or even a caring member of society, you are responsible for the knowledge you impart and the impact it will have on others. Your job is to provide knowledge that will empower others to make good choices.

One of my heroes, Nelson Mandela, wisely said, *"Education is the most powerful weapon which you can use to change the world."* His own education empowered him to affect substantial change in his country of South Africa. As its first Black president, he believed education to be one of the greatest equalizers available to humanity.

He added: *"Education is the great engine of personal development. It is through education that the daughter of a peasant can become a doctor, that the son of a miner can become the head of the mine, that the child of farm workers can become the president of a great nation."*

That's why the Educate & Counsel pillar is quite possibly the most important one I'm sharing in this book. Counseling goes hand in glove with education. Being a counselor can be as simple as giving advice or helping to create a plan of action. It can be helping someone make an important decision or offering a divergent opinion. When counseling others, we're able to help them in their quest for knowledge. It's where all of us become teachers.

Allies in Education

As noted in prior chapters, I'm a big believer that our actions need to

13. Educate & Counsel

align with our values. When it comes to education, I'm a deeply committed advocate. For more than 25 years I've worked tirelessly for every child's right to a quality public education, first as chair of the Shelby County Board of Education, then as president of the Tennessee School Boards Association (TSBA), later as president of the National School Boards Association (NSBA) and now through the work of the American Public Education Foundation (APEF).

During my years advocating for public education, I've had the privilege of striking up friendships with high-character individuals who've been incredible counselors and allies to me as we worked to provide the best education possible for America's youth. Among those people were John Aitken, who loved his job as a principal so much that he personally greeted each of his 2,000 students by name, and Tracy Speake who has built a career around mentoring others and bettering the community through his involvement with senior citizen programs.

Another friend and mentor who immediately comes to my mind is Joe Clayton, a shining beacon for public education in suburban Memphis. After years of serving as a principal in both public and private schools, he won a seat on the Shelby County Board of Education the same year I was elected. We quickly became fast friends and each other's greatest advocate!

Joe fought numerous budget battles alongside me, and we could always count on his holding steadfast for what he thought was right. His life bore witness to the strength of his character and his commitment to education. Working with Joe and countless others, I've learned there's no limit to what strong individuals with a shared passion can accomplish when they collaborate.

While our primary focus was on public education advocacy, securing adequate and equitable funding was a cornerstone of our efforts through our work with businesses, elected government bodies and private enterprise. I was involved with creating multiple educational funding foundations.

When serving on the Shelby County School Board, I declined to take a paycheck or to accept travel-expense reimbursements. Instead, with the approval of the board, I directed those funds toward the creation of the Shelby County Schools Education Foundation, a non-profit that among other things funded two college scholarships annually to high-achieving local students. After the merger and subsequent demerger we talked about in Chapter 2, the funds I had contributed to the Shelby County Schools Education Foundation became seed money for our non-profit organization, American Public Education Foundation (APEF). It supports powerful causes such as workforce development and financial literacy to this day.

When then Superintendent John Aitken of the newly formed Collierville Municipal School District asked for my support in raising funds to build a new high school that would provide enhanced learning opportunities for the students, I wholeheartedly agreed. He explained the new Collierville High School would need to accommodate 2,500 kids.

John visualized creating a new kind of school that could offer students an education unlike the typical high school, and he knew additional funding would be needed to make his dream a reality. After John secured $125 million in funding through the "One Town, One School" capital campaign to fund construction of the new school, he asked me to create a not-for-profit program that would tap into outside resources to fund enhancements for the school.

Expanding Workforce Development Opportunities

I enthusiastically moved forward with a capital campaign for what would be the largest and most innovative high school in the Southeastern United States. As part of the fund-raising process, we created the Partners in Education (PIE) foundation to enlist the support of businesses to help make John's dream a reality. We raised more than $1.5 million through PIE for enhancements to the new Collierville High School.

At the beginning of the process, we donated the services of our law and accounting firms to legally establish the foundation; after the school was built, we continued to support the fund-raising initiatives of the district. More recently we loaned Cassie Foote, our APEF Assistant Executive Director, to serve as executive director for the new program.

Eventually, PIE evolved into APEF's Workforce Development program. As a major initiative, it aligned with our belief that while college was and still remains a worthy goal for many students, public education must embrace the challenge of a rapidly evolving global marketplace. In fact,

13. Educate & Counsel

it's reported that 60% of the most in-demand jobs of tomorrow won't require a bachelor's degree.[1] Instead, a growing number of jobs will require advanced certification, creating a demand for training for those types of jobs.

We viewed our relationship with the new Collierville High School as an opportunity to beta test this new approach. We wanted to offer students technical, vocational or professional development skills that would better equip them to compete in a quickly evolving marketplace.

We brought local business owners together with curriculum leaders and teachers to discuss workforce development needs. We explained how a partnership could benefit everyone involved. Students would learn emerging technology and vocational skills, schools would gain additional training and funding from the businesses and the business owners would gain access to the next generation of workers and play a role in preparing them for the workforce.

Soon, more than 250 area businesses pledged their support to the program that gives our students access to training for jobs as airplane mechanics, pilots, drone-aviation specialists, welders, commercial-kitchen builders, nurses and hospice-care workers with clinical medical assisting (CMA) certification, and cosmetologists. Since the program started, hundreds of students at Collierville High School have participated in internships, externships and have been employed by partner firms as part of this vocational training program.

One of the most surprising success stories of the program, however, has been in the field of agriculture technology. In today's world, agriculture goes well beyond tractors, planting and harvesting crops. It requires science and technology to improve land productivity. For instance, "smart" combines can detect differences in yield from one field to the next. Soil maps reveal soil structure and chemical properties. Today's farmers also rely on high-tech advances to track weather patterns, soil erosion and biodiversity. Through our partnership with several agricultural companies we built a teaching farm on the Collierville High School campus so kids could learn firsthand about some of these new technologies. It has

---

1 Highest Paying Jobs with an Associate Degree; TBS Staff; May 24, 2022; https://thebestschools.org/careers/highest-paying/associate-degree-jobs/

given the students a different perspective on agriculture as well as an introduction to the skills needed for success in that field.

The collaborative efforts of the Partners in Education Foundation and APEF's Workforce Development program have proven so successful that schools throughout the state have begun replicating our efforts. Companies such as Ford Motor and FedEx now champion this innovative partnership. They've helped us reimagine public education and develop a more capable workforce. The program has even been touted nationally, and a number of states have adopted similar programs. Furthermore, we created the West Tennessee Workforce Collaborative, a division of our American Public Education Foundation, to establish a constant communication pipeline between businesses and education and ensure schools in our state continue to offer courses relevant to the ever-evolving marketplace.

I'm proud of our contributions to reshaping and redefining public education. With the collective efforts of local businesses, government and public education, we're trying to change the world by taking students beyond the books into real-life learning.

Enhancing the Teaching Profession

While our work in education often focuses on raising standards and securing funding, we can't lose track of a vital human element—the teachers themselves! Teachers are some of America's most unsung heroes. As Henry Adams, 19th Century historian and author once said, *"A teacher affects eternity. You can never tell where [their] influence stops."*

> *"A teacher affects eternity. You can never tell where [their] influence stops."*
> – Henry Adams

13. Educate & Counsel

We can't educate our children without educated, devoted teachers. That may seem like common sense, but many people take our teachers for granted or even have a negative view of teaching and the teaching profession.

While a study reported most teachers (nine out of 10) are satisfied with their jobs, and nearly eight in 10 would choose it as a profession again, fewer than one in three teachers believe it is a valued profession in society.[1]

It has taken a pandemic and schools going "virtual" for many families to realize just how important the relationship between student and teacher is and to understand the societal significance of the teaching profession. Writer and producer Shonda Rhimes tweeted this after spending a little over an hour each day homeschooling her kids during that time: *"Teachers deserve to make a billion dollars a year ... or a week!"* I'm sure lots of parents in similar situations would wholeheartedly agree.

It's past time to elevate the level of professionalism in teaching, to have it recognized as a revered and influential career. As president of NSBA, I spent time in Finland studying their education system. Finland is regarded as the No. 1 country globally for education. This is primarily due to the fact that it is a small country, relatively affluent and ethnically homogenous. Its socialist government gives all Finnish school children access to quality education.

The fundamental difference between our two countries is the level to which Finnish teachers are revered as professionals. To be an elementary school teacher in Finland, you must earn a four-year degree in education. If you want to teach middle or high school, you must have an advanced degree in education. While teachers are paid no more than factory workers, they are given respect and have tremendous influence in the community.

During my association with our local school board and NSBA, I became and still serve as a board member of the National Board for Professional Teaching Standards (NBPTS), an organization whose certification process is seen as the gold standard in teaching excellence—every child deserves an accomplished teacher. Similar to the process of a doctor becoming board certified in a specialty area, the NBPTS certification is an exhaustive program that takes four years to complete and provides

---

[1] OECD.org; *The OECD Teaching and Learning International Survey*; https://www.oecd.org/education/school/talis-2013-results.htm

continuing education to help teachers be their absolute best. Tests have shown that a student taught by a national board-certified teacher enjoys the equivalent of four additional months of learning overall and three more months of reading skills. It's a game changer.

With national efforts to encourage a professional teaching standard, more teachers today are pursuing board certification. I've felt passionate about this for a long time—to be part of a national movement to raise the stature of teaching as a profession. I was proud to be chair of the NBPTS' resource development committee, where we sought funding from corporations, government and private entities to seed the efforts. To date we have secured over $30 million in private grant funding for the work of NBPTS. And I'm happy to say we've worked as a team to provide incentives and benefits for teachers to pursue board certification. Over the past several years, we have seen over a dozen states provide funding and incentives.

Fundamentally, I believe the future of our nation depends on preparing America's 54 million public-school children for engaged citizenship and global competitiveness. Finding and supporting great teachers gives more students the benefit of a great education. It's something we can all agree on.

In the words of former Supreme Court Justice Felix Frankfurter: *"The public school is at once the symbol of our democracy and the most pervasive means for promoting our common destiny."*

Public education is more than a civil right. It is a vital national security interest. The future of our nation will be largely determined by our ability to prepare our children for civic engagement and global competitiveness.

One local organization that promotes such common destiny is Porter-Leath Children's Home, a not-for-profit organization where I serve as a trustee and board vice chair. Porter-Leath has multiple centers in underserved areas throughout the Memphis community. The centers help children, from ages two to five, gain a pre-kindergarten experience that will better prepare them for success when they start school.

A study found that too many kids show up to kindergarten never having been read to nor introduced to the joy of reading a good book. Additionally, there is a significant chance that kids who couldn't read would never

13. Educate & Counsel

graduate from high school. Nearly 85% of the kids who end up in juvenile court are functionally low literate, and 70% of all incarcerated adults can't read at a fourth-grade level.[1] In the criminal justice system, administrators often lament how they can predict how many prison beds they are going to need based on the number of kids in third grade who are not reading at grade level.

As you can see, the process of dropping out starts long before high school. For many kids, success boils down to teaching them to love reading. It's about preparing them to learn prior to entering kindergarten. It's all about early childhood experiences that can encourage and support their success.

Financial Literacy

Just as reading is a necessary skill for competing in our highly evolved workplace, I've come to realize financial literacy is an absolute necessity for achieving a successful life, not only for students, but for our clients and the public in general. Today, lack of financial literacy has created a national crisis as so many families sink into a sea of debt and financial dependency. However, if students can have the opportunity to learn important financial skills in the classroom at an early age, the next generation will be better prepared for life. Financial literacy can change the course of the future for them and for our country. It is literally the essential element for workforce development.

Our foundation, APEF, created the Nation's Report Card on Financial Literacy to assess the quality of financial education for grades K-12 school children. It grades each state's dedication to financial literacy instruction, assesses whether the state requires a personal finance course for graduation and whether it created grade-specific learning standards in personal finance. Sadly, nearly 70% of the states are earning a "C" grade or less. They are failing their children by not providing them with this vital education. (To see your state's grade, go to: https://www.thenationsreportcard.org/)

While convincing educators and legislators to prioritize financial education remains a daunting challenge, our foundation hopes to provide

---

[1] *The Relationships Between Incarceration and Low Literacy*; Literacy Mid-South; https://www.literacymidsouth.org/news/the-relationship-between-incarceration-and-low-literacy/

schools with some of the resources they need. To do this, we created a free digital library of personal finance content and curriculum available to all teachers, students and parents throughout the country. It contains some of the best financial literacy content from across the web. (https://www.fllibrary.org/) We've also created the first National Standards for Financial Literacy that will soon be adopted throughout the United States.

We were pleased when, in 2019, the APEF received the Catalyst Award given by the "Invest in Others" charitable foundation. The award recognized our commitment to promoting positive change and displaying entrepreneurial vision and leadership. It also acknowledged our efforts in developing the first national standards for financial education in grades K-12, as well as the corresponding curriculum and learning activities that we make available to every school, teacher and family in America at no cost. The recognition included a substantial, much-appreciated donation that will be used to continue promoting high-quality public education to the 54 million children in America's public schools.

Financial Literacy for Clients

Just as I want school children to be informed about financial topics, I'm constantly striving to help raise the overall financial literacy of my clients to empower them.

As noted earlier, we spend a fair amount of time updating clients on their progress and counseling them about the details of their accounts, but a significant portion of what we do also involves educating them about money. We want them to understand the important dynamics of the stock market and its impact on their portfolio. We want them to know we're watching the market and we're prepared to act when needed.

In an effort to better educate our clients and the community, we developed a number of educational campaigns to share our knowledge on important topics. This journey began with the creation of the bull mascot and logo that have since become symbols for our firm and a fun introduction to our education programs.

In 2016, we started our quarterly *BullTalk* calls for clients. These calls are friendly, fireside chats where I demystify financial topics and educate

13. Educate & Counsel

clients about the state of the market and the economy. After 30 minutes, I open the call up for any questions and concerns listeners might have. It's exciting how quickly attendance to these calls has grown as clients invite their family members, friends and neighbors to participate.

When the pandemic hit in the spring of 2020, we increased the frequency of these "BullTalk" calls to a weekly basis to help calm clients' nerves. These weekly calls continue to this day and give us the opportunity to take intimidating topics that people often avoid and make them understandable and applicable to the listeners.

As special circumstances have arisen, we also have conducted special

---

Taking the Bull by the Horns

In 2009, we began the process of developing a company icon, a brand that would become symbolic of our firm and the services we offer to clients. It was to become a core element of our marketing communications.

After several enthusiastic brainstorming sessions, we decided to use the bull for our icon. It not only characterizes favorable economic prospects, but is a symbol of strength, stamina, determination and steadfastness. It's a true representation of our company's values and our ethical approach to doing business.

Throughout the years, our creative juices have kicked in. Our first bull, the Elvis Bull, was followed with more than 100 different versions, some impersonating super heroes in the Marvel movies and Broadway shows such as Hamilton. Others are a takeoff on trendy artwork and well-known works of literature.

Today, the Bull adorns all of our marketing materials and has become an iconic image for our firm. We take the bull by the horns to "make a difference in the lives of our clients. We celebrate their achievements and support them in times of challenge and adversity, helping them navigate through life's turbulent waters."

broadcasts, podcasts and town hall meetings to keep our clients informed. When the presidential election loomed, many clients felt uncertain about how the election might affect the economy. To keep clients informed, our chats became town-hall meetings where we talked about political and economic history and explored how the market might fare depending on which party won the election.

Over the past few years, we've expanded our communication to include *BullCast*, a podcast uploaded to our social media accounts each week and made available on our website. These casual conversations appeal to a younger demographic, e.g., Millenials and Gen Zs. Hosted by my daughter, Katie Pickler, and staff members Cort Winsett and Cameron Spann, the podcasts break down personal finance topics into engaging, bite-sized topics. (https://www.bullcastpodcast.com/episodes) We were honored when Pickler Wealth Advisors, as the producers of the BullCast podcast, was selected in 2022 and 2023 as only one of 10 firms in the nation to receive the Invest in Others Charitable Foundation's Charitable Champions award for giving back to the community and successfully promoting a culture of philanthropy in our organization.[1] In 2023, BullCast was nominated for the ThinkAdvisor LUMINARIES Awards in the Thought Leadership & Education category.[2]

Through our Partners in Education (PIE) initiative (discussed earlier in the chapter), we founded *BullTV*, a monthly broadcast produced and edited by high school students as part of our Workforce Development initiative. The PIE foundation provided the funding to build a television studio in the school to give students real-world television production experience. Consistent with our firm's commitment to community engagement, I interview influential people who are making a difference in the community, including elected leaders and heads of organizations. These student-run productions have given high schoolers real-life experiences and have pro-

---

[1] 2022 IiO Charitable Champions, Created by Invest in Others. This award is based on companies that successfully promote philanthropy and not specific to financial services and does not imply an endorsement, recommendation, or otherwise reflect the performance of the advisor. https://www.investinothers.org/charitable-champions/

[2] 2023 ThinkAdvisor LUMINARIES Award, Thought Leadership and Education Individual-Finalist: David Pickler, created by ThinkAdvisor. Finalists announced in June 2023 for the preceding 12 months. Over 300 Advisors were considered, advisors pay a fee to hold out marketing materials. Not indicative of advisor's future performance. Your experience may vary. https://event.thinkadvisor.com/luminaries-awards

13. Educate & Counsel

pelled some of them to pursue careers in television production.

In addition to the "Bull" entities, we also write a weekly blog called *My Two Cents* distributed to more than 10,000 people. Taking a more relatable approach, we share family pictures and talk about happenings in our lives and with the business. Sometimes we'll include opinions on politics or education. Other times we share updates on our philanthropic events. I like to think the blog gives our clients an inside look at who we are and what we stand for.

But we don't stop there. Our wildly popular Lunch-and-Learn workshops that we've held regularly over the last two decades cover a wide range of topics for clients and prospects, including identity theft, bucket-list goals, gardening tips, and our own spin on Antiques Roadshow. For some older attendees who don't get out much, the Lunch-and-Learn workshops are a much-appreciated social event. Clients often show up early to these workshops to reserve seats for friends and to network. The friendships forged at these events often last a lifetime. One client, who moved back to Memphis after living in Florida, remarked to our amazement that one reason she'd returned was because she missed friends she'd made at the luncheons.

Another example of an educational opportunity we've offered our clients is The Fiscal Academy. A more structured educational opportunity, we invited two-dozen clients to join us for one evening each month for an entire year and taught them about the stock market and finance. We covered topics such as financial planning, retirement and estate planning, as well as tax laws. Upon completion, we celebrated with an enjoyable graduation ceremony and dinner. We look forward to welcoming future classes to this academy.

To support and encourage community members who are entering their third chapter of life, we developed The PowerYears Network. In this endeavor, we provide presentations to empower and enlighten those who are 50-years old and older to help them thrive as they enter a new phase in their lives.

Educating clients is one of the most important parts of my job, and I have to say it's also the most rewarding. I love to educate, enlighten and encourage clients to expand their interests and knowledge. I love to provide insight and knowledge about the topics we discuss and encourage informative interactions.

The Only Constant is Change

Just as our firm has regularly had to adapt to changing market conditions and the way we communicate with clients, we encourage clients to adapt to all the changes in their lives. To again quote Albert Einstein, one of the greatest and most influential physicists of all time, *"The measure of intelligence is the ability to change."*

The world is in constant flux. If you don't believe it, visit your childhood home and see if it appears just as it did when you were young, if it is still standing. Tour the community where you spent your youth. Has anything changed? Of course it has. Time doesn't stand still, and to keep up, neither should we. However, keeping pace with ever-evolving changes requires a commitment to lifelong learning.

As mentioned in the preface, the most significant part of my job as an advisor is ongoing professional education and growth, or as I'm fond of saying, "sharpening the saw." If you've ever attempted to chop wood with a dull blade, you know what I'm talking about. And you likewise know that if you spend time sharpening the blade before you begin sawing or chopping, your work will be substantially easier. As President Abraham Lincoln famously said, *"If I had six hours to chop down a tree, I'd spend the first four hours sharpening the axe."*

"Sharpening the saw" means stepping away from our immediate tasks and pursuing something less tangible that could help us do our jobs better. In some cases, sharpening the saw means leaving our comfort zones and exploring new ideas and even contrasting views. I'm a firm believer that if we only seek opinions that align with our own, we're limiting our growth potential. Contrasting views can help us expand our own.

To lead a life of true significance, ongoing education should be among our highest priorities. We should find ways to systematically improve our skills, including in our professional lives. Over the past three decades, I'm proud to have earned degrees and certificates from The Wharton School, the American College, Yale University and the Investments & Wealth Institute.

13. Educate & Counsel

The Role of Counselor

I believe the role of counselor goes hand in glove with education. Anyone who takes on the role of educator needs to provide the best possible counsel to others. Ongoing education gives us the wisdom to more effectively advise others on important matters in their lives. However, to give meaningful and appropriate advice, we have to be aware of our own shortcomings and learn new skills.

Too many professionals are too entrenched in their habitual ways of doing things. They find it easier to conduct "business as usual" than to learn a new and more effective way of working. They're stuck in their rut, and they believe their way is the only way. As they limit their learning opportunities, they fail to use their brains the way the Good Lord intended them to be used.

I mention that as a cautionary reminder for clients seeking financial advice and counseling. In much of society, it's still the Wild West for advice. Anyone can hang up a shingle claiming to be an expert in his or her field. While doctors have to go to medical school, complete a residency and pass the medical board exam to become an M.D., other professionals are not nearly as tightly regulated. In fact, almost anyone can rent a nice office and hand out engraved business cards to promote their services without having to prove their competency.

So how do you know if you can trust the professional you choose? How do you know if they have the knowledge and experience to stand among the best? Ask them!

Find out if they are continually expanding their knowledge base. Ask if they are taking additional classes. Have they earned certifications attesting to a desire to increase their knowledge? No one wants to work with a professional whose education ceased the day they graduated from college.

That's why my team and I work hard to earn industry certifications and continue taking college classes. We want to eliminate the fearful "shot in the dark" when a prospect is considering whether they want to work with us. Instead, we want them, as potential clients, to understand how they will benefit from our commitment to lifelong learning.

Pillars of Purpose

Yes, You Can Teach an Old Dog New Tricks

Expanding my knowledge through continuing education ensures I stay current on changes that occur in our business and in the world. I consider it my responsibility as a fiduciary to provide the best counsel possible to my clients. If at any time I'm unable to do that, I'll direct them to someone who can.

As I've gotten older, I find it comforting to know I still have the capacity to learn. I don't believe the adage, "You can't teach an old dog new tricks." In fact, a recent study found the mental capacity of adults aged 58 to 86 improved significantly after taking several classes over a three-month period, rivaling the mental abilities of younger people, some even 30 years younger.

Once a person's mind expands, it never retracts. That's why each of us should continue to grow and expand our knowledge. As McDonald's founder Ray Kroc often replied when asked how he was doing: *"I'm green and growing."* If you are green and growing, you're willing to take chancs and you're willing to put yourself out there. You're in a constant state of learning.

However, true wisdom comes not just from hitting the books but from applying our knowledge and gaining perspective. Regurgitating facts will never be a productive educational activity. I'm reminded of a former colleague who was an engineer by training. He had a near-photographic memory and could recite all sorts of facts and details. Some might even consider him to be a genius. Confident in his knowledge, he started his own advisory practice. Unfortunately, he was out of business in less than a year.

He had a great education. He had knowledge. He had everything a person should need to succeed. But he didn't have the ability to connect. Knowledge is fine, but to truly counsel others we have to find a way to mold it into something meaningful. We need wisdom to provide meaningful counsel. It's the essence of everything we do. To quote Anthony Douglas Williams, consultant, researcher and author, *"Knowledge comes from learning. Wisdom comes from living."*

Imparting that wisdom in a way that is easily digested and applicable to the situation is a key ingredient for effective counseling.

13. Educate & Counsel

The Learning Process

Often, in my efforts to counsel clients, I need to put myself in their shoes and see where they are on their personal "learning curve" just as I assess my own. In Chapter 8, we talked about the four stages of learning:

1. Unconscious incompetence
2. Conscious incompetence
3. Conscious competence
4. Unconscious competence

In stage one, we are unaware of any problem: "We don't know what we don't know." In stage two, we become aware we have a problem, but we're not sure how to fix it. In stage three, we know how to fix it and are consciously working toward a solution, and in stage four, the solution has become an ingrained part of our process—something we automatically do without thinking.

So how do we overcome the first, most difficult stage—unconscious incompetence? With continuous learning. As our knowledge base grows, we become more aware of what we don't know, and we're able to work toward a solution.

While we should aspire to achieve the fourth stage—unconscious competence—attaining it can put us in a "danger zone." As we become more competent, we become creatures of habit and can fail to recognize the need to change course. Often, we fall into the "it's always been done this way" rut. It's similar to sinking deeply into a comfortable, over-stuffed sofa and then physically finding you're unable to get back up. Your comfort becomes your nemesis.

When this happens, it's time to burst out of our comfort zone. We all need to evolve as times change just as other professionals must evolve in their work practices. For instance, accountants no longer keep records on a hand-written ledger. Instead, they now use accounting software programs on their computers. Doctors have changed dozens of their treatment protocols over the years. No longer do they prescribe aspirin for a child's fever knowing it can cause Reye's Syndrome. Instead, they're now prescribing Tylenol. They've evolved by keeping current with medical advances.

Pillars of Purpose

The Knowledge Evolution

No matter your occupation or your status, knowledge continues to evolve, and we must change with it. Whenever we challenge the way things are done and explore greater possibilities, we're enlarging our sphere of knowledge—ensuring that we're not in a stubborn rut. This is not to say it's not a difficult process at times.

As case in point, we recently hired a consulting professional to come to our office to assess our marketing efforts. It was an interesting dialogue and somewhat uncomfortable to have her challenge the way we were marketing our business. However, after a deeper conversation, we began to realize her approach held merit and should be considered. She brought a fresh perspective to our old way of doing things.

The process of seeking outside counsel doesn't have to involve hiring an expert, however. Sometimes the best experts are our own peers, as is the case when business owners join a mastermind group to help them learn new ideas. The mastermind concept originated with steel magnate Andrew Carnegie, who rose from poverty to become the richest man in the world. He said his business was ruled by a "master mind," which he defined as being *"the sum total of all these minds that I have gathered around me."* He credited the mastermind with being the key to his success.

Members of mastermind groups share their challenges and successes. However, the real value comes in pushing each other to think bigger.

In Napoleon Hill's book, *Think and Grow Rich*, he describes mastermind groups as *"A friendly alliance with one or more persons who will encourage one to follow through with both plan and purpose."*

After interviewing Andrew Carnegie, Hill spent the next 20 years interviewing affluent people to learn the secret to their success. The "mastermind alliance" was one of the 13 secrets he discovered and occurred when successful people got together to brainstorm ideas and make them happen. Each member of a mastermind alliance provides counsel and encouragement to the others.

I'm reminded of my work with the Service Corps of Retired Executives (SCORE) which provides mentorships for aspiring entrepreneurs and

13. Educate & Counsel

business owners. To help SCORE rise out of a challenging situation (it lacked participants), we reached out to our firm's contacts, got our clients involved, hosted gatherings at our office and encouraged people to seek out mentorships with the executives and business owners on our hand-picked roster. We partnered with the chamber of commerce to create programming and workshops. Word of our successful program spread rapidly. Our once-struggling SCORE chapter now has so many entrepreneurs wanting its services, it's only limited by its ability to recruit volunteers to serve as mentors.

What does mentoring have to do with educate and counsel? It goes back to John Donne's most famous quote …*"No man is an island."* We all rely on others to work more effectively and efficiently. Theologian Thomas Merton, a Trappist Monk, further explained, *"We are not all weak in the same spots, and so we supplement and complete one another, each one making up in himself for the lack in another."*

Our efforts to educate and counsel can bless lives, including our own. After all, what good is knowledge if it's not shared with others?

Consider these questions as you apply the principles in this chapter.

As a lifelong learner:

- Do you seek ways to expand your knowledge base?
- Do you listen to opposing views with an open mind?
- Do you "pay it forward" by sharing your knowledge with others?
- Do you eagerly participate in mastermind groups or informal mentor programs to learn from others?

As a counselor and teacher:

- Are you committed to continuing education?
- Are you aware of the power of your words and actions?
- Do you strive to communicate clearly and succinctly without jargon or cliches?
- Do you actively listen to others' questions without interrupting?
- Do you put yourself in the shoes of your learner and teach them

on their level?

- Do you provide others with a wider scope for overcoming a challenging situation?
- Do you consider yourself a wise counselor?

If you can answer "yes" to most of these questions, you're solidly building this pillar of success in your life, and I can confidently assure you that there is no greater joy than using your knowledge to help transform another person's life for the better.

Knowledge is one of the only things you can give away and immediately get more back in return. Sachin Ramdas, Indian writer and producer, once expressed, *"Human beings' biggest wealth is knowledge because it cannot be robbed and always increases by sharing."*

I encourage you to commit to lifelong learning and to cultivate the wisdom necessary to counsel others. What we give away comes back to us many times over. Sharing what we learn helps make the world a better place.

Chapter 14
MAIN STREET VALUES

"The greatness of community is most accurately measured by the compassionate actions of its members."
– Coretta Scott King

We've explored the previous eight Pillars, and now it all culminates in the last one—Main Street Values. In most small towns, the principle commercial street is traditionally called Main Street, and it is the focal point for activity and commerce. "Main Street" has also become shorthand for describing a local economy, the mom-and-pop shops and the small business owners who are committed to serving their neighbors and friends. Main Street is essentially the heartbeat of a community.

If Main Street is the heart, then Main Street Values are the lifeblood. Main Street Values are demonstrated by neighbors looking out for each other—bringing a casserole to a sick friend or helping a stranded driver change a tire. They are values reflected in civic-mindedness. such as a local business owner getting involved in the chamber of commerce, or someone seeing a need and sacrificing time and resources to make it

Pillars of Purpose

happen. They're manifested in volunteerism—the parent who serves in the local PTA and participates in bake sales to raise funds for good causes or the young college student who reads to an elderly widow.

I genuinely believe Main Street Values make America great.

It's why we hope that Main Street Values permeate everything we do. We like to think we're a cause, not a business. We invest in the dreams of families, the hopes of small business owners and the independence of our senior citizens. We are strong believers in "giving back and paying it forward" in our community.

While you may have your own notion of Main Street Values, I've created a list of 12 virtues we adhere to that reflect Main Street Values. I believe they could benefit every business owner, family member, friend or neighbor who embraces them:

1. **Loyalty.** Being devoted and faithful
2. **Honesty.** Known as being straightforward, truthful
3. **Integrity.** When you are consistently trustworthy in all your actions
4. **Ingenuity.** Skilled in being clever, original, inventive, innovative
5. **Accountability.** Demonstrating that you are responsible and dependable, even to yourself
6. **Simplicity.** Characterized by being easy to understand, not confusing
7. **Respect.** Showing admiration, deference and professionalism
8. **Passion.** Acting with strong emotion, belief and enthusiasm, a zeal for a cause
9. **Compassion.** Exhibiting care, concern for others, being people-centric
10. **Boldness.** Having a willingness to take risks, to act confidently and courageously
11. **Servant Leadership.** Defined by self-sacrifice, humility and desire to lead by example
12. **Humor.** Not taking yourself too seriously, embracing fun and laughter

14. Main Street Values

Main Street Values encompasses all of these virtues. They are *all about* making a difference, serving the needs of others and engaging in community service. It's a belief that you are your brother's keeper.

Community Engagement

One of the ways you can demonstrate Main Street Values is through community service, e.g., becoming involved in the fabric of your community not just in name only but with a desire to shake things up. As Mom Culture® founder Sarah Komers wisely observed about her efforts to create a supportive community for mothers, *"Community is much more than belonging to something: it's about doing something together that makes belonging matter."*

I couldn't agree more. After all, what good is doing something if you're not fully committed to it?

When thinking of Main Street Values, I'm reminded of Geoffrey Canada, the founder of Harlem Children's Zone (HCZ). Geoffrey grew up in the South Bronx in a poor, sometimes violent neighborhood. Against all odds, he went on to achieve academic success, receiving a bachelor's degree from Bowdoin College and a master's degree from the Harvard Graduate School of Education.

However, his most significant achievement was returning to his community roots to help children who, like himself, grew up in distressed neighborhoods. While I'm sure he could have earned much more in academia at the more elite schools, he instead spent his career teaching underprivileged children and tapping into their often-unrecognized potential.

The organization he founded, the HCZ, has become the national model of neighborhood-based innovation, and has been called, *"One of the most ambitious social-policy experiments of our time."* It is being replicated in many cities across the country, and it's truly an example of Main Street Values at work.

Another prime example of giving back to the community is my friend Erin Gruwell. As a young teacher, Erin was hired to teach high school students who were already labeled "unteachable." At that time, Long Beach, California, was a racially-divided community filled with drugs, gangs and homicides. The tension had spilled into the hallways of the school, making teaching a challenging and sometimes terrifying job.

However, Erin believed her students were capable of far more than anyone expected, even the students themselves. She just needed to reach deep to help them discover the joy of learning. Using a wide variety of literature and media, she found voices and stories that resonated with disadvantaged teenagers. She introduced them to the writings of Anne Frank, and to Ziata Filipovic, a young Bosnian diarist who chronicled the tragic Bosnian War from Sarajevo in the 1990s. Many of the students responded positively to these poignant written works as they put down their weapons and picked up pens and pencils. Having found a new way to express themselves, they embraced history and humanity and were given hope.

Today, many of Erin's students have pursued higher education and now have successful careers. Under her leadership and vision, she and several of her students operate the Freedom Writers Foundation. It was formed to help educators replicate the success of this innovative program and to provide scholarships.

Both of these educators believed in servant leadership and backed their beliefs with action. These stories clearly demonstrate what I like to think of as Main Street Values. They epitomize love, caring, giving and being a good neighbor. In each of the above examples, the teachers' commitment to disadvantaged kids sprang from authentic concern about the students they knew and eventually radiated far beyond their own communities.

These values are what make America great. They are at the core of what I've tried to do in my professional capacity as well as my philanthropic efforts. Just as Geoffrey's and Erin's small seeds grew to benefit thousands, small deeds of kindness and authenticity can affect not only your personal and professional life, but also your community and our world.

To quote Academy Award winner and philanthropist, Denzel Washington, "At the end of the day it's not about what you have or even what you've accomplished ... it's about who you've lifted up, who you've made better. It's about what you've given back."

14. Main Street Values

A Community Effort to Save Lives

As in the stories above, most grand accomplishments start with taking ownership of a problem. And that has certainly been the case with one of my philanthropic efforts: my work with Kiwanis International. Now more than a century-old, Kiwanis is a global service organization dedicated to changing our world one child and one community at a time. Local chapters organize food drives, build playgrounds, reach out to sick children and honor veterans among other service projects in their communities.

After serving as president of our local Kiwanis club, I was then elected to serve as Governor in 2007, serving the Great and Historic Louisiana, Mississippi, West Tennessee District of Kiwanis International, one of 20 districts throughout the world. This position gave me a chance to lead something quite special for a number of communities.

Traditionally, every newly inducted Governor selects a service project that resonates among the clubs in their district. After discussing needed services within our communities, we decided to pursue a goal to place automated external defibrillators (AEDs) in each of our local schools—a worthwhile cause given that more than 300,000 people die of cardiac arrest every year. It's the leading killer in the United States. When a person suffers sudden cardiac arrest (SCA), CPR alone often can't get the heart back into rhythm. Every minute in these situations matters. When blood stops pumping to the brain, you have roughly three-and-a-half minutes to get it flowing again, or you won't make it. Each minute you are in atrial fibrillation, you lose up to a 10% chance of survival. Consequently, fewer than 10% of individuals survive sudden cardiac arrest when they are given compressions and mouth-to-mouth resuscitation alone.

Fortunately, an on-site defibrillator can make a huge difference, shocking the heart back into rhythm as the patient awaits further medical care. A study estimated 1,700 lives are saved each year from bystanders using these devices, although at the time of our project, there still weren't many AEDs around.

Our leadership team agreed to take on the project, and I began coordinating with more than 250 clubs with the expressed goal of putting at least one AED in each school in every school district in the three states we served. I relished seeing the combined efforts of these clubs enthusiastically pursuing this goal over the next year.

By the end of my term in 2009, we had raised more than $300,000 to place more than 1,500 AEDs (valued at $2,000 per unit) in schools throughout our districts and coordinated training on these devices for staff members and employees. It felt great knowing our efforts might help save the lives of a student, parent, teacher or school visitor having a heart attack.

Then the stories started pouring in. One day, not long after the placement of the AEDs, I got an emotional phone call from a woman saying she just wanted to thank me. Her husband had driven over to the elementary school to pick up their daughter. While at the front desk signing her out, he suddenly dropped to the floor. He had experienced sudden cardiac arrest. Fortunately, the office staff knew what to do.

"The AED saved his life," the wife gushed, adding that by the next day, "He was fine."

I received 25 to 30 letters with similar stories. It was humbling when the school honored me, along with the teacher who had actually saved the father's life, and several members of the office staff during an award assembly.

Although not every Kiwanis club in my area raised enough money to meet our goal, I carried the AED project forward in my role as chair of the Shelby County Board of Education. Partnering with the Parent-Teacher Association (PTA), the Girl Scouts and Boy Scouts, we continued our fundraising efforts to ensure every school had this life-saving device.

Every member of these participating groups put their hearts and souls into an effort to raise money to potentially save a person's life. No amount of recognition or awards will come close to the feeling of changing or saving a life. Just knowing a father will be going home to his children at night or a teacher will be able to teach another day is reward enough.

Main Street Heroes

Everyone has a chance to be a hero, to exert influence. It can be that random act of kindness, volunteering or donating money to a great cause. However you choose to empower other people or causes, you can be sig-

14. Main Street Values

nificant. As the famous statesman Sir Winston Churchill once said, *"You make a living by what you get; you make a life by what you give."*

Too often we define success by the amount of money we make, the house we live in or the car we drive. Instead, true success results from being significant in other people's lives and in our communities. Each of us has a chance to be significant—to actively participate in making life better for others and for future generations.

More than that, I believe it's our obligation as citizens of this planet to give back. The greater our good fortune in life, the greater our responsibility to bless others. Just as teachers show a commitment to their community through education, it behooves people from all backgrounds to strengthen the fabric of their communities.

To become a "Main Street Hero," you don't need a fortune. Nor should it be something that sucks the energy out of you. Instead, it should be something that fills your soul. It could be something as simple as driving an elderly neighbor to a doctor's appointment. It might be as small as brightening a person's day by telling them how much you admire them or as large as advocating for changes that will make your community a better place to live. It's about living a life of purpose.

Of course, being trustworthy is a driving force behind Main Street Values. Just as the first pledge in the Boy Scout oath is to be "trustworthy," I believe making and keeping promises are essential for building a life of significance. As political philosopher, author and Holocaust survivor Hannah Arendt once said, *"Promises*

> *"You make a living by what you get; you make a life by what you give."*
> —Sir Winston Churchill

are the uniquely human way of ordering the future, making it predictable and reliable to the extent that it is humanly possible."

Knowing you can depend on someone is a vital ingredient for building trust. Similarly, when people know you as a person who keeps his or her word, the relationship is strengthened.

As wealth managers and fiduciaries, we know our clients rely on us to keep our promises. We strive to be trusted advisors in everything we do. We have built our business around serving the needs of others according to our values, beliefs and moral principles.

I'm always amazed when people in business or politics portray themselves to be something they're not. They brag about their achievements but can't authenticate their veracity. Their actions don't align with their words. In contrast, trustworthy people don't have to prove anything. They go quietly about their work knowing their actions speak much louder than words. They're known for doing what they say and saying what they'll do.

Our firm is proud to represent Main Street America—people living across the nation who support the mom-and-pop shops, work hard to put their kids through college, save for retirement and are always ready to lend a helping hand when needed. They represent the *real* economy.

Main Street Values and Client Service

Along with being trustworthy, it takes character and authenticity to be a Main Street "Hero," especially in a small town where everyone knows everyone. They will soon be found out if someone is betraying their neighbors. That's why we often make the distinction between Wall Street Values and Main Street Values in my industry.

As fiduciaries for our clients, we believe the personalized services we provide to our clients are the essence of small-town character. We want our clients to talk about us favorably and refer us to their friends and associates. Previously, I mentioned how I started my wealth advisory practice when I became discouraged with the way Wall Street firms frequently treated their advisors and their clients. I wanted to start a firm where clients were always the priority and where, as fiduciaries, we

14. Main Street Values

would always put their interest ahead of our own.

No matter what business endeavor you're engaged in, customers respond to how you act. I passionately believe that if you reflect Main Street Values, you will build a successful, long-term business, and you will be able to sleep at night.

If you're a business owner, you might ask yourself: Do I embrace Main Street Values? Do I walk the walk and talk the talk? Am I willing to take the time to build a strong foundation and do the right thing? It's about holding yourself to a standard that is consistent with who you are ... and that may not always be easy. Taking shortcuts will dilute your efforts.

As fiduciaries, we know our job is to earn the trust of our clients, not just at the first meeting, but each and every day. Unlike big firms that see clients as interchangeable commodities, we see them as our neighbors, friends and even our extended family. Our goal is to keep every client for life, to inspire them to refer us to their friends, family and co-workers, and to always reward their trust when they *do* refer friends to us.

We simply think of this as our three R's:

- **Retain.** We strive to provide world-class service bringing authenticity to every encounter. Each year we review every client relationship to gauge if it's great, good or needs to be improved. We then meet with clients on a systematic basis, at least semi-annually, to keep up to date on what is happening in their lives and to assist them with any changes that need to be made. Additionally, we strive to never over-promise and then fail to deliver. Instead, we do our utmost to be trustworthy, honest and open about what we can do. We're more prone to under-promise and over-deliver.
- **Refer.** Nearly every new client to our firm arrives via a referral from existing clients. They gladly refer us to their friends and family members as they have faith and confidence that we will provide the best counsel possible for the individual they refer. We take our responsibility for those referrals seriously. While some advisors establish an account minimum that new clients must meet, we accept any referral sent our way—no matter who they are or how large or small their investment account. We treat all clients

with respect, recognizing that this benefits everyone. We know we sometimes have to plant small seeds to grow giant oaks, and we never know when that germinated seed might turn into something more than we initially considered.

- **Replicate.** We recognize the huge degree of trust involved when a client refers their friend or family member to us. We never want them to regret the trust they place in us. We never want a client to leave us because we failed to dot the i's or cross the t's. Working as a team, we have created a repeatable process that ensures we're all working on the same page, and that nothing falls through the cracks. We strive for consistency in client service, and we are committed to doing things the right way. We're always aware that trust must be earned.

When clients visit our office, we want them to feel comfortable, like they're slipping into that old cardigan sweater that makes them feel warm and fuzzy. This feeling can only come if they have total trust in us. We want them to get that small-town feeling. As former Canadian Prime Minister Brian Mulroney aptly said of his countrymen: *"This country is made up of small towns and big dreams."* We focus on our clients' big dreams and treat them like our small-town friends and neighbors.

Honoring the Real Heroes Among Us

While I encourage you to become a Main Street Hero in your town, there are heroes walking among us who have sacrificed so much on our behalf. They are our military veterans. Some have been deployed around the world and separated from their families for long stretches of time. In some cases they're engaged in dangerous combat missions.

I'm a true patriot. I believe deeply in our country and have unabashed respect for those who have fought for our freedom. When I founded our law firm, I wanted to find a way to give back to our courageous military veterans. I knew this effort would need to involve more than just me. It also would take a commitment from members of our team who were equally enthusiastic about giving back to the community.

After much brainstorming, we created the Planning for Patriots program. Since 2010, The Pickler Law Firm has offered free estate planning ser-

14. Main Street Values

vices to active duty or retired members of the military. The complimentary package (valued at $750 to $1,000) includes a will, healthcare power of attorney and other necessary documents. In the first 10 years of the program, we gave away more than $2 million worth of pro bono legal services. As the vets sign paperwork, they sometimes ask me what they owe. Our response is always: "Your bill has been paid in full by your service to our country."

During the pandemic, our staff enthusiastically expanded our pro bono estate planning work to give back to first responders, including our police, firefighters, ambulance drivers, EMTs, paramedics and nurses. Since we started this program, staff members have given freely of their time to make this possible. We believe in Main Street Values, in showing our appreciation for the services these people provide. We know by doing this, we're making a real difference in their lives.

The Spirit of Volunteerism

Volunteering is a huge part of Main Street Values. It's also the secret to a happy life. As Jesus said, the best way to find our life is to lose our "self" in the service of others. (Matthew 10:39)

My best example of selfless service is my wife. When Beth came into my life, everything changed. She directed my efforts outward to others through her loving example. Beth enjoyed close relationships with her family. Growing up, their house had been the center of their community, hosting many large gatherings. Her father was president of the local bank until his death at the young age of 52, and her mother taught school for 40 years. Upon retirement, she volunteered at the school for another 20 years, until in her 80s, and was voted Arkansas Citizen of the Year. Beth's family radiated the spirit of volunteerism. The strength and closeness of her family strongly influenced the direction of our own young family.

When my son, Chris, began kindergarten, Beth became involved in the PTA. She participated continuously in activities for the kids and served five terms as PTA president. Her commitment to the PTA began to change my world, too. I became an enthusiastic advocate for public education in large part because of her volunteerism. Beth also inspired our family and employees' involvement with the Memphis Oral School for the Deaf

(MOSD). This was discussed in Chapter 3.

Beth is the epicenter for our family's and firm's community involvement and philanthropic efforts. While she has never been one to look for recognition, her real reward is seeing others benefit. She understands people's emotions and listens to their viewpoints. She is trustworthy and nonjudgmental. Beth is the person others go to for advice, and she resolves conflicts as a peacemaker. Beth epitomizes Main Street Values, and she has helped me become the man I am today.

Children Open the Doors to Community Service

Beth and I have been fortunate to have two children ... and they couldn't be more different. Chris is analytical and technically oriented while Kate loves people and looks more at the big picture. Despite their personality differences, both have embraced our love for community service and have provided entry to various community organizations that we may never had been involved with if it weren't for them.

I became involved with Boy Scouts of America (BSA) because of Chris. As a parent and later as a Scout leader, I attended three BSA National Jamborees with Chris. Every summer, from 1996 to 2001, I took his troop on high-adventure camping experiences such as scuba diving at the Florida Keys, canoeing at the Canadian Boundary Waters in Minnesota and a 100-mile hike at the Philmont Scout Ranch located in Cimarron, New Mexico.

During his 12 years in Scouting, Chris earned 100 merit badges, an almost unprecedented accomplishment. For his Eagle Scout project, Chris converted an unusable 50 x 60-foot center courtyard, which was surrounded on all four sides by glass and covered in asphalt, into an outdoor environmental garden. For three years Chris organized volunteers to help transform the area. They built a waterfall, created a teaching area, added interesting architectural features and planted wildflowers.

After completion, we were thrilled when a family of ducks chose to make their home in the garden, seemingly conferring God's stamp of approval on the project. For his efforts, Chris was recognized as the American Legion National Eagle Scout of the Year, and on his 18th birthday, his last

14. Main Street Values

day of scouting, Chris earned his 100th and final merit badge.

My daughter, Katie, has also caught the service bug and inspired our family's volunteering efforts. A social butterfly with a college degree in organizational communication, she started her career in the not-for-profit world. Fresh out of college, she interviewed with the local chapter of the Juvenile Diabetes Research Foundation (JDRF) and was hired as the director of development in charge of fund raising. Lacking experience or a strong background in fund raising, she impressed her employer immediately with her passion and sincerity, which gave her an edge in the job.

Through Katie, we became more aware of the challenges facing children with diabetes. Born healthy, these juveniles usually develop Type 1 diabetes at 10 to 12 years old when their pancreases stop working effectively. This condition requires checking their blood as often as 10 to 12 times a day and taking insulin to regulate their glucose levels.

As part of her job, Katie organized the JDRF youth ambassadors, a group of 25 kids diagnosed with Type I diabetes. Serving as ambassadors, they made presentations at community events. While most were teenagers, some were as young as seven years old. Spending a lot of time together, they became like family to each other, even enduring heartbreak together. One day, a 22-year-old ambassador named Blac experienced a sudden drop in his blood-sugar level and went into a coma from which he never awoke. It was devastating to everyone. Katie got an early education on the tragic impact of this disease, which still has no cure. Researchers are making progress, in part from work at St. Jude Children's Research Hospital and other entities, thereby increasing these kids' chances of leading a normal adult life.

For many years our firm sponsored a gala event to raise funds for this important cause. And we can't forget that our experience running those crazy races at Disney World was, in fact, to raise money for JDRF. For Katie, her work with JDRF was more a passion than a job.

While she no longer works there, our firms still sponsor and volunteer for events to help raise funds to fight Type 1 diabetes. I am proud to say, my wife, Beth, and son-in-law, Daniel, have both been named Volunteer(s) of the Year for JDRF. They are true examples of how volunteering can better the lives of others and of the community.

Pillars of Purpose

Our little charitable operation of four has now been extended to the people who work in our firms and the not-for-profit American Public Education Foundation. As volunteers, they're no longer just employees, but fellow concerned citizens. Along with being exceptional at their jobs, my staff members have selflessly contributed their time and energy to many of the philanthropic projects my family supports. They have personally embraced that passion.

I would be remiss if I didn't also mention the hundreds, perhaps thousands, of people who have collaborated with me on local, state and national service projects. They have inspired me, and without them I wouldn't have been able to accomplish a fraction of what we've accomplished.

Darren Rowse, blogger and professional speaker, gives this advice for improving our community: *"Be the community you want to have."*

Main Street Values bring groups of people together to make great things happen. I've shared just a few examples of how my family and colleagues have contributed to our community. There are so many ways to get involved and to help others in need, whether it's actively participating in your community or assisting individuals on the other side of the world.

For instance, you might choose to:

- Serve in a soup kitchen
- Aid in church activities
- Volunteer at local schools
- Mentor a child
- Tutor students
- Donate to a homeless shelter
- Visit the elderly or volunteer at a senior citizen center
- Volunteer at hospitals
- Help at the local food bank
- Walk dogs at an animal shelter
- Help build homes (Habitat for Humanity)
- Coach a youth sports team

14. Main Street Values

- Support your school's extracurricular programs
- Collect presents for a Sub-for-Santa program
- Join a community service organization
- Assist with voter registration
- Help at a library or museum

As you can see, the list is endless. Giving back to the community not only improves others' lives, but also will help you grow as a person. You may think you're not qualified or you don't have the time, but remember the wise words of spiritual author Elizabeth Andrew: *"Volunteers don't necessarily have the time; they have the heart."*

Faith as Small as a Mustard Seed

Without faith, action seems futile. To contribute to others and commit to making your community a better place, you need to believe you can make a difference. Sometimes we all feel discouraged by geopolitical events happening in our states, in Washington D.C. or around the world. At times we feel helpless to change the situation. After all, we're just one person.

But one individual can achieve great things with faith. As Jesus reminded us, *"Truly I tell you, if you have faith as small as a mustard seed, you can say to this mountain, 'Move from here to there,' and it will move. Nothing will be impossible for you."* (Matthew 17: 20-21)

While your faith may be as small as a mustard seed, if you start sprinkling it with action, you are on the road to accomplishing great things. Start small by lending an ear to a friend or family member who is anxious, depressed or stressed. Then search your neighborhood for those in need. Eventually, your efforts may extend to your community, just like Erin Gruwell's and Geoffrey Canada's did. It may eventually have a positive effect on people throughout the world.

> *"We have this day and the rest of our lives, however long that may be, to make a difference, change our behavior, **take action**, and do the things we've always dreamed of."*
>
> – Scott Allan, author of the self-help book, *Do It Scared*

Pillars of Purpose

Have faith you can make it happen, and with action you can contribute to making the world a better place. "Action" makes the difference.

Here are some action steps you can take to embrace Main Street Values:

- **Find a need.** What would you most like to change in your community? (Perhaps something that has touched your family's life personally, like having a family member with special needs.)
- **Discover opportunities.** Are you looking around your neighborhood and community for an opportunity to serve? (Sometimes community service organizations can introduce you to others who are already involved in the need you'd like addressed.)
- **Improve efforts.** What can you do to improve areas you're already serving in and to affect more lives positively? (Raising more money, spending more time, brainstorming better solutions, being more prepared before board meetings, recruiting more volunteers.)
- **Inspire others.** How can you inspire others to join in the causes you've embraced? (Social media campaigns, word-of-mouth, outreach to co-workers, family members.)
- **Define success.** How do you define success in your service efforts? (Dollars raised, number of volunteers recruited, people served.)

Leaving a Long Shadow

As we close our discussion of the pillars that contribute to a life of significance, I want to impart one final story, one that has stayed with me for many years and illustrates the value of both community and service.

Ray Olachia lived a life of service and had a passionate commitment to the Boy Scouts of America. My friend's dedication to scouting was ultimately rewarded in a very dramatic manner.

Ray is a member of the Sioux Nation and a retired oil executive living in Houston. Every four years, he generously donates his time to appear in full Native American regalia at the National Boy Scout Jamboree in Virginia and helps hundreds of boys earn their Native Lore badge.

Ray patiently teaches the boys how to make arrowheads with traditional

14. Main Street Values

tools and then gives them one as a souvenir. He also has honored hundreds of scouts by handcrafting a special arrow that he gives to those who have *truly* earned their Eagle Scout badge.

I met Ray at the 1997 BSA National Jamboree, and we immediately developed a fast friendship. We would talk about our love for the Boy Scout organization and about our families. One day Ray told my son, "When you have *truly* earned the right to be awarded your Eagle Scout badge, call me. I'd be honored to participate in your Eagle Scout Court of Honor ceremony."

Ray knew full well the arduous journey a boy has to travel to become an Eagle Scout, a pathway similar to the concepts we've included in this book. They first have to identify their *why* (the five Bedrock Principles). Why do they want to become an Eagle Scout? How will it affect their lives and the lives of those around them? What is the driving force that makes them want to succeed? They then need to integrate the *how* (the nine Pillars) into their internal constitution or code of action. Only after building this strong foundation are they able to reach a point of realization and actualization that leads to a life of significance and success.

As the date for the ceremony approached, we called Ray, but our calls went unanswered for three weeks, leaving us alarmed. Finally, Ray called us back, anxiously explaining, "We've had some issues." This turned out to be the understatement of the century. Shockingly, Ray's daughter had been kidnapped and taken to Mexico where she had been held prisoner in a cave. Our government seemingly couldn't do anything about it.

At that point, a core group of Boy Scouts and their leaders came to the rescue. In what I can only imagine was like a scene from a *Mission: Impossible* movie, they organized a trek across the border, and in an astonishing and daring rescue, "kidnapped" his daughter back. They risked their lives to save hers. It was an amazing story that gives me goose bumps to this day. What a tribute to the character of those scouts and their leaders and to their lasting friendship with Ray, born of service!

True to his promise, Ray made the trip from Houston to our hometown of Germantown, Tennessee. Ray delivered my son's Eagle Scout ceremony at Farmington Elementary School, which was the location of Chris'

Pillars of Purpose

Eagle Scout project. He performed the ceremony in full Native American attire, complete with many special elements he had customized for the event, including the presentation of the ceremonial arrow which he had made for Chris. The evening before the event, we had the opportunity to get to know him even better. At dinner he told us about his experience as a young man, preparing to leave and serve in Vietnam. His family gathered to say their goodbyes. Trying to be a brave young man, Ray reached out to shake his father's hand. However, his father refused his hand and instead stepped closer to embrace Ray in his arms. He knew he might never see his son again, and that hug represented all his fears, hopes and the love he felt for Ray.

When Ray returned from Vietnam, it became a tradition for father and son to hug each other. This simple embrace represented the love and appreciation they felt for each other and the knowledge that tomorrow is never promised.

Ray shared with us a mantra he had learned from his father: "*No matter how long we live, we should strive to leave a long shadow for others to follow.*"

At dinner he talked about how these words had influenced him throughout his life. He explained how each person leaves a trail—the work we engage in—and how throughout our lives, our works and the authenticity with which we embrace our passions leaves a shadow that is a signature of our lives. He symbolically compared the long shadow to an arrow on a compass that always points true North toward our purpose. Leaving a long shadow is dependent on finding our purpose and then striving to live it each day. More importantly, he stressed how

> *"We will be known forever by the tracks we leave."*
> –Dakota saying

14. Main Street Values

our efforts will make the path easier for those who follow.

Those words have stuck with me for more than two decades, and Ray's life truly exemplifies his message. In essence, we should all aspire to leave a long shadow, a composite of the sum of our lives. Leaving a long shadow is truly a characterization of Main Street Values.

Humanity is My Business

I share these stories about how my family and others have contributed to the betterment of humankind, as I feel these experiences have helped to make me a better person.

I'm reminded of the words from Charles Dickens' *A Christmas Carol* when the ghost of Jacob Marley tries to warn Scrooge about pursuing an empty life of "business" without compassion for his fellow human beings. Marley, now in the chains of eternal damnation, laments: *"Mankind was my business: Charity, Mercy, Forbearance! The deals of my trade were but a drop of water in the comprehensive ocean of my business!"*

I encourage you to make humankind your business. Find a passion as deep as the sea, and let your devotion carry you to amazing places. Once you know your *why*, the *how* will become apparent. In the end, your life will be transformed, and you'll make the world a better place.

Pillars of Purpose

SECTION III
THE PINNACLE OF SUCCESS

Accountability

Leading a Life of Significance

Pillars of Purpose

Chapter 15
ACCOUNTABILITY

"The buck stops here."
– President Harry S. Truman

In the first section of this book, we talked about the five Bedrock Principles—Power of the Possible, Perseverance, Passion, Integrity and Discipline—which help us create a rock-solid foundation, connect us with our *why* and inspire us to pursue a vision of who and what we want to become.

In the second section, we explored the nine Pillars of Purpose: Trust, Peace of Mind, Problem Solving, Advocate & Partner, Order & Control, Objectivity, Navigate Life, Educate & Counsel and Main Street Values. These comprise the life skills and tools (the *how*) we use to accomplish our life's vision and potential.

In this section, we'll bring it all together by discussing Accountability and how it makes all of this happen. Accountability is the "joist" that supports our life's structure. It's the glue that joins the *why* with the *how*. Accountability helps us actualize our *why*. Without personal accountability, we can never reach our most-cherished goals or become the person we envision.

Unfortunately, however, the word "accountability" doesn't always inspire people. In fact, it often carries a negative connotation. An early edition of Webster's Dictionary, for instance, describes accountability as *"the obligation to bear the consequences for failure to perform as expected."* The word accountability has been historically used to assign blame for a failed task or an unsuccessful venture. Just hearing the word *accountability* in that sense can produce an *"Oh no, what have I done now?"* reaction.

Given this negative association, accountability has come to be seen by many as something to avoid or dread. A fear of accountability often predisposes people to "pass the buck," to point fingers or to shift the blame when things go wrong.

In contrast, I equate accountability with a more positive connotation. Instead of something on the "back end" that happens to us when we fail, I think of it more as a "front-end" activity that facilitates success. Accountability (to me) means doing everything in our power to prevent something from going wrong in the first place instead of merely trying to avoid blame when it does. Accountability means accepting responsibility upfront and throughout any process, and it truly is a fundamental part of building a life of significance and success.

True client advocates will resolutely hold themselves accountable for the tasks they perform for their clients. Their front-end approach should include:

- Setting expectations and parameters before they begin the assignment.
- Accepting individual responsibility for a task and completing it to the best of their ability.
- Giving everyone complete ownership of their assigned task or job.
- Affording team members freedom to determine the approach they'll use to reach the desired results.

By giving full ownership of the task to team members and setting pa-

15. Accountabililty

rameters for what needs to be accomplished, each person's value to the company increases. They're more confident in their ability to perform the task and more diligent in completing it. They're free to utilize their creativity and talents, accepting full responsibility for the result. Consequently, they take more pride in the outcome.

How'm I Doing?

While we must accept accountability for ourselves, it's just as important to ask others to hold us accountable for doing what we say we'll do. I'm reminded of the late mayor of New York City, Ed Koch. While famous for his brash and blustery remarks, Ed was just as well known for standing on street corners or subway stops and asking constituents, "Hey! How'm I doing?"

In an interview with an NPR (National Public Radio) reporter, he insisted this was more than just shtick. He really wanted to know. He explained: *"Some people have said that's a mark of insecurity. Gee, I have to be patted on the back, how'm I doing."* Continuing, he queried, *"... think about this: Do you know people in public life who are sufficiently secure to ask people to rate them?"*

Ed's diligent probing for honest feedback and his ability to openly listen to people's responses worked for him. He served three terms as mayor of America's largest city (1978 to 1989), winning endorsements from both Democrat and Republican leaders.

During a particularly stressful time as mayor, Ed received a call from noted American clergyman John Joseph "Cardinal" O'Connor, who consoled the weary mayor, saying, "Everyone knows you're an honest man." What a tribute to a politician who was living his life in the public eye! He was a man who said what he'd do and did what he said. He was a man of integrity.

In an interview with cinematographer Sean Patrick Ferrell in 2007, Koch explained it this way: *"I want to be remembered as being a proud Jew who loved the people of New York City and did his best to make their lives better."*[1] When he died in February 2013, Mayor Michael R. Bloomberg

---

1 Sean Patrick Ferrell; *Last Word, Ed Koch*; February 2013; https://www.nytimes.com/video/obituaries/1194834046901/last-word-ed-koch.html?action=click&module=RelatedCoverage&pgtype=Article&region=Footer

Pillars of Purpose

praised him as *"an irrepressible icon, our most charismatic cheerleader and champion."*

Ed Koch lived a life of purpose. To this day and for many more to come, he'll be remembered for his endearing question, "How'm I doing?"

> *"Accountability is the acceptance of responsibility for one's own actions, and implies a willingness to be transparent, allowing others to observe and evaluate one's performance."*[1]
>
> – Will Kenton, culture writer

Just as Mayor Koch regularly sought feedback from his constituents, we strive to create a culture in our office where clients feel comfortable telling us how we're doing. We encourage them to share any concerns and to keep questioning us until they fully understand everything we're doing for them and why we're doing it that way. We appreciate feedback as it helps us improve and grow professionally. Ultimately, we want clients to feel good about who we are, what we stand for and to feel confident that we're committed as fiduciaries to doing the best possible job for them.

Accountability Factors

As I've journeyed through life, I've observed that individuals who excel at accepting responsibility go further in life because they're committed to continuous improvement. Here are some tips for improving your own Accountability Factors:

- **Actively solicit feedback.** Create an environment around you where people feel comfortable providing feedback. You might encourage this with a customer survey, through brainstorming sessions or simply by asking people you work with, clients and others close to you, "How am I doing?" Turn off your defense mechanisms and be prepared to openly listen.

- **Be reliable.** Develop a reputation for doing what you say you'll do. Don't over-promise or exaggerate. Keep your promises and if you fall short, accept responsibility. Never make excuses or trivialize responsibilities. Reliability breeds trust, and trust sustains positive re-

---

1 Will Kenton; *Accountability;* Investopedia; 07/25/2022; https://www.investopedia.com/terms/a/accountability.asp

15. Accountabililty

lationships. Moreover, and perhaps more importantly, when you're reliable, you trust yourself and exude confidence in your ability to get the job done. When you trust yourself, you're unstoppable.

- **Invite others to hold you accountable.** Even those of us who thrive on personal accountability sometimes need a little help keeping our commitments. Even as the boss, you can ask others to hold you accountable. For instance, if I tell my staff I'm preparing for a meeting and they catch me casually reading a newspaper, I want them to call me on it, to hold me accountable. I'll thank them for it. Welcome constructive criticism, as it will make you better.

- **Expect great things.** Approach each new challenge or opportunity with hope and optimism, anticipating a good outcome. As former Secretary of State Colin Powell once said, *"Perpetual optimism is a force multiplier."* Defaulting to your fear or anxiety will only hamper your performance. Instead, be confident in your ability to get things done. Hold yourself to high standards and work to consistently learn new skills or to refine existing ones.

- **Respect the "power of intention."** When holding others accountable, we must recognize their capacity for improvement. Never expect someone to work at the same level or speed as you if they lack skills or training. Instead, patiently work with them, believe in their ability and help them achieve a higher level.

> *"Criticism, like rain, should be gentle enough to nourish a man's growth without destroying his roots."*
> – Frank A. Clark, 19th century lawyer and politician

These strategies can help you become more accountable in your daily life and inspire those around you. We cannot sustain success without accountability.

As a youth, I participated in DeMolay, a leadership and character-building organization for young men. There I learned the word "fidelitas" meaning faithfulness—the importance of my word being my bond. To me that means when I make a promise, it should be something people can "take to the bank and earn interest on." Likewise, I encourage you to be trustworthy and to consistently hold yourself accountable for doing what you say

Pillars of Purpose

you'll do. Only then will you earn the trust of those around you.

A Yellow-Brick-Road Journey

In the international best-selling book *The Oz Principle*, authors Roger Connors, Craig Hickman and Tom Smith compare accountability to the journey Dorothy took in L. Frank Baum's popular children's book, *The Wizard of Oz*. In the beginning, Dorothy tearfully wailed about missing her home, family and friends, while the lion bemoaned his inability to be brave, the scarecrow lamented his lack of a brain and the tin man grieved his perceived absence of a heart. Self-victimized, they each felt helpless to solve their own difficulties.

However, as they continued their journey down the yellow brick road, each began to take accountability for their life. The lion mustered the courage to overcome fearful obstacles, the tin man experienced emotions that proved he had a heart, and the scarecrow exhibited wisdom as he solved problems. Even Dorothy found that what she wished for was within her reach. With just the click of the heels of her ruby red slippers she was transported back home to be with family and friends. Each found that what they desired existed within their own capacity to make it happen.

Visualize a horizontal line, and then place the steps these characters took to accept accountability above the line, in the achievement section. Now, below the line (the non-achievement area) list the initial opposite reactions to their problems, e.g., making excuses, blaming others, feeling helpless and refusing to accept responsibility. These negative emotions hindered their growth and provided no workable solution to their problems. Only when they changed their approach and accepted personal responsibility for their woes were they able to overcome the obstacles in their pathway.

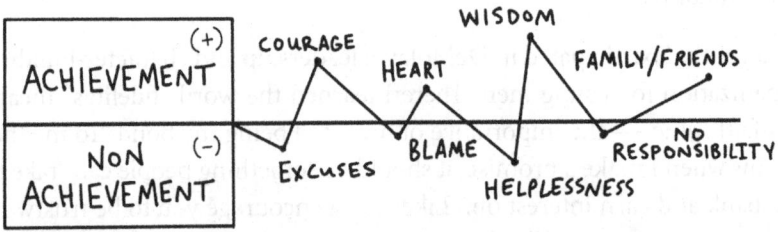

15. Accountabililty

The Oz Principle teaches some valuable lessons:

- **Don't get stuck on the yellow brick road.** If you're not making progress as you travel down the road, don't be afraid to change course, explore alternatives or seek counsel from a trusted friend or mentor. It worked for scarecrow, who was stuck on a nail, the tin man, who was rusted and the cowardly lion, who was caught in a counter-productive cycle of fear and bullying. Each allowed Dorothy to help free them and suggest a new course.

- **Don't blame others for your circumstances.** Dorothy could have easily blamed her problems on the ornery neighbor who kidnapped Toto, an insanely powerful tornado or the wicked and vindictive witch. However, in the end, she only had to click her heels together to go back home. It just took personal accountability.

- **Don't wait for the wizard to wave his magic wand.** Like relying on a fraudulent wizard, people often look to others for solutions that never materialize. They don't bother to check out a person's credentials and may get fooled by smoke and mirrors. Instead, we need to hold ourselves accountable for the things we want to accomplish and always choose potential advisors and mentors carefully.

- **Don't expect all your problems to disappear.** We need to accept reality. There will always be problems in life. However, if we're not part of the solution, we're part of the problem. A quote from the Wizard of Oz proclaims, *"Experience is the only thing that brings knowledge, and the longer you are on earth the more experience you are sure to get."* Commit to seeking solutions and embrace the process.

Accountability is a person's ability to accept an obligation and a willingness to take responsibility for one's actions. It's about preventing something from going wrong instead of accepting blame when something does.

The Last Lecture

I'm always inspired by the story of Randy Pausch, a beloved professor of computer science at Carnegie Mellon University in Pittsburgh. Students loved his lectures because they didn't feel like they were being forced to learn. They were just listening to someone incredibly passionate, interesting and entertaining. A former high school athlete and devoted Star Trek fan, Pausch had been known to perform push-ups on stage, while engaging students about electronic arts and virtual reality.

In April 2008, Pausch was diagnosed with pancreatic cancer and was told he only had six months to live. In what would eventually be called the "Last Lecture," he shared a story about how at one of his most grueling high school football practices, the assistant coach approached him and said, "Coach Graham rode you pretty hard, didn't he?" to which Randy replied, "Yeah."

The assistant coach responded, "That's a good thing … When you're screwing up and nobody's saying anything to you anymore, that means they gave up."

In his speech, Pausch summarized this experience by saying, *"When you see yourself doing something badly and nobody's bothering to tell you anymore, that's a very bad place to be. Your critics are your ones telling you they still love you and care."*

Pausch was a true believer in living life in such a way that your dreams and aspirations will come true. *"It's not about how to achieve your dreams, but how to lead your life. If you lead your life the right way, the Karma will take care of itself. The dreams will come to you."*

Until the end, Pausch was determined to live life to the fullest. He bravely accepted the inevitable: *"That is what it is. We can't change it. We just have to decide how we'll respond. We cannot change the cards we're dealt, just how we play the hand."*

Almost as an afterthought, the inspiring "Last Lecture" was videotaped and posted to social media where it quickly went viral. So far, more than 10 million people have downloaded it, and thousands have written to say how it has changed their lives.

Randy Pausch died on July 25, 2008, at the age of 47. Along with his wife, Jai, and three young children, he left behind a legacy of hope, grace and optimism. His ability to accept and transcend life's challenges left a lasting impact on all who have been inspired by his cheerful outlook and the way he took responsibility for the days he had left. Author Geoffrey

15. Accountabililty

Meland summed it up when he wrote, *"(Randy) lived an extraordinary life, and in dying he inspired others on how to live."*

What if you knew you were about to die? What would you say that could encapsulate everything that is important to you? Are you in control of the direction you want your life to go in? Do you accept responsibility for your decisions and actions? Are you fulfilling your "purpose?"

Passing the Buck

At the beginning of this chapter, I shared one of my favorite quotes, *"The buck stops here."* President Harry S. Truman popularized the expression, keeping an engraved 13-inch wooden plaque with those words mounted on a walnut base on his desk in the White House during his two terms (1945 to 1953). The plaque was a gift to him at the beginning of his presidency, and he referred to it in public statements, including at an address at the National War College on December 29, 1952, when he said, *"You know, it's easy for the Monday morning quarterback to say what the coach should have done, after the game is over. But when the decision is up before you—and on my desk I have a motto which says, 'The Buck Stops Here'—the decision has to be made."*

Not only does the decision have to be made, but also the person making it must hold himself accountable for following through with that decision and the resulting consequences.

And so it goes ... "the buck stops here."

I encourage you to step it up and take accountability for your thoughts, your actions ... your life. To do this:

- **Be trustworthy.** Are you doing things for the right reason or do you have ulterior motives that are self-serving? Founding father Thomas Payne once said, *"A body of men holding themselves accountable to nobody ought not be trusted by anybody."* Holding yourself accountable will increase your trustworthiness in the eyes of others. Be transparent. Be open and honest with others no matter how challenging it might be. Be straightforward and lead by example.

Pillars of Purpose

- **Establish measurable expectations.** Write down daily, weekly and monthly goals to ensure you are continually moving in the right direction. Every morning at 6 a.m. I write my daily accountability goals, knowing that at the end of the day, I'm the person who has to hold myself accountable for accomplishing them. It works for me.

- **Commit to being a better person.** Each day is a new day and a new chance to move a step closer to your life's purpose. As spiritual leader Joel Osteen once said, *"It doesn't matter what your present circumstances look like, today is a brand-new day, and God wants to do a new thing in your life and in your relationship with Him every day."* Don't waste this opportunity.

- **Be willing to accept feedback.** Ask people you trust, "How am I doing?" Create a safe environment where they are comfortable providing feedback on what you could be doing better. As you expand your network of critics, your opportunities for growth will increase exponentially.

I'm not telling you the process is going to be easy. It takes hard work, humility, sacrifice and self-evaluation. It takes holding yourself responsible for the decisions you make, actions you take and the tasks you complete. Just remember, every day is a new day filled with possibilities. You are accountable for making it the best day it can be.

Chapter 16

LEADING A LIFE OF SIGNIFICANCE

"The key to realizing a dream is to focus not [only] on success but significance—and then even the small steps and little victories along your path will take on greater meaning."
– Oprah Winfrey

We've come to the final chapter of our journey. Throughout this book I've shared my thoughts, stories and advice for achieving a life of success and significance. However, there's one more important brick to be laid before sending you on your way.

To truly become the best version of ourselves, we need to appreciate the difference between *success* and *significance*. Now, you may be thinking success and significance basically mean the same thing. However, while they are similar and often coincide, there are notable, important differences. When we aim only for *success*, we're attempting to create something of value that mainly benefits ourselves or those within our immediate circle. When we pursue a life of *significance*, we gain the opportunity to bless countless lives beyond our own regardless of how much money we wind up with or fame achieved at the end of this game we call Life. Significance is the end goal, the pinnacle of what we're working toward.

Pillars of Purpose

A life of *significance* extends beyond our lifetime. It transcends the present to become a lasting, edifying *presence* in our community and in the world. While success is ephemeral—fleeting and short-lived—significance is eternal.

Separating success from significance can sometimes be difficult. In our society we tend to worship those who have achieved fame and covet the fortune some have acquired. We become obsessed with our favorite entrepreneur, Hollywood star, singer or professional athlete. They captivate us with their accomplishments, and for many, these individuals represent the height of worldly success. While some of these "celebrities" have worked hard to develop their God-given talents, and some have overcome obstacles and displayed an inordinate amount of determination to succeed, their success is often fleeting and can sink into oblivion in the blink of an eye.

Freethinking artist Andy Warhol said that anyone can enjoy 15 minutes of fame, but few can sustain the longevity of success. Instead, he wisely suggested, *"The idea is not to live forever; it is to create something that will."*

While success is something to pursue and to work toward, it is only a stepping-stone on the path to achieving a life of significance. A person can be successful yet never be significant, while a significant person is always successful. Being significant doesn't depend on the wealth you've gained or the celebrity you've achieved. Instead, it's about who you are, what you've become and the impact you've had on others. It's achieved with the "power of intention" by applying the lessons you've learned and wisely using the time you've been given.

In the first section of this book, we laid the foundation. We explored the process of identifying your *why*. The Bedrock Principles help you to reach deep inside yourself to discover your true purpose and embrace it with passion.

In Section II, we discussed the Pillars of Purpose, the *how*. We outlined the skills needed to build that life of purpose. Each skill contributes something vital and valuable. Our blueprint for achieving a life of purpose requires knowledge, motivation and action to make it all happen. When we internalize or personalize knowledge, it motivates us to act.

16. Leading a Life of Significance

Action forces us out of our comfort zone so we can make a difference in our own life and the lives of others.

Now, in our final stage of creating a life of significance, it all comes down to "intention." It's what binds the *why* with the *how*. Along with holding yourself accountable, being intentional requires you to make some important decisions. Now don't get me wrong, that doesn't mean it comes down to making one big decision. Instead, it's the thousands of small decisions you make. It's the little things you do when no one is looking and without even thinking about it. It's about living a life dedicated to becoming the best we can be.

Who Will You Fight For?

> *"With great power comes great responsibility."*
> – Uncle Ben in Spiderman (the movie)

I believe becoming the best we can be means recognizing our power and our responsibility to use it for good. The "power" referred to in the above Spiderman quote has nothing to do with being famous or making lots of money. It's *who* you are. You have the power to change the direction of your life, to decide how you'll use the tools you've been given to help others.

As a fan of the *Rocky* movies starring Sylvester Stallone, I'm inspired by the *Rocky IV* storyline where Rocky takes on Soviet boxer Ivan Drago, who was billed as "the most perfectly trained fighter in history." Preparing for their upcoming bout, Drago had access to the best of everything —an indoor, immaculate, temperature-controlled facility, a huge staff of doctors to monitor every vital sign and countless technological advances.

In stark contrast, Rocky's training took place in the freezing Russian countryside and inside a barn that wasn't much warmer. Because he's pursuing an unsanctioned fight, he had to give up his heavyweight title. He was quite literally going it alone with only his trainer for support. With no fancy training equipment, Rocky chopped wood and ran up and down mountains, often treading through deep snow.

As usual, nobody gave Rocky much of a chance against the younger, bigger Drago, who after all, was "a killing machine." However, during their epic 15-round battle, Rocky showed his trademark tenacity as he took beating after beating but refused to surrender. In a pivotal scene toward the end of the fight, Rocky rallied and started landing body blows of his own. As the formerly hostile Russian crowd began cheering him on with chants of, "Rock-y! Rock-y!" Drago's boss, a Soviet politician, berated Drago, telling him he was an embarrassment to his country. Enraged, Drago shouts back, *"I fight to win. I fight for me!"*

As the two fatigued fighters traded punches in the final round, the TV announcers summed it up: *"Forget technique. Forget strategy. This is a street fight—it's a question of who wants it most."*

Of course Rocky, the big-hearted hero, wanted it most. Unlike Drago, who was fighting for himself, Rocky was fighting for others. He was fighting to avenge his friend and mentor Apollo Creed's death at the hands of Drago. He was fighting to make his wife and son proud. And by the end of the fight, he realized his cause was even bigger than that. He was representing his country's ideals in this Cold War sporting rivalry between the world's two most powerful nations. Far from his hometown of Philadelphia, Rocky was giving hope to people he'd never met before, people he had always thought of as enemies before that moment. Through his bravery and will to fight, Rocky showed everyone that change was possible. He became a true hero.

Choosing to be a Hero Every Day

It's easy to spot the heroes and the villains on the big screen. We're captivated when the fictional hero faces a moment of truth, as was the case in another of my favorite movies, *Star Wars*.

Star Wars creator George Lucas described his original three-part space adventure as the "Redemption story of Anakin Skywalker." Anakin, you'll recall, was the gifted young Jedi knight who, over a period of time, gave in to the dark side and became the iconic villain Darth Vader, terror of the galaxy. It was only in his final moments, when he sacrificed himself for his son, Luke, and overthrew the Emperor, that Anakin redeemed himself.

Likewise, Anakin's brooding grandson, Kylo Ren, battled his own dark side. In his final moments, he sacrificed his life to save his friend, soul-

16. Leading a Life of Significance

mate and fellow Jedi, Rey. He achieved his own redemption as a Jedi in restoring her, using his powers for good.

I like the symbolism in *Star Wars*. We can liken "the dark side" to our own fears, resentments and selfishness that leads us away from our potential to do good. And just like Vader and Kylo Ren transformed from villains to heroes on the big screen, we can all change. We all have our moments of truth, and we all must sacrifice something to achieve our full potential. Even if we fall to the darkness, we can find the light. Each of us can be transformed into a hero, and each of us can have our own redemption story.

What will you choose in your life? How will you hone your natural abilities to become a force for good in the world? While we'll no doubt be tempted by "the dark side" one time or other, it's making a conscious decision to become the best, or most heroic version of ourselves that truly counts.

Commit to a Cause

As you've learned throughout this book, my family and I are passionate about community service, leadership and working with non-profit organizations. Over my career, I intentionally developed life skills that would allow me to give back to the causes I truly believed in. The capstone of this ongoing professional development occurred when I pursued and received the Chartered Advisor in Philanthropy® (CAP®) designation in 2021. It was one of the most unique educational processes I've gone through, and it provided me with the knowledge and ability to effectively help others with their legacy planning.

Since then, I have used these intentional skills to develop "planned giving" programs for the Cecil C. Humphreys School of Law at the University of Memphis, Maui United Way, Boy Scouts of America, Porter-Leath Children's Home and TEEN ARTS NJ. It's always inspiring to collaborate with patrons who are eager to give to the causes important to them. While some of them may have an abundance of wealth to contribute, others are just ordinary people of lesser means, but who are just as passionate about their causes.

My journey with planned giving began when I became a board member of the Orpheum Theatre in Memphis, Tennessee, in 2008. I'd always believed the heart and soul of a community is expressed by its commitment to the creative arts. My wife, Beth, and I have been theater patrons for more than 35 years and have shared these amazing experiences with our children, Katie and Chris. We've enjoyed productions of *Cats, The Phantom of the Opera, Les Misérables, Wicked* and countless other productions. In fact, when Katie married Daniel in 2019, their wedding was held at the Orpheum Theatre.

Our love of theater led to my becoming Director of Planned Giving, a volunteer role that allows me to develop giving programs for the Orpheum Theatre. Planned Giving empowers donors to show their commitment to the theatre's future by creating a legacy gift. Along with counseling potential donors to explain the process and benefits of planned giving, we offer the services of our law firm to draw up the required legal work. Including the Orpheum Theatre Group in their estate plans helps individuals establish a memorial or tribute gift. Most of these gifts won't transfer until the donors pass on, but the legacy they leave behind will be remembered for years to come.

> *"The ultimate test of man's conscience may be his willingness to sacrifice something today for future generations whose words of thanks will not be heard."*
>
> Gaylord Nelson, former Governor of Wisconsin

Microsoft founder Bill Gates is a great example of someone whose philanthropic efforts will benefit people for generations to come. As a young child, Gates was bullied by the other kids because of his small size. However, growing up in a family that valued competition and winning, Bill shrugged aside those negative experiences to excel in school and to immerse himself in the world of computer programming.

To make a long story short, Gates and childhood friend Paul Allen went on to found Microsoft, the world's largest personal computer software company. The company changed the way we work, and its software can be found on nearly every computer worldwide. When Gates was only 31 years old, the company went public and overnight he became the world's youngest billionaire.

16. Leading a Life of Significance

While Gates' contribution to the technology era has been significant, the time and money he has given to charitable foundations is equally impressive. In 2000, he and his wife co-founded the Bill & Melinda Gates Foundation, a nonprofit organization that fights poverty, disease and inequity around the world. As their initial commitment to the foundation, the couple donated $20 billion worth of Microsoft stock. Since 2000, the foundation has spent $53.8 billion to make a difference in the lives of others. Most recently, more than $2 billion has been given to the global COVID-19 response alone.

In 2010, Gates extended his philanthropic efforts even further. Planning to eventually give away almost all his money to the foundation, he launched the Giving Pledge, asking America's wealthiest people to make a similar commitment. Today, more than 40 of America's wealthiest people have followed the Gates' example by agreeing to give the majority of their wealth to nonprofit organizations to address some of society's most pressing problems.

While Gates is truly one of the most successful people in the world today, contributing a huge portion of his fortune to help others exemplifies a life of significance.

However, I must remind you that it doesn't take a fortune to be a philanthropist! Most of the contributors to Orpheum Theatre's Planned Giving program are just average people who appreciate the arts and want to show their support to the theatre for years to come. Giving a little is sometimes giving a lot. It's about using your time and talents, your power, to make a difference in the lives of others.

You probably recall the Bible story of the widow who only had two mites:

> [41]Now Jesus sat opposite the treasury and saw how the people put money into the treasury. And many who were rich put in much. [42]Then one poor widow came and threw in two mites..."
>
> [43] So He called His disciples to Himself and said to them, "Assuredly, I say to you that this poor widow has put in more than all those who have given to the treasury; [44]for they all put in out of their abundance, but she out of her poverty put in all that she had, her whole livelihood." — Mark 12:41-44

Pillars of Purpose

Giving extends far beyond a dollar amount. It can be as simple as giving your time to listen to a young child talk about his first day of school, bringing a meal to a sick friend or mentoring a colleague. However you choose to enrich the lives of others is a step toward living a life of significance.

> *"Humanity's greatest advances are not in its discoveries but in how those discoveries are applied to reduce inequity. Whether through democracy, strong public education, quality health care, or broad economic opportunity, reducing inequity is the highest human achievement."*
>
> – Bill Gates

Three Valuable Gifts

As you strive to live a life of significance, the Good Lord has given you three gifts: Time, Talent and Treasure, each being of equal importance. When shared, they will enrich your life and the lives of others. Let's explore them in more detail:

- **Time.** People who create a life of significance give freely of their time in activities that can make a difference. I'm a believer in "engaged philanthropy." It means that when I choose to get involved with a cause, I don't just write checks. I pay with sweat equity as well. I show up! Showing up matters as we can see firsthand the people we're helping, and we become emotionally involved in our communities. In the United States, it's estimated that Americans spend an average of 52 hours a year volunteering, including time spent at food banks, doing fundraising projects, tutoring and helping at organizations such as Habitat for Humanity. Where would we be without these people who are willing to sacrifice their time and talents to make life a little better for others?

    We all possess the same amount of time each day. Yet we often squander it on trivial pursuits. At the end of our lives, will we look back on wasted opportunities and wish we had taken more time to spread our influence?

    As self-help author Zig Ziglar once said, *"Lack of direction, not lack of time, is the problem. We all have 24-hour days."* To be significant,

16. Leading a Life of Significance

we must attempt to do more with the time we have. By sacrificing our time to causes we love, we make our time on Earth more meaningful. When you give of your time, you're demonstrating engaged philanthropy—the most powerful form of charitable giving.

- **Talents.** Creating a life of significance is also about sharing your talents with others. When you use your God-given gifts to enrich the lives of others, you'll also grow and flourish. Mozart's concertos would have been for naught if he'd kept them locked in a safe. Italian tenor Andrea Bocelli's beautiful voice would have been wasted if it had never escaped the confines of his shower. And Rembrandt's art would never have inspired generations if left to deteriorate in a dark and damp closet. While all were enormously successful in their own rights, they inspired others with the joy and beauty of their individual talents.

According to 20th Century artist Pablo Picasso, *"The meaning of life is to find your gift. The purpose of life is to give it away."*

You don't have to be a famous figure to share your talents with others. While you may not describe your ability to organize a closet, cook a special meal or to grow a weed-free garden as talents, they are. Everyone has talents. What you choose to do with the ones you've been given is what truly matters. Using your talent to help a handicapped person clean their home, to bake cookies for a fundraiser or to assist a neighbor in building a shed are all part of living a life of significance.

Kahlil Gibran, author of the best-selling book *The Prophet*, wisely suggests, *"You give but little when you give (only) your possessions. It is when you give of yourself that you truly give."*

- **Treasure.** When you think about the philanthropic efforts of people like Bill Gates, you might say, "If I had all that money, I'd be more than happy to give to others." Certainly, it's easy to give when you have abundance. However, I'm reminded of the power that comes from true sacrifice. Again, remember the Bible story of the widow who only had two "mites." It was a trivial sum, but she contributed all of it to something she believed in, drawing praise from the greatest giver of all.

Pillars of Purpose

There is an ennobling power that arises from true sacrifice. Treasure takes many forms. Your treasure might be the excess food you have in your pantry, the furniture you no longer need or the car you were going to trade in on a new one. Donating these items or even the bag of clothes you were ready to throw out can make a difference in another person's life. You don't have to be wealthy to donate your treasure. in some cases, what seems like a small amount or an insignificant item to you could be a fortune to others. True sacrifice is the unselfish act of giving up something of value to a cause outside yourself with the purpose of fulfilling another person's needs.

What are you willing to sacrifice to create something of more lasting value? Would you contribute to an enterprise that will not benefit you personally? Would you sacrifice some of your comfort to make a better tomorrow for someone else?

As 18th Century writer John Bunyan, author of Pilgrim's Progress, put it: *"You have not lived today until you have done something for someone who can never repay you."*

As mentioned in Chapter 9, Mother Teresa is an excellent example of a woman who sacrificed everything for the welfare of the sick and orphaned. Moved by the plight of people living in the slums of Calcutta, she made the decision to leave the serene and cloistered environment of the convent to live and work amongst the poorest of the poor. When awarded the Nobel Peace Prize in 1979, she humbly said, *"I am unworthy."* Then, referring to the $190,000 prize she won, she said, *"Thank God for this gift for the poor. God's blessings will be with the people who have given the prize. I hope it will be real means of bringing peace and happiness in the world of today."*

As you search for worthwhile projects to which you can donate your time, talents or treasures, remember to pick ones you are truly passionate about. Just as my family and I are passionate about the arts and public education, you will find you're more committed to your cause if it is something that interests you and reflects your values. Dig deep to understand your motivation. Then select causes for which you feel you can truly have influence.

16. Leading a Life of Significance

"Whoever seeks to preserve his life will lose it, but whoever loses his life will keep it." —Luke 17:33

It's All About Character

Living a life of significance is all about character. Becoming a person of character and significance means making important decisions and sticking to them. It means being disciplined and holding yourself accountable for your decisions and actions. A person of character is selfless, considerate, loyal and loving—all the qualities we're striving for as we pursue a life of significance.

While we admire these universal character traits and embrace them, it's important that our actions be sincere. We can be most significant when we are true to ourselves and our values, instead of trying to become an exact replica of someone else. To live a life of purpose and significance, we must:

- **Be authentic.** Be genuine and let your actions speak louder than your words. If you are honest and trustworthy, no one can question your motives. While successful people *try*, significant people *are*. Your authentic self is transparent. People will recognize you for who you are and what you do. You'll never have to convince them to acknowledge your value, they'll just know.

- **Be purposeful.** If you act with intention, your purpose will be magnified. A purposeful person is focused on a cause and committed to making it happen.

- **Have faith.** Often, people feel stymied in their actions thinking they can't make a difference. But even small acts can lead to positive change. You've heard the phrase, "pay it forward." One small act of kindness can lead to an avalanche of change.

- **Be trustworthy.** An empty promise leads nowhere. Instead, be consistent. Be committed.

- **Be present.** Be there for others, not just when "big things" are involved but for the "little things" as well. As film director, writer and actor Woody Allen once said, *"Eighty percent of life is just showing up."* Be a trusted warrior for your cause ... not just today but every day.

Pillars of Purpose

As we discuss purpose and significance, the term "servant leadership" comes to mind. While it's a common and perhaps overly used term, servant leadership lies at the heart of all the traits previously mentioned. Servant leaders bring energy to their positions and find genuine joy in making lives better. A servant leader can be a mom who is organizing a PTA fundraiser, a grandfather who is actively involved in his church, a business owner or philanthropist. It can be anyone whose actions spring from their heart while never focusing on bank balances, the benefits they'll reap or the connections they'll make with the "right" people.

Servant leaders:

- Support good causes because it's the right thing to do, not because they will benefit from them.
- Are always eager to help those around them meet their goals. They never feel threatened by competition, but instead rejoice in the accomplishments of others.
- Get involved in good causes to serve, not to be served.
- Bring energy to every project and find joy in making the lives of others better.
- Provide encouragement, guidance and counseling to others without expecting anything in return.

As professional advisors, we consider ourselves to be servant leaders. Sir Winston Churchill's famous quote is our mantra: *"We make a living by what we get, and we make a life by what we give."* When clients experience serious difficulties or life-changing events, they sometimes just need to talk. Although we may be pressed for time, we make it a priority to listen, to let them know we're present and that we care. We give them the dignity of our time and attention, and we feel enriched by the bonds we develop with our clients during those situations.

We've gone out of our way to give a stranded client a ride home. We've comforted families who have experienced the loss of a loved one. We don't do this so they'll invest more money with us. We don't even need a pat on the back. Instead, we do it because they're our friends, and many are like family members to us. We do it just because it's the right thing to do.

16. Leading a Life of Significance

The Gift of Giving

Ordained minister Steve Goodier, publisher of the *Your Life Support System* newsletter, wrote: *"Money is not the only commodity that is fun to give. We can give time, we can give our expertise, we can give our love, or simply give a smile. What does that cost? The point is none of us can ever run out of something worthwhile to give."*

While giving can take many forms, often we don't give ourselves credit for the simple gifts we give on a daily basis. It's about those little things. It's about showing you care, listening and just being present.

If you've ever watched the movie, *Mr. Holland's Opus*, you probably know what I'm talking about.

The movie depicts the true story of a teacher named Glenn Holland, played by Richard Dreyfuss. As a young man, Mr. Holland takes a high school teaching job thinking it will just be a temporary means to support his family. He believes his real purpose lays in composing music. Over the next 30 years, however, he slowly loses faith in his dream and reluctantly accepts teaching as his destiny.

During his teaching career, he helps students cope with social turmoil, such as the assassination of President John F. Kennedy and the onslaught of drugs and school violence. He also helps them navigate personal issues, build self-confidence and find their true selves. Meanwhile, he continuously fights budget wars with the principal and school board as he advocates for students and his programs. Ultimately, he loses the battle when the school board decides to eliminate programs for the arts, including his music classes. In spite of his impassioned plea to the Board of Education, his teaching career has ended. In losing his job, he comes to the realization that his "temporary" job has become a huge part of who he really is and all he ever wanted to do. He realizes how much he loves the job, yet he feels like a failure. He doesn't believe he has made a difference.

After helping him clear out his office, his wife and son start to lead him out of the school for the last time. Suddenly, Mr. Holland hears a commotion in the high school auditorium. To his total surprise he finds it is packed with his current and former students, who greet him with a standing ovation, and later publicly praise him for all the help and encouragement he has given to each of them over the past 30 years. As the ceremony reaches its crescendo, they hand him the baton to lead them as they perform, for the first time ever, his opus, *The American Symphony*.

Mr. Holland thought his purpose was to compose music—to write the perfect symphony. While over time he did complete his symphony, more importantly, he finally realized he had accomplished something more lasting and far reaching. He realized how significant he had been in his students' lives. He finally understood his opus was much more than the music he composed. It was about the lives he touched and the significant role he played in the lives of the students.

Similarly, you are probably already taking those small steps (and maybe some large ones) that will help you reach the ultimate goal of living a life of significance. In a previous chapter, I talked about the importance of "leaving a long shadow," a path that makes it easier for others to follow. It's not just the big things that cast a shadow of our lives, but the accumulation of smaller things. These simpler steps, taken over time, help us accomplish our life's purpose. Being significant is what we do when no one is looking. It's what we do without needing recognition or even expecting a "thank you."

Your edifying presence is about being there ... making yourself available for those times when someone just needs to be uplifted and their lives made a little easier. It's about living a life that exudes love in every thought and action you take.

Make the music of your life your masterpiece—your personal opus.

***

Special Acknowledgements

As I've shared my personal journey and those of others, I hope you've been inspired by the lessons taught and the accomplishments achieved. In reflection, I know my life would not be the same without the love of my wife, Beth. You may have heard the quote, "Behind every great man is a greater woman." I prefer the quote by the Muslim philosopher Tariq Ramadan, *"Behind every great man is not a woman, she is beside him, she is with him, not behind him."* I feel truly blessed and honored to walk beside Beth. She inspires my footsteps and helps make dreams come true for our family and all the causes to which she has dedicated her life.

My love and enthusiasm for serving the youth of America as president of the local and state school boards and then as president of the National School Boards Association was flamed by Beth. She also enlarged our family's scope of appreciation by introducing us to the Memphis Oral School for the Deaf (MOSD) and the great work they do.

Our kids, Katie and Chris, have often forced me out of my comfort zone (remember the Dopey Challenge at Disney World) and their influence has been far reaching. I became a Scout leader because of Chris, and my deep appreciation for JDRF and serving children impacted by Type 1 diabetes was because of Katie.

I've also been fortunate to have so many other wonderful people in my life who have believed in me and my passion to get things done, such as the campaigns to raise money for the new Collierville High School, to enlist Steinway to place pianos in the Arkansas State University music department and to make Collierville High School the first "All Steinway High School." There are those who stuck with me during the merger and subsequent demerger of the Memphis and Shelby County School Boards, making a very arduous journey a little less bumpy.

My experiences working on election campaigns and in the trenches of the school board helped me to realize the importance of sticking to my guns when I knew what I was doing was right and to never negotiate a lesser solution. My time working at Xerox helped refine my skills and prepared me for my true purpose in life, helping others to identify and reach their personal goals.

At Pickler Wealth Advisors, The Pickler Law Firm and Pickler Accounting Advisors, I've had the privilege of working with some of the finest and most professional people in America. With their support, expertise and attention to detail, we're able to provide life-changing solutions for our clients. Our team has "gone the extra mile" (beyond their day jobs) as they've donated their time and talents to a variety of charitable causes —raising money for MOSD, JDRF, public education and providing complimentary legal documents for our vets and first responders to name just a few. Their enthusiasm for "giving back and paying forward" helps me to continually stay positive and ready for whatever life throws our way.

And last, but certainly not least, I'm so thankful for the relationships we've developed with our clients. Without them, I would never be able to fulfill my life's mission, my true purpose of delivering solutions to families and truly being there for them. As we've helped them navigate life's unpredictable and sometimes tumultuous journey, we strive to make their lives a little better and to help them reach their long-term goals.

As you travel your personal journey, realize the road is not without challenges, and there are no shortcuts. We all begin our lives with hopes and dreams, but sometimes we lose sight of our purpose along the way. Life can and does happen. When life throws us a curve, we have to adjust and adapt.

Just remember, we're all in this together. It takes a unified effort of a family, town or a country to make the world a better place. However, it all starts with one small step and YOU! Through self-examination and steadily striving each day to better yourself, you can be one step closer to reaching your final destination—achieving a life of significance.

I hope the words I've shared in our time together provide insight and inspiration to help you reach that goal and to make the lives of others a little easier. I hope you are continually inspired and rejuvenated by your *why* and follow the course of your *how* to realize your full potential—to reach your pinnacle. In the end, those you've helped along the way will be the beneficiaries of your life of significance.

Special Acknowledgements

Each of us has the capacity to lead a life of significance, to give back and pay forward. Each of us can leave a long shadow for all to follow. We can be the composers of our own opus as we let the music of our life and the passion of our purpose change our world, one person and one community at a time.

May God bless you on your journey.

David Pickler

PILLARS OF PURPOSE

LEADING A LIFE OF SIGNIFICANCE

ACCOUNTABILITY

- TRUST
- PEACE OF MIND
- PROBLEM SOLVING
- ADVOCATE & PARTNER
- ORDER & CONTROL
- OBJECTIVITY
- NAVIGATE LIFE
- EDUCATE & COUNSEL
- MAIN STREET VALUES

THE BEDROCK PRINCIPLES

- POWER OF THE POSSIBLE
- PERSEVERANCE
- PASSION
- INTEGRITY
- DISCIPLINE

About the Author

David A. Pickler, Esq., CFP®
President & CEO, Pickler Wealth Advisors
dpickler@picklerwealthadvisors.com

David Pickler began his career in the investment business over 30 years ago. He graduated with Highest Academic Honors from Arkansas State University with a Bachelor of Science in Business Management degree in 1980 and from Cecil C. Humphreys School of Law, University of Memphis, with a Juris Doctor Degree in 1985. He was admitted to the Tennessee Bar in 1986 and maintains an active practice emphasizing Tax and Estate Planning. He is a CERTIFIED FINANCIAL PLANNER™ professional, a CERTIFIED PRIVATE WEALTH ADVISOR®, a Chartered Financial Consultant (ChFC®), and a Certified Divorce Financial Analyst® practitioner.

David has built his personal and professional life on the principles of community service, civic leadership, and philanthropic investment. His greatest passion is in promoting high-quality public education for every child, which he says, "will help ensure America's economic and vital national interests."

David began his community involvement with the PTA in his children's schools. David was elected to the Shelby County School Board of Education in 1998 and served as chairman for 12 years. He was then elected as the Tennessee School Boards Association President. In April 2013, David became the President of the National School Boards Association. He has twice been honored as Tennessee School Board Member of the Year.

In July 2012, David was honored by the Academy of Education Arts and Sciences as a recipient of the "Educators Voice Award," and in September of 2013 he received the prestigious Bammy Award as "School Board

About the Author

Member of the Year." In 2019, David was awarded the Invest in Others "Catalyst Award" for his work in public education through his non-profit, the American Public Education Foundation—a 501(c)(3) in which he serves as Executive Director.

David has twice been named among the top 1,000 financial advisors in the U.S. in *Barron's* magazine. He has been named a Five Star Wealth Manager multiple years in a row, and in 2015, David was selected to the *Financial Times* 400 Top Advisors List. He has been honored in *Forbes'* Best-in-State Wealth Advisors list numerous times. In 2021, Pickler Wealth Advisors was named *Memphis Business Journal's* Small Business of the Year, and, in the same year, was listed as one of the fastest-growing private companies in America by *Inc.* magazine. David was also named the 2022 and 2023 Charitable Champion by Invest in Others Foundation for promoting a culture of philanthropy.[1]

---

1 To read more about these awards and view disclosures, please visit: https://www.picklerwealthadvisors.com/recognitions-and-accolades